Caroline Bingham was born in Hampstead in 1938. She was educated at Cheltenham Ladies' College and Bristol University, where she read history. She married in 1958, and has a daughter, born in 1961. She held a research fellowship at Royal Holloway College, University of London, 1984–86, and wrote the official centenary history of the college. Most of her other books are on Scottish subjects, and besides *Darnley*, they include her two-volume biography of his son, King James VI and I, and a life of Mary Queen of Scots's father, *James V, King of Scots*.

By the same author

The Making of a King: The early Years of James VI and I
James V, King of Scots
The Life and Times of Edward II
The Crowned Lions: The Early Plantagenet Kings
James VI of Scotland
James I of Scotland
The History of Royal Holloway College, 1886–1986
Beyond the Highland Line: Highland History and Culture

DARNLEY

A LIFE OF
HENRY STUART, LORD DARNLEY
CONSORT OF MARY QUEEN OF SCOTS

CAROLINE BINGHAM

A PHOENIX GIANT PAPERBACK

First published in Great Britain by
Constable and Company Limited in 1995
This paperback edition published in 1997
by Phoenix, a division of Orion Books Ltd,
Orion House, 5 Upper St Martin's Lane,
London WC2H 9EA

A CIP catalogue record for this book
is available from the British Library.

ISBN: 1 85799 779 4

Printed and bound in Great Britain by
Butler & Tanner Ltd, Frome and London

To the Memory of my Parents

MURIEL WORSDELL
1904–1992

CEDRIC CONYERS WORSDELL
1902–1995

'Grace and rememberance be to you both'

CONTENTS

ILLUSTRATIONS

ACKNOWLEDGEMENTS

It is a pleasure to record my gratitude to Mr James Lomax, curator of Temple Newsam, for his kindness in giving me a tour of the house, and providing me with valuable information and material on its history. For assistance with the illustrations I should like to thank Mrs Sarah Wimbush of the Courtauld Institute Photographic Survey Department, and Mrs Enid Nixon, then Assistant Librarian of Westminster Abbey, who was kind enough to arrange for a new photograph to be taken of the monument of Lord Darnley. My thanks to Miss Kate Shearman, for editing the paperback.

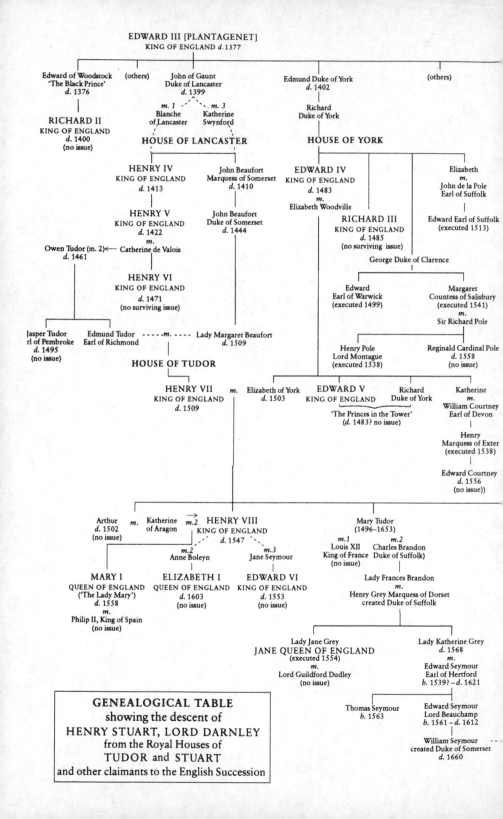

EDWARD III [PLANTAGENET]
KING OF ENGLAND d.1377

Edward of Woodstock 'The Black Prince' d. 1376 — (others) — John of Gaunt Duke of Lancaster d. 1399 — Edmund Duke of York d. 1402 — (others)

RICHARD II KING OF ENGLAND d. 1400 (no issue)

m. 1 Blanche of Lancaster / m. 3 Katherine Swynford

Richard Duke of York

HOUSE OF LANCASTER

HOUSE OF YORK

HENRY IV KING OF ENGLAND d. 1413

John Beaufort Marquess of Somerset d. 1410

EDWARD IV KING OF ENGLAND d. 1483 m. Elizabeth Woodville

Elizabeth m. John de la Pole Earl of Suffolk

HENRY V KING OF ENGLAND d. 1422 m.

John Beaufort Duke of Somerset d. 1444

RICHARD III KING OF ENGLAND d. 1485 (no surviving issue)

Edward Earl of Suffolk (executed 1513)

Owen Tudor (m. 2) d. 1461 ←— Catherine de Valois

George Duke of Clarence

HENRY VI KING OF ENGLAND d. 1471 (no surviving issue)

Edward Earl of Warwick (executed 1499)

Margaret Countess of Salisbury (executed 1541) m. Sir Richard Pole

Jasper Tudor rl of Pembroke d. 1495 (no issue) — Edmund Tudor Earl of Richmond - - - - -m.- - - - Lady Margaret Beaufort d. 1509

Henry Pole Lord Montague (executed 1538)

Reginald Cardinal Pole d. 1558 (no issue)

HOUSE OF TUDOR

HENRY VII KING OF ENGLAND d. 1509 m. Elizabeth of York d. 1503

EDWARD V KING OF ENGLAND / Richard Duke of York

Katherine m. William Courtney Earl of Devon

'The Princes in the Tower' (d. 1483? no issue)

Henry Marquess of Exter (executed 1538)

Edward Courtney d. 1556 (no issue))

Arthur d. 1502 (no issue) m. Katherine of Aragon m.2 HENRY VIII KING OF ENGLAND d. 1547

Mary Tudor (1496–1653)

m.1 Louis XII King of France (no issue)

m.2 Charles Brandon Duke of Suffolk)

m.2 Anne Boleyn

m.3 Jane Seymour

Lady Frances Brandon m. Henry Grey Marquess of Dorset created Duke of Suffolk

MARY I QUEEN OF ENGLAND ('The Lady Mary') d. 1558 m. Philip II, King of Spain (no issue)

ELIZABETH I QUEEN OF ENGLAND d. 1603 (no issue)

EDWARD VI KING OF ENGLAND d. 1553 (no issue)

Lady Jane Grey JANE QUEEN OF ENGLAND (executed 1554) m. Lord Guildford Dudley (no issue)

Lady Katherine Grey d. 1568 m. Edward Seymour Earl of Hertford b. 1539? – d. 1621

Thomas Seymour b. 1563

Edward Seymour Lord Beauchamp b. 1561 – d. 1612

William Seymour created Duke of Somerset d. 1660

GENEALOGICAL TABLE
showing the descent of
HENRY STUART, LORD DARNLEY
from the Royal Houses of
TUDOR and STUART
and other claimants to the English Succession

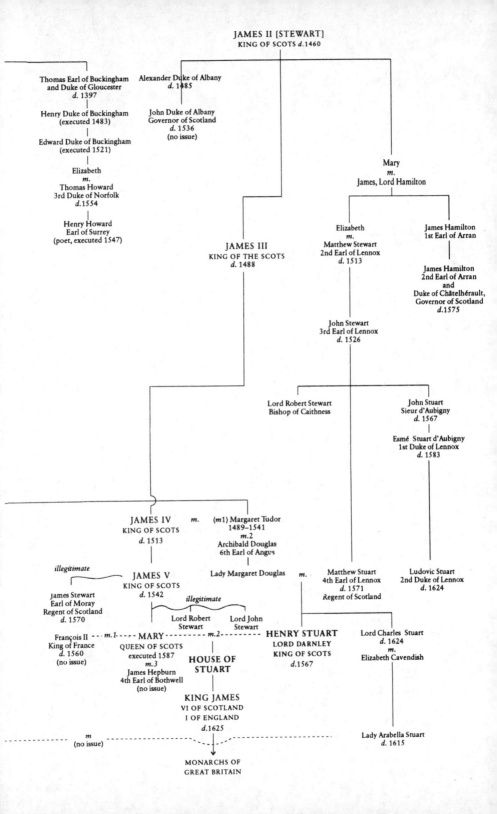

JAMES II [STEWART]
KING OF SCOTS d.1460

Thomas Earl of Buckingham
and Duke of Gloucester
d. 1397

Henry Duke of Buckingham
(executed 1483)

Edward Duke of Buckingham
(executed 1521)

Elizabeth
m.
Thomas Howard
3rd Duke of Norfolk
d.1554

Henry Howard
Earl of Surrey
(poet, executed 1547)

Alexander Duke of Albany
d. 1485

John Duke of Albany
Governor of Scotland
d. 1536
(no issue)

Mary
m.
James, Lord Hamilton

Elizabeth
m.
Matthew Stewart
2nd Earl of Lennox
d. 1513

James Hamilton
1st Earl of Arran

James Hamilton
2nd Earl of Arran
and
Duke of Châtelhérault,
Governor of Scotland
d.1575

JAMES III
KING OF THE SCOTS
d. 1488

John Stewart
3rd Earl of Lennox
d. 1526

Lord Robert Stewart
Bishop of Caithness

John Stuart
Sieur d'Aubigny
d. 1567

Esmé Stuart d'Aubigny
1st Duke of Lennox
d. 1583

JAMES IV   m.   (m1) Margaret Tudor
KING OF SCOTS   1489–1541
d. 1513   m.2
                    Archibald Douglas
                    6th Earl of Angus

illegitimate   JAMES V   Lady Margaret Douglas   m.   Matthew Stuart   Ludovic Stuart
                  KING OF SCOTS   4th Earl of Lennox   2nd Duke of Lennox
James Stewart   d. 1542   d. 1571   d. 1624
Earl of Moray   illegitimate   Regent of Scotland
Regent of Scotland
d. 1570   Lord Robert   Lord John
                    Stewart   Stewart

François II --- m.1 ---- MARY ---------- m.2 --------- HENRY STUART   Lord Charles Stuart
King of France   QUEEN OF SCOTS   LORD DARNLEY   d. 1624
d. 1560   executed 1587   KING OF SCOTS   m.
(no issue)   m.3   d.1567   Elizabeth Cavendish
                    James Hepburn   HOUSE OF
                    4th Earl of Bothwell   STUART
                       (no issue)

                              KING JAMES
                              VI OF SCOTLAND
                              I OF ENGLAND
                              d.1625

      m   Lady Arabella Stuart
(no issue)   d. 1615

                              MONARCHS OF
                              GREAT BRITAIN

PROLOGUE

HENRY STUART, LORD DARNLEY, less frequently called Henry King of Scots, is a central figure in the history of the British Monarchy. His birth gave him a significant position in the succession to the thrones of both Scotland and England. He became King of Scotland through his marriage to Mary Queen of Scots, by whom he was the father of King James VI of Scotland and I of England. He is therefore the ancestor of all the ensuing sovereigns of Great Britain. He was also a murderer, and the victim of one of the most famous unsolved murders of history. It is astonishing that Darnley has never been the subject of a biography, but the lack needs to be explained before it is redressed.[1]

It is not a question of oversight. Darnley has not been ignored by historians and biographers, but he has been overshadowed by his wife. Mary Queen of Scots is one of the favourite biographical subjects of all time. Lady Antonia Fraser, author of the best-known biography of Mary to be written in modern times, commented that in the Collection Blis, in the Bibliothèque Nationale in Paris, 'there are about twenty thousand books listed in the catalogue on Mary Queen of Scots, ranging from John Knox to Jean Plaidy'.[2] In other words, this massive total covers the whole spectrum from contemporary polemics to historical novels. The Queen's most recent biographer, Dr Jenny Wormald, added that 'As the subject of historical studies, and the heroine of romantic fiction, Mary Queen of Scots has a massive lead over all other earthly Maries, only the Virgin scoring more heavily – as even the most cursory glance at the British Library Catalogue of Printed Books makes clear'.[3]

One must ask the reason for this abiding fascination. It is not only that Mary was a queen, and a very beautiful woman, whose life was dramatic and tragic, convulsed by passion and murder, and ended by execution. Though these are the ingredients of a compelling story they are not enough to explain the enduring quality of its fascination, or to account for its endless retelling and reinterpretation. The explanation is in the controversy, for there is no consensus on Mary Queen of Scots, and so far as one can see, there never will be. This is because there was no consensus among her contemporaries.

As a Catholic queen she was vilified by Protestant writers. Though her religion played only a contingent part in her downfall, religious division provided the terminology of sixteenth-century conflict. Adultery and murder – the murder of Darnley – were the charges brought against her by George Buchanan, the mouthpiece of her half-brother James Stewart Earl of Moray, and his supporters, who forced her abdication and ensured her imprisonment in England. At the same time, Moray's public character as a 'godly' nobleman and a defender of Protestantism, and Buchanan's reputation as a leading Protestant scholar, assisted in casting Mary in the role of a papist villainess, a role overtly assigned to her in John Knox's *History of the Reformation*, though during her reign in Scotland she did little to combat the advance of Protestantism.

Mary's defenders inevitably were Catholic writers, and their defence of her changed to praise as her alleged crimes faded from public memory and her misfortunes increased. Long before her death she was represented as a prisoner suffering for her religion; her execution made her, in the eyes of her sympathizers, a Catholic martyr.

Against her, Buchanan's *Detectio Mariae Reginae Scotorum*, also published in Scots as *Ane detectioun of the doinges of Marie Quene of Scottes* (1571), and the relevant chapters of his *Rerum Scoticarum Historia* (1582), and John Knox's *History of the Reformation*, and for her, John Leslie's *A Defence of the Honour of. . . Marie Quene of Scotland* (1569) and Adam Blackwood's *Martyre de la Royne D'Escosse* (1587) and *La Mort de la Royne d'Escosse* (1588), formed the two opposed images of her on which generations of later writers, influenced by their own faith or prejudices, relied.[4] A third image, that of the beautiful *femme fatale*, derived from the Abbé de Brantôme's *Vie des Dames Illustres*, or Book of the Ladies. Brantôme, who had known Mary at the court of France, described her beauty, her idolization by the court poets, and also recounted the tragic story of Châtelard, who followed her to Scotland, maddened beyond reason by his passion for her, and was executed for his presumption in hiding in her bedchamber and attempting to make love to her.

PROLOGUE

Brantôme's portrayal, though it was intended entirely as eulogy, could be utilized either by Mary's detractors or supporters. The adulteress and murderess of the Buchanan/Knox tradition could be represented as a wicked *femme fatale*, a Jezebel or a Clytemnestra. The martyr queen of the Leslie/Blackwood tradition could be represented as a wronged and blameless beauty, a Lucretia (aptly, since she was also by her own account a rape victim), or as any female martyr saint.[5]

William Camden, who wrote his *Annales* (1615) under the aegis of James VI and I, presented the most impartial portrayal of Mary Queen of Scots to appear before the twentieth century. Camden was pressurized by James to write a direct refutation of Buchanan, but he resisted the King's directive, and attempted to rehabilitate Mary's reputation without entering into controversy or stressing her Catholicism. But Camden's attempt at impartiality was premature, for the religious passions at the source of the Marian controversy were still unquenched.[6]

It was not until the polemical inspiration began to fade, and modern biography, with its study of the interaction of causation and character, began to develop, that the stock images of Mary also began to change, and even to blur. Then it became possible to present her as innocent of the crimes imputed to her, but not beyond criticism, or even as guilty of those crimes, but not beyond sympathy. But the result of this breakdown of the old alignments of 'pro' and 'anti' was not consensus but diversification of interpretation. There are now as many Mary Stuarts as there are biographers.

A sample taken from some of the most famous biographies will illustrate the diversity of the resulting literary portraits. To Agnes Strickland, whose *Lives of the Queens of Scotland and English Princesses* (1850–59) is a biographical series dominated by Mary Queen of Scots, the Queen is a blameless, almost saintly figure, as pure in mind and genteel in manners as the feminine ideal of Strickland's own century. To T. F. Henderson, in *Mary Queen of Scots: Her Environment and Tragedy* (1905) and in *The Royal Stewarts* (1919), in which he distils his views on Mary in a biographical essay, Mary is intelligent, courageous and energetic, impassioned with Bothwell, and guilty of complicity in Darnley's death. To Stefan Zweig, in *The Queen of Scots* (1935), Mary is a *grande amoureuse*, aroused to passion and sexual fulfilment by Bothwell, and guilty with him of plotting Darnley's death. To Lady Antonia Fraser, in *Mary Queen of Scots* (1969), Mary is cultivated, intelligent, humane and merciful, innocent of involvement in Darnley's murder, and the victim of Bothwell's ambition; Fraser's is a more sophisticated characterization than Strickland's of a blameless woman. To Professor Gordon Donaldson, in *Mary Queen of Scots* (1974), Mary is an intelligent queen, gifted with religious tolerance beyond the grasp of her contemporaries, guilty not of crimes but of follies, which lead her to a downfall unfortunate for being on the whole undeserved. To Dr Jenny Wormald in *Mary Queen of Scots: A Study in Failure* (1988), Mary is a negligent ruler, guilty of irresponsibility and incompetence, and also guilty of complicity in Darnley's death. The impression derived from reading these biographies (and many more) must be that while Mary Queen of Scots is one of the best-known characters in history, she remains one of the most unknowable. Consequently there will always be more historians and biographers (and novelists and playwrights) eager to explore, and hoping to solve, the enigma of Mary Stuart.

With Darnley the case is entirely different. His contemporaries all stressed the same characteristics in portraying him: his dazzling good looks and unusual height, his accomplishments and his arrogance, his violent temper, and the weakness and instability of his character. These contemporary descriptions will be quoted in their contexts in his lifestory. When pro-Marian and anti-Marian writings began to appear the characterization of Darnley differed very little, because his character did not affect the argument: if Mary were innocent it made her all the more blameless that she had patiently endured an intolerable husband; if she were guilty, then she had wickedly sought to rid herself of an intolerable husband, whom she ought to have endured as virtuous women were expected to do. Thus neither side in the debate had any particular interest in attempting to improve the image of Darnley. Even George Buchanan, who as a Lennoxman was a hereditary supporter of Darnley's father, the Earl of Lennox, did not attempt to credit Darnley with good qualities which he did not possess. The most that Buchanan did was to refrain from speaking any evil of him.[7] Only to Lennox himself, who adored his son, was Darnley an 'innocent lamb'.[8]

As personal rather than polemical biographies of Mary began to appear, presenting her character with such remarkable diversity, the characterization of Darnley remained consistent. As a principal

[4]

character in her story he could never be neglected, yet he was never reconsidered.

Agnes Strickland, basically charitable in her outlook, could find some, if not many, excuses for his conduct:

> When he arrived in Scotland he was but a precocious stripling, deeply versed in classic learning, a proficient on the lute, singing well, and capable of penning a sonnet to his lady's eyebrow; excellent at dancing a galliard, unrivalled at riding at the ring, preeminent in games of strength or skill, but deficient in the royal science of governing himself or others. Proud, passionate, selfish and presumptuous, he had considered it highly derogatory to his marital dignity that the executive power of the realm, whereof he had become titularly joint sovereign, should be directed by the Queen rather than himself . . . The family motto of this unfortunate Prince, AVANT DARNLÉ – DARRIÈRE JAMAIS, having been impressed on his mind from infancy, had flattered him with the notion that his will, if obstinately persisted in, was to carry everything before it. But as he possessed not the qualifications which lead to such results – firmness of purpose, founded on reason, united with conciliating manners, a knowledge of the human heart, and just consideration for the rights of others – he provoked everyone by his presumptuous selfishness, and provoked enmities among the nobles of Scotland which nothing but his death could satisfy.[9]

T. F. Henderson was more magisterially condemnatory:

> A tall and athletic youth of some nineteen years of age [at his first arrival in Scotland], remarkably well set up by the diligent practice of manly exercises, Darnley had also been carefully trained in music, dancing and the more graceful accomplishments; and his late attendance of Queen Elizabeth must have helped to give ease and readiness to his address. His appearance and manner were at first rather prepossessing, and, until his head had become turned by the success of his visit [to the Scottish court] his courtesy gained him general approval. But his essential defects of character could not long be hid; and his new circumstances acted with the artificial power of a hothouse in developing them. On a first acquaintance he was, to use Randolph's phrase, 'well liked for his personage';

but so soon as he became familiar he generally aroused hostility mingled with contempt. His bodily size and strength belied the character of his personality. Though expressing a certain physical vigour, his self-assured, yet babyish countenance, crowned by its close cropped yellow hair . . . was both intellectually and morally weak; and while doltish, proud, obstinate and passionate, he yet, physically strong though he was, possessed, as Mary, to her utter contempt was to discover, 'a heart of wax'.[10]

To Stefan Zweig, Darnley was merely the object of Mary's illusion, and an unworthy one, at that:

The object of her first passion was, strangely enough, no other than the man who was a suitor for political reasons . . . Proneness to illusion was part of the fiery and impatient temperament of Mary Stuart . . . Thus it came to pass that Mary, in her quickly kindled liking for the tall, smooth-chinned young Darnley, failed to perceive that beneath the comely surface there was no depth; that there was no moral strength to this man of powerful muscles, no intellectual culture to back up his courtly manners . . . The young man was crude, vain, with nothing to commend him but good looks. Like countless other men who have been passionately loved by women of outstanding intelligence, Darnley's only merit, his only magic, was that he chanced to be the man who, at the decisive hour, presented himself to a young woman whose will-to-love had been long pent up.[11]

In 1928 Dr Karl Pearson published a curious study entitled *The Skull and Portraits of Henry Stewart, Lord Darnley*, in which he endeavoured to authenticate the portraits of Darnley by comparing them with his purported skull. His conclusion on Darnley's appearance and character from his observation of the skull was:

Darnley was a man with broad brows, a large roundish face . . . and a long nose flattish at the bridge and narrow at the wings, a deep upper lip; of the chin we can say nothing, for the mandible was not with the skull – to judge from the best portraits it was small, semicircular and somewhat recedent . . . We must not off-hand condemn any man for the shape of his skull, but if ever there was a skull which the man in the street would describe as that of a moron or fool, it must certainly be Darnley's and his every action confirms such a judgment.[12]

Lady Antonia Fraser formed a better impression of Darnley's looks, from examination of two of his portraits, but detected a hint of depravity:

> The contemporary portraits by Eworth . . . show that Darnley at the age of eighteen was nothing if not outwardly good-looking. In these portraits Darnley appears at first sight like a young god, with his golden hair, his perfectly shaped face with its short straight nose, the neat oval chin . . . But on closer inspection the god appears to be more Pan than Apollo: there is something faun-like about his pointed ears, the beautiful slanting hazel eyes with their unreadable expression, and even a hint of cruelty in the exquisitely formed mouth with its full rosy lips.[13]

The character sketch which follows stresses his ambition, his vanity, which led him to 'seek solace in the admiration of low company'; and his pursuit of pleasure 'which led him inevitably on to fresh excitements, and thus to more vicious enjoyments as simple pleasures failed'. But 'none of this was apparent to Mary Queen of Scots at her first meeting with her cousin in Scotland . . . She merely saw and admired his charming exterior, which, like a delightful, red, shiny apple ready for the eating, gave no hint of the maggots which lay inside'.[14]

Darnley probably reached the nadir of authorial contempt in Edith Sitwell's *The Queens and the Hive* (1971), an account of the reigns and the relations of Mary Queen of Scots and Queen Elizabeth I, which sometimes wanders into the literary no-man's land between fact and fiction. Sitwell describes Darnley as:

> The long and boneless Waxworks King . . . with his white, flaccid, meaningless face, like the taffeta mask he was so soon to be obliged to wear, with his curling marigold-coloured hair, and his long hands like satin gloves filled with damp sand . . .[15]

Beneath the varieties of literary style, and approach, the characterization of Darnley remains constant: he is superficially attractive, but on closer acquaintance he is revealed as an unpleasant and vicious fool. The only change in the portrayal to be discerned in these selected quotations is the progressive tendency to stress his foolishness and viciousness. Professor Gordon Donaldson's description of him does not reverse the trend, but it concludes with a comment which strikes a slightly different note:

> He was indeed tall, like the Queen herself, and good-looking in a soft kind of way . . . but Mary may have found his smooth mouth and cheeks more attractive than those of more hirsute Scottish nobles. Her susceptibilities may have been intensified by the failure of other marriage plans, for Darnley at least offered a practicable match. In fact Darnley might have been the ideal husband if only he had had a brain to match his birth.[16]

My intention, in the ensuing biography, is to re-examine the man who might have been the ideal husband, and who had the wit to seize the opportunity if not to play the role; to re-examine the familiar events of the reign of Mary Queen of Scots, but with Darnley, instead of the Queen, as the central figure; and to discover, if possible, what was his view of the events in which his participation was disastrous, and his end was murder.

1

DANGEROUS INHERITANCE

Young Darnley is the nearest person in the regal succession to both realms – by right of his father in Scotland, if Mary Stuart . . . has no issue; likewise he is the next heir to the throne of England through his mother, Margaret, Countess of Lennox.[1]

TOWARDS NOON ON 22 August 1485, Henry Tudor, Earl of Richmond, surveyed the carnage on Redmoor Plain, near the village of Market Bosworth in Leicestershire. The casualties of battle belonged mostly to the enemy, and included their commander, King Richard III. The Earl of Richmond was surrounded by his soldiers who shouted 'God save King Henry! God save King Henry!' Then his stepfather Lord Stanley approached with a gold circlet, the 'crown of ornament' which had fallen from King Richard's helm, and placed it on Henry's head. Later tradition added that Stanley had pulled it from a thorn bush, a detail that seemed appropriate in an age attuned to symbolism.[2] The Battle of Bosworth ended simultaneously the Wars of the Roses and the Plantagenet dynasty, and the impromptu crowning acknowledged the victor as the first Tudor King, Henry VII. Darnley was his great-grandson.

The Tudor dynasty was inaugurated with the rituals of Church and State. The accession of Henry VII was confirmed by Act of Parliament and sanctified by coronation. But the impression remained that he was a usurper and a parvenu. Undoubtedly he had usurped the throne of Richard III, which he had won by battle, but he was no parvenu, for his blood was royal though his claim to the succession was tenuous. His mother, Lady Margaret Beaufort, was a great-great-granddaughter of Edward III, but she descended from the third marriage of the King's third son, John of Gaunt, Duke of Lancaster, a line of dubious legitimacy, debarred from the succession by Act of Parliament. Henry's father, Edmund Tudor, Earl of Richmond, was the son of Henry V's widow, Catherine de Valois, by her second husband, Owen Tudor, an impoverished Welsh nobleman who claimed descent from the mythic British King Cadwallader. Royal blood, however dubious and diluted, gave Henry of Richmond his claim to the throne. The rituals of crowning and anointing conferred on him a semi-divine status. Under the Tudors the status of monarchy grew so exalted that when one of Elizabeth I's ministers declared 'She is our God on earth', he was merely affirming what everyone believed.[3]

His kingship established, Henry VII married Elizabeth of York, eldest daughter of Edward IV, a marriage that was celebrated as the union of the White Rose and the Red, a reconciliation that promised an era of peace. But peace seemed perpetually threatened by the uncertainty of the succession, for the Tudor bloodline ran thin. Henry VII was the only son of an only daughter, and his father was the only one of three brothers to beget a child. Henry himself fathered several children, but they in turn were not prolific. The death of his elder son left the male line once again represented by a single life. The younger son was Henry VIII, whose six wives produced only three children, and those three produced none. It was not surprising that the Tudor sovereigns viewed all their relatives with suspicion. These were kinsmen or kinswomen who might win the Crown if the established succession failed, but must not be seen to plot or even to hope for it. Henry VIII endeavoured to protect his line by desperate efforts to beget heirs. It was the imperative of the succession rather than unusual uxoriousness which drove him from marriage to marriage. Four of his wives might have expected the status of mistress rather than queen, had not his quest for an heir led him to formalize his liaisons.

Henry VIII also sought to protect the succession by eliminating potential rivals. He executed many descendants of Edward III whose only offence was their possession of Plantagenet blood. While Henry VII contented himself with the execution of Edward, Earl of Warwick, nephew of Edward IV, and Perkin Warbeck, the pretender who claimed to be Edward IV's younger son, both in 1499, Henry VIII executed Edmund, Earl of Suffolk in 1513, Edward, Duke of Buckingham in 1521, Henry, Lord Montague and Henry, Marquess of Exeter in 1538, Margaret, Countess of Salisbury in 1541 and Henry, Earl of Surrey in 1547 (for their relationship to the Tudors, see Genealogical Table). Edward Courtney, son of the Marquess of Exeter, survived this slaughter and was canvassed as a possible husband for Elizabeth, but he died a natural death in 1556, two years before her accession.

Ten years later, when she received the news of the birth of a son to Mary Queen of Scots and Darnley, Elizabeth famously described herself as 'a barren stock'. Probably this was the moment of truth at which she recognized that the Tudor dynasty would end with her; yet she continued until she could no longer sustain the pretence that she might bear children to exact the maximum political advantage from her diplomatic courtships. Even when Elizabeth was conclusively cast in the role of the Virgin Queen she refused to make an official pronouncement on the succession, though during the last years of her reign it became increasingly obvious that the son of Mary and Darnley would succeed her.

The succession problem which bedevilled the Tudor dynasty for most of its existence in the end resolved itself with easy acceptance of the strongest claimant, but not before it had cost many lives and endangered many more. Tudor blood and proximity to the succession was Darnley's dangerous inheritance.

In the early years of the dynasty the Tudor succession seemed securely established. Elizabeth of York bore Henry VII seven children, four of whom reached adulthood: Arthur (born 1486), Margaret (born 1489), Henry – the future Henry VIII (born 1491) – and Mary (born 1496). These children provided the means of dynastic aggrandizement, through the negotiation of prestigious marriages. In 1501 Arthur was married to Katherine of Aragon, daughter of the Spanish sovereigns Ferdinand of Aragon and Isabella of Castile, and in 1503 Margaret was married to James IV of Scotland. Both these alliances helped to consolidate the Tudor dynasty, for Spain, unified by the marriage of Ferdinand and Isabella, was emerging as one of the great powers of Europe, and under the Stewart dynasty Scotland had steadily increased its prestige among the smaller kingdoms. The particular purpose of the Scottish marriage was to secure perpetual peace between England and Scotland, which had spent centuries intermittently at war.

Princesses were not consulted about their marriages. Though canon law required that their consent be publicly asked and given, it was unthinkable that they would refuse. They were dynastic sacrifices to their fathers' policies. Katherine of Aragon was so great a prize to England that when Arthur died in 1502 Henry VII retained her as a diplomatic pawn until his death, and even considered marrying her himself. In 1509 Henry VIII succeeded and married the Spanish Princess, with ultimately tragic consequences.

Meanwhile, Margaret adapted herself to life in Scotland, with the husband to whom she had been married by proxy when he was thirty and she thirteen. James IV was an able and popular ruler, with a wide range of talents and interests – a linguist, musician, athlete and soldier, and a knowledgeable patron of the arts and sciences. He was also a lover of beautiful women, and unfortunately Margaret was no more than averagely pretty, though Scottish courtly poets dutifully hailed her as 'fairest of every fair' and 'Freshest Queen of Flowers'. Once she had overcome her early resentment of James's mistresses and illegitimate children, she was able to admit to her brother Henry VIII, 'our husband is ever the longer the better to us'.[4]

The deepest emotion James and Margaret shared was probably sorrow, for of their five children only one reached adulthood, the son who reigned as James V. But Margaret's greatest misfortune was political. The Anglo-Scottish alliance which her marriage had been intended to cement broke down under the stress of international conflicts, and in a war largely provoked by the bellicosity of Henry VIII, her husband was killed in the disastrous defeat of Flodden, in 1513. Her son became King at the age of seventeen months, and her appointment as his tutrix, or guardian, granted her by the will of James IV, was much resented since she was a representative of the enemy power which had caused the death of a much-loved King. It was a situation which might have defeated the most resourceful of women, and though Margaret possessed courage and resilience she lacked the political skill to conciliate or dominate the opposition. She felt the need of comfort and protection, and may even, with pathetic optimism, have hoped for happiness. In 1514 Margaret married – 'for her pleasure' in the general opinion – Archibald Douglas, sixth Earl of Angus. He was a handsome and attractive young man, though his uncle the Bishop of Dunkeld described him as 'a young witless fool'.[5] However, this is a commonplace criticism of the younger generation by the elder, and if Angus, like many young people, was high-spirited and light-hearted, he would have attracted the unhappy Margaret. But she may also have hoped that he would bring her political support, for he was the nominal head of the great house of Douglas, one of the most powerful families of Scotland, and had mature kinsmen to teach him how to use his power. It was not long before he surprised Margaret with the ruthlessness of his ambition; but by then they had quarrelled, and the power that she had hoped would support her was deployed against her.

Margaret's remarriage enabled her opponents to claim that she should forfeit her guardianship of the King, under the terms of James IV's will. They invited the King's nearest kinsman, John, Duke of Albany, to assume governership of the realm, which accorded with earlier Scottish custom. He was the son of Alexander, Duke of Albany, brother of King James III, who had been banished for plotting against the King, and had gone to live in France, where he had married and died, leaving a son who grew up as a Frenchman. Thus, the invitation extended to the younger Albany implied a renewal of Scotland's 'auld alliance' with France, and a repudiation of the English influence represented by Margaret.

When Albany arrived in Scotland in May 1515, he demanded custody of the King, to secure his authority in the kingdom, though he did not intend to deny Margaret access to her son. Margaret initially refused to relinquish the child who was also the symbol of her own authority. But she could not long resist, and having lost custody of the King and seen her own chance of retaining power evaporate, she resolved to flee the country and take refuge in England. Her pregnancy by Angus provided the opportunity. As its full term approached she went to Linlithgow Palace and ceremonially entered her 'lying-in chamber' in accordance with royal custom, to await the birth of her child. Thence she slipped away secretly and, escorted by Angus, crossed the Border, to seek the protection of the English Warden of the Marches, Lord Dacre, at Harbottle Castle, in Northumberland. On 8 October 1515 'she was delivered and brought to bed of a fair young lady' – the Lady Margaret Douglas, who was baptized the following day with a haste that suggests anxiety for her survival. But anxiety was unnecessary, for Lady Margaret lived long enough to see her son Lord Darnley become King Consort of Scotland, and her grandson crowned as James VI, King of Scots, though not long enough to witness the ultimate triumph of his accession to the throne of England.

Queen Margaret, who always suffered in childbed, was slow to recover after the birth of her daughter, and too weak to resume her journey to England as worsening weather increased the difficulties of travel. She and her child moved from Harbottle to more comfortable quarters at Morpeth, and remained there until the spring. They left Morpeth on 8 April 1516, and travelled slowly south. Angus, who had been allowed to visit his wife at Morpeth, but not to stay with her, returned to Scotland and capitulated to Albany, to save his estates from confiscation for his 'rebellious' support of Margaret. His return also enabled him to resume his affair with his mistress, Janet Stewart of Traquair.

On 4 May Margaret made her state entry into London, riding a white palfrey, side by side with her brother King Henry, and escorted by a procession of courtiers. At the English court Margaret formed a trio of queens, with her sister-in-law Katherine of Aragon and her younger sister Mary, the widow of Louis XII of France, who was still known as 'the French Queen', though she had recently married Charles Brandon, Duke of Suffolk.[6] All three queens gave birth to daughters in successive years. Lady Margaret Douglas was the eldest, followed by Queen Katherine's daughter, Princess Mary, born in February 1516. In 1517 the Queen-Duchess of Suffolk gave birth to Lady Frances Brandon, who would become the mother of Lady Jane Grey, the nine days' Queen. The destinies of these three cousins might have been happier had Henry VIII been able to succeed in his current ambition to arrange a marriage between Princess Mary and Margaret's son James V. However, Albany favoured a French marriage for him, and negotiated a treaty which promised him a French bride.

Margaret was reluctant to leave the English court, where pleasure without responsibility was very much to her taste, but early in 1517 Henry ordered her back to Scotland to attempt to reassert English influence there, and to make her peace with her husband, whose defection had greatly offended her. Margaret's arrival in Scotland immediately followed Albany's departure on a visit to France where he remained until 1521. He had left Scottish affairs in the hands of a Council of Regency, of which Angus was a member. Margaret was formally reconciled with Angus, but the reconciliation foundered, presumably when she discovered his liaison with Janet Stewart. A power struggle between Angus and Margaret followed, soon embittered by Margaret's resolve to seek a divorce. Henry VIII, shocked by such an ungodly and immoral proceeding, transferred his sympathy to Angus, as the wronged husband. Angus expressed his gratitude, 'with much effusion and in excellent Scots'[7]:

> Maist excellent and redoutit prince, it lyis not in my little possibili-
> tie to rendir thankis unto your maist nobill hynes, that has intendit
> and procurit sa excedand wislye this my pure [poor] causs . . .
> Quhairfor, besyde the rewarde of God, quhilk I doute nocht bot
> youre grace sall ressaif for sa meritable labour, I sall endevour and
> abandoune perpetually my pure service in every behalf and sort
> to me possible, unto youre maist nobill excellence . . . and salbe
> all tymes reddy eftire my pure power, althoucht it was sua that
> youre hienes commandit me furthwith to pas one fute to Jerusalem,
> and fecht with the Turkis to the dede [death] for youre causs . . .

The absence of Albany was marked by violent strife between the members of the Council of Regency, street fighting between their supporters, and continuing quarrels between Margaret and her hus-band. In 1520 Angus seized their daughter Lady Margaret Douglas and placed her in the Douglas stronghold of Tantallon Castle on the east coast of Scotland, with a household of Douglas ladies. Angus, like many estranged fathers, wanted possession of his child, a pretty little redhead whom he loved devotedly, but he was also aware of her potential value in the international marriage market, as the half-sister of the King of Scots and niece of the King of England. He brought her up to regard herself as a Princess of Scotland, but 'deriv-ing from her English birth claims in regard of the neighbouring king-dom beyond those of her royal brother James V'.[8]

Angus's letter to Henry VIII gives the flavour of the language that Lady Margaret Douglas would have heard and learnt to speak in her father's household. During her first five years of life she had been surrounded by both Scots and English speakers, but henceforward the predominant language would be Scots. Between 1522 and 1524 the household removed to France, an honourable exile imposed by Albany to rid Scotland of Angus's disruptive presence. Angus knew no French, and on his arrival in Paris, the English diplomat Sir Thomas Cheyne, who assumed he had come as ambassador, wondered how he would manage to perform his duties.[9] Presumably, in the course of two years' residence in France, Angus learnt some French, and it is likely that his daughter did so too, as modern languages were considered suitable subjects of study for women.

The Duke of Albany finally left Scotland in 1524, and his departure cleared the way for Angus's return. On his arrival Angus found that Queen Margaret, supported by his enemy the Earl of Arran, had seized power, and on the pretext that the twelve-year-old James V was now of age to rule, they had invested him with the symbols of sovereignty and were ruling in his name. Exile had matured Angus. His ambition remained, but he pursued it with more finesse. He had returned home by way of the English court, to assure himself of the support of Henry VIII, who was persuaded that he would serve English interests more efficiently than Margaret and 'better than five earls of Arran'. Angus further ingratiated himself with Henry by seeking a new reconciliation with Queen Margaret, but she refused his advances, as she was now hoping to obtain her divorce through the assistance of Albany, who had influence with the Pope.[10]

While Queen Margaret awaited the result of her petition she acted in an outwardly friendly fashion towards Angus, who might yet make enough trouble to ruin her plans. In March 1525 he was admitted as a member of her Council. In July it was arranged that a rota of lords – Angus, Arran, Lennox and Argyll – should be responsible for the King's safety, each guarding him for a quarter of the year. Angus took responsibility first, but when the time came for him to give way to the next member of the rota, in November 1525, he refused to do so. The coup by which he gained power was both simple and bloodless. He followed it by employing his younger brother, Sir George Douglas of Pittendriech, his constant supporter and adviser, to pressurize the young King to write to Queen Margaret to assure her that 'with none more cheerfully, willingly and contentedly could he live and spend his time than with the Earl of Angus'. This was far from the truth, but if Angus hoped to cast the opprobrium on his brother by using him to bully the King, he failed completely. James, whose mind had been poisoned against Angus by his mother already, thenceforward regarded his stepfather with a loathing that assured Angus's downfall sooner or later. However, Angus remained *de facto* ruler of Scotland until 1528.

Queen Margaret gained her divorce in 1526, and married her third husband, Henry Stewart, younger son of Lord Avondale. James V later created him Lord Methven, to honour his mother; but it was reported that Henry VIII 'never carried such respect to his sister as he had done before'. He now relied upon Angus, whom he continued to regard as his lawful brother-in-law, to look after English interests in Scotland. But Angus's anglophile regime had the long-term effect of ensuring that James V would react by favouring the auld alliance with France. In the meantime Angus planted his kinsmen in key positions in the administration and in the King's household, while their wives continued to attend on Lady Margaret Douglas. It seems likely that Lady Margaret would have met her half-brother the King at this time, but with the estrangement of her parents she never saw her mother again.

Angus proved a competent ruler whose regime survived two attempts to rescue the King by force of arms. The second culminated in a battle near Linlithgow on 4 September 1526, in which John, third Earl of Lennox, to whom James had appealed for deliverance, was defeated and captured, and disgracefully murdered after his surrender.[11] Eventually James V, a resourceful youth, arranged his own escape towards the end of May 1528, and immediately won widespread support from the nobility, who had resented the Douglases' monopoly of power. Angus resisted the downfall of his family, and fought a vigorous rearguard action. The castle of Tantallon was besieged, and Lady Margaret and her ladies escaped to wander the countryside as fugitives. King James sent out scouts to find his sister and restore her to her mother, but Angus spirited her across the Border and found refuge for her in Norham Castle, and later placed her in the protective custody of Captain Strangeways, in Berwick, the walled town that was England's northern outpost. In July 1529 Strangeways reported that he had been warned that Margaret might be 'stolen and withdrawn into Scotland, which caused me to take more labour for her sure-keeping; yet I know well she was never merrier nor more pleased and content than she is now, as she ofttimes repeats'.[12] No doubt she was thankful to be safe, and grateful to Strangeways for protecting her from delivery to her mother. Angus had monopolized the affection of his daughter, as had Margaret that of her son.

*   *   *

Finally acknowledging defeat, Angus retired to England, where he lived for many years as the pensioner of Henry VIII. At the beginning of 1530 Lady Margaret was also in England, first as the guest of her aunt Mary, Queen-Duchess of Suffolk, and then at Newhall in Essex, with her cousin the Princess Mary. The two young girls, who had spent a brief time together as babies, now formed a lasting friendship which benefitted Margaret when Mary became Queen. For the present she was fortunate in winning the affection of her terrifyingly capricious uncle Henry VIII. This did not prevent her from offending him, but it probably saved her from the worst consequences of her offences.

Lady Margaret Douglas arrived in England at a time of crisis, when the King had entered his long struggle with the papacy to obtain the annulment of his marriage to Katherine of Aragon. The Queen continued to preside at court, accorded hollow honours, while Anne Boleyn appeared openly as the King's companion. Lady Margaret's first friends in England were the women who were about to suffer eclipse: Queen Katherine herself, the Queen-Duchess of Suffolk, who would withdraw from her brother's court when Anne Boleyn became his Queen, the Princess Mary, and the Lady Governess of her household, the Countess of Salisbury, who would lose her head in 1541. Lady Margaret quickly learnt to keep her balance in the shifting sands of the court. While maintaining her friendship with Princess Mary, she did not reject the overtures of the future Queen and her relations. As a dependant on Henry VIII's charity, she wisely recognized that she could not afford to insult those whom he favoured. She must have possessed remarkable tact to retain the friendship of both groups.

During 1532 and 1533 Princess Mary kept her establishment as the King's legitimate daughter and heiress, with the Countess of Salisbury as Lady Governess and Lady Margaret Douglas as First Lady of the Household. But the world was changing around them. Step by step the King dismantled the powers of the papacy in England and substituted his own. The process culminated in the Act of Supremacy of 1534 which declared that the King 'is and ought to be Supreme Head of the Church of England'; but even before that the Act in Restraint of Appeals of 1533 had declared that all cases dealing with wills, marriages, and other 'spiritual' causes should be settled in England, and not carried by appeal to Rome. Under this Act, on 23 May 1533, Henry's marriage to Katherine of Aragon was annulled by the new Archbishop of Canterbury, Thomas Cranmer; but on 25 January, without awaiting the annulment, Henry had secretly married Anne Boleyn, who was already pregnant. She was crowned and anointed Queen on 1 June, now visibly and proudly carrying the infant which she and the King were sublimely confident would be the Prince for whose sake the King was transforming the relationship of Church and State.

The child, born on 7 September 1533, was a daughter, the future Elizabeth I, an appalling disappointment when she entered the world, and a bastard in the eyes of almost everyone except the father who had framed his own laws to legitimize her. In October Henry ordered that Princess Mary's household at Newhall should be disbanded, and Mary, her status now reduced from that of princess to 'the Lady Mary', should enter the household of her new half-sister, the Princess Elizabeth. Lady Margaret Douglas was appointed First Lady of the newborn Princess's household, which gave her precedence over the Lady Mary. But even this humiliation of the former Princess, a profound one in a period imbued with respect for hierarchy, did not disrupt their friendship.

In the circle of the new Queen was a young courtier with whom Lady Margaret fell in love, and he with her. He was Lord Thomas Howard, the Queen's uncle, though he was scarcely older than she. Anne Boleyn's mother was Lady Elizabeth Howard, daughter of the second Duke of Norfolk by his first marriage. Lord Thomas was a son of the Duke by his second marriage. As Norfolk had married for the first time in 1472 and for the second time in 1507 and fathered twenty-two children, his family was sufficiently spaced out for Queen Anne to have an uncle young enough to be her brother.[13]

An attachment between the Queen's kinsman and the King's niece seemed suitable, but was unequal enough to be considered a 'disparagement' to Lady Margaret. Lord Thomas Howard lacked both wealth and prospects: his father had died in 1524, and his eldest half-brother was third Duke of Norfolk. He was not much of a match for a royal lady, and his genuine love for Lady Margaret would have had little chance of success if Queen Anne had not seen the advantage of another link between the royal house and her own family. Through her persuasions the King permitted Lady Margaret Douglas and Lord Thomas Howard to be betrothed. A sixteenth-century betrothal was more formal than a twentieth-century engagement. It was a legal contract, not simply a personal commitment. There were two forms of betrothal, *per verba de futuro* and *per verba de praesenti*, the one promising future marriage, the other immediately binding. Betrothal *per verba de praesenti* could be consummated at once, with a church ceremony to follow. Whichever form of betrothal Margaret and Thomas solemnized, and whether or not they cohabited, the outcome was disastrous.

Queen Anne's heyday was short. Her downfall was threatened when she bore the King a daughter instead of the promised son, and certain when her miscarriage of a son convinced the King that their marriage did not enjoy the blessing of God. Anne was arrested on 2 May 1536, accused of multiple adultery and of incest with her brother, Lord Rochford. The trials and executions of all the accused followed speedily. The purpose of a State trial was not to prove guilt but to demonstrate it, so the verdict was a foregone conclusion. On 17 May the marriage of Henry VIII and Anne Boleyn was annulled, and on 19 May Anne was beheaded. Within two weeks the King married one of her ladies-in-waiting, Jane Seymour. The new Queen was one of ten children, and it was hoped that her mother's fecundity was an indicator of her own.[14]

On 15 June Henry and Queen Jane attended the feast of Corpus Christi in Westminster Abbey, and the Queen's train was borne by Lady Margaret. Her position at court seemed assured, but disaster struck when suddenly the King perceived a new significance in the recent sequence of events. The annulments of his first two marriages had *ipso facto* rendered the daughters of those marriages illegitimate. This meant that until Queen Jane produced a child his heir was either his nephew James V of Scotland or his niece Lady Margaret Douglas, whose claim might be preferred since she was not an 'alien', having been born in England. Suddenly the innocent love affair of Lady Margaret and Lord Thomas Howard assumed a sinister aspect in the King's eyes: surely, in wooing Lady Margaret, the ambitious young man had been aiming at the throne!

Lord Thomas Howard was impeached for having 'traitorously contracted himself by crafty, fair and flattering words to and with the Lady Margaret Douglas . . . by the which it is vehemently to be suspected that the said Lord Thomas falsely, craftily and traitorously hath imagined and compassed . . . by reason of marriage in so high a blood . . . [to] . . . aspire by her to the imperial crown of this realm . . .'[15] The impeachment was followed by a statute making it high treason for anyone to marry or seduce any lady related to the blood royal within specified degrees, which included the children of the King's brother or sister. An additional enactment extended the penalty for treason to 'the woman so offending, who shall suffer suchlike death and punishment as appointed to the man so offending'.[16]

On 18 July the unfortunate lovers were arrested and imprisoned in the Tower of London, subject to sentence of death under the new legislation. The danger of proximity to the succession, especially when there was no direct heir, had never been so clearly demonstrated. In this terrifying situation Margaret and Thomas did not despair. Though incarcerated separately they managed to communicate. Someone who was kindly or corruptible, or possibly both, delivered their missives, which were poems. The courtiers of Henry VIII habitually wrote poetry. Two of them, Sir Thomas Wyatt and Henry Howard, Earl of Surrey, were major poets of their time. Others wrote poems of varying quality, but it was part of their culture to express their emotions in verse, as cultivated people of later generations would express them in diaries.

Lord Thomas Howard wrote:

> Now may I morne as one off late
>   Dryven by force from my delyte,
> And can not see my lonely mate
>   To whom for ever my hart ys plyte . . . [plighted]

> I wyll not swerve I yow insure [assure]
>   For gold nor yet for worldly fere;
> But lyke as yerne [iron] I wyll indure
>   Suche faythful love to yow I bere . . .

> And I wyll promyse yow agayne
>   To thynke off yow I wyll not lett [cease]
> For nothyng cowld relesse my payne
>   But to thynke on yow my lover swete.[17]

Lady Margaret replied with a confidence which must have been wonderfully encouraging:

> I may well say with joyfull harte
>   As never woman myght say beforn [before]
> That I have takyn to my part
>   The faythfullyst lover that ever was born.

> Great paynes he suffereth for my sake
>   Contynually both nyght and day,
> For all the paynes that he doth take
>   From me hys love wyll not decay.

> Wyth thretnyng great he hath ben payd
>   Off payne and yke [also] off punnysment,
> Yet all fere asyde he hath layed;
>   To love me best was hys yntent.

> Who shall let me then off ryght [deny me the right]
>   Onto myself hym to retane
> And love hym best both day and nyght
>   Yn recompens off hys great payne?

> Yff I had more, more he shold have,
>   And that I kno he knowys full well;
> To love hym best unto my grave,
>   Off that he may both bye and sell . . .[18]

It will be noted that the diction of this poem is anglicized. Though Lady Margaret would have been accustomed to Scots in her father's household, and probably would still have spoken with a Scots accent, she was now writing in English. Her poem breathes a remarkable spirit of confidence, both in her lover's fidelity and in her own capacity to defend him. His reply was appreciative of her poem and her sentiments. It also contains an acknowledgement that their relationship was socially unequal ('Synce ye desende from your degre'), but was equalized by the quality of his devotion:

> To yowr gentyll letters an answere to resyte,
>   Both I and my penne there to wyll aply,
> And thowgh that I can not your goodnes aquyte
>   In ryme and myter [metre] elegantly
>   Yet do I meane as faythfully
> As ever dyd lover for hys part,
> I tak God to record whych knowyth my hart.

> And where as ye wyll contynew myne
>   To reporte for me ye may be bold,
> That yff I had lyves as Argus had yne*,
>   Yet soner all them lyse [lose] I wold
>   Then to be tempte for fere or for gold
> Yow to refuse or to forsake
> Wych ys my faythful and lovyng make [mate]

> Wych faythfulnes ye dyd ever pretend [claim]
>   And gentylnes as now I see
> Off me wych was yowr pore old frend,
>   Yowr lovyng husband now to be;
>   Synce ye desende from your degre
> Take ye thys unto yowr part
> My faythful, true and lovyng hart.

> For terme off lyfe thys gyft ye have.
>   Thus now adwe myn one [mine own] swete wyfe
> From T.H. wych nought doth crave
>   But yow, the stay off all my lyfe;
>   And they that wold other bate or stryfe [either oppose or resist]
> To be tyed wythyn ower lovyng bandys,
> I wold they were on Goodwyn Sandys.[19]

* Argus or Argos was a monster in Greek mythology, who had many eyes, which were taken by the goddess Hera to deck the peacock's tail.

If the concluding reference to the notorious quicksands is intended as a metaphor for the quicksands of the court which had engulfed Thomas himself and his beloved, then his poem gains an extra dimension; but even without this it gives the poem a sombre conclusion. Lord Thomas Howard lacked the lyric genius of his nephew the Earl of Surrey, but both his verses and Lady Margaret's have a poignant sincerity.

In August news reached Queen Margaret in Scotland that her daughter was imprisoned in the Tower. She wrote King Henry an impassioned plea for her daughter's pardon and release, and suggested that Margaret should return to Scotland 'so that in time coming she shall never come into your Grace's presence'.[20] Henry ignored both the plea and the suggestion. He had no intention of losing control of his niece, though he intended to reduce her status, which could not be permitted to remain superior to that of his daughters. He instructed his ambassador in Scotland, Lord William Howard (a brother of the imprisoned Lord Thomas), to find Janet Stewart of Traquair, and attempt to prove that Queen Margaret's marriage to Angus had been invalid, either because of precontract or bigamy. Though Angus was highly embarrassed at being publicly reminded of Janet's existence, there was no evidence that she had been an impediment to his marriage with the Queen. However, Henry decided that Janet's relationship with Angus sufficed for his purposes, and Margaret was pronounced illegitimate, removing her for the present from the English succession. But when Queen Margaret died in 1541 she made a deathbed declaration that Angus had been her lawful husband, which removed the stigma from Margaret's birth. In any case, the succession now seemed to be assured in the person of Prince Edward, born to Queen Jane on 12 October 1537.

By this time Lady Margaret had been in prison for over a year. The previous autumn she had fallen ill in the Tower and believed herself to be dying. Her earlier optimism had vanished, and now the prospect of death seemed welcome:

> Thys touer ye se ys strong and hye,
> And the dooris fast barred have I
> That no wight my pairpose let shold:
> For to be quen of all Ytaly
> Nat on[e] day lenger leve I wold.[21]

But Margaret recovered and was transferred to Syon Abbey, a Bridgettine convent in Middlesex, on the banks of the Thames. Here she showed some recovery of spirit by wrangling with the Abbess, Dame Agnes Jourdain, over the number of servants permitted her. She had arrived with a gentleman usher, a gentleman-in-waiting, a groom of the chamber and a chaplain, and had added two servants of Lord Thomas Howard, who had come to her pleading destitution. This dispute, which shows Lady Margaret in a creditable light, attempting to help the unfortunate men in the midst of her own misfortunes, was interrupted by a letter from Thomas Cromwell, the King's chief minister, and at this time Lord Privy Seal, offering her pardon and restoration to the King's favour, if she would agree to renounce Lord Thomas Howard.

As Margaret was still under sentence of death, and had abandoned the hope that she would ever be reunited with Lord Thomas, it was not surprising that she grasped at the offer of restoration to favour. She wrote Cromwell an abject letter:

My Lord,

What cause I have to give you thanks, and how much bound I am unto you, that by your means hath gotten me, as I trust, the King's grace and favour again! Besides that it pleaseth you to write and give me knowledge wherein I may earn his Grace's displeasure again . . . I assure you, my lord, I will never do that thing willingly that should offend his Grace . . .

Of Lord Thomas Howard she wrote '. . . I beseech you not to think that any fancy doth remain in me touching him, but that all my study and care is how to please the King's Grace and to continue in his favour . . .' She concluded this pitiful letter by asking Cromwell 'to be so good as to get my poor servants their wages . . .'[22] She did not date it, so there is no knowing how long elapsed between her writing it and her liberation.

She was set free almost immediately after the birth of Prince Edward, on 12 October. Queen Jane died of puerperal fever on 24 October, and Margaret's first public duty was to ride in her funeral procession on 12 November. Dressed in black and mounted on a horse caparisoned in black, she was accompanied by the Lady Mary, and her cousin Frances, daughter of the Queen-Duchess of Suffolk. Margaret had a private reason for wearing mourning more compelling than the public one: on 31 October Lord Thomas Howard had died in the Tower. The contemporary chronicler Wriothesley reported that she 'took his death very heavily', and no doubt she blamed herself for having escaped by repudiating him, if not directly for his death. His nephew the Earl of Surrey had no doubts that he had died for love of her:

> For you yourself doth know
>   It is not long ago
> Sith for his love one of our race
>   Did end his life in woe,
> In Tower both strong and high
>   For his assured truth,
> Wherein with tears he spent his breath,
>   Alas, the more the ruth [sorrow].[23]

With the death of Lord Thomas Howard, Margaret was left in the embarrassing position of official doubt as to whether she was a widow or a virgin. Thomas had addressed her as 'myn one swete wyfe', but when she repudiated him she stressed to Cromwell that she was 'a maid'.[24] She was named among Queen Jane's mourners as 'Lady Margaret Howard, the King's niece'. But possibly King Henry reflected that her value as a marriageable young woman was greater as a virgin than as a widow, and chose to believe her. It was as Lady Margaret Douglas that she was appointed First Lady to Henry's fourth Queen, Anne of Cleves, a brief arrangement, as the King's disappointment with Anne of Cleves, and the collapse of the political alliance against the Emperor Charles V which had made it seem desirable, led to a speedy declaration of nullity, and also to the fall of Thomas Cromwell, who was blamed for the marriage and the alliance, and went to the block. Lady Margaret was immediately appointed First Lady to Henry VIII's fifth Queen, Katherine Howard.

On 28 July 1540 the King, on the rebound from disillusionment, married for love a pretty young woman he called his *rutilans rosa sine spina* – 'blushing rose without a thorn' – a daughter of Lord Edmund Howard, yet another son of the prolific second Duke of Norfolk. She was thus the niece of Lord Thomas Howard and the first cousin of Anne Boleyn. Queen Katherine Howard was expected to advance her family's fortunes, and one of the early beneficiaries was her brother Sir Charles Howard, who was appointed to the King's Privy Chamber.[25] The young man at once paid court to Lady Margaret, and she unwisely encouraged his advances. Was she attempting to recapture the happiness that she had lost, or obscurely seeking to make amends for having rejected another Howard? Or was she frightened that time was passing her by? She was approaching twenty-five, an age at which most royal and aristocratic ladies were already married. She must have assumed that Queen Katherine could make the King look favourably on her brother's courtship. But apparently she could not. This time there was not even a brief period of sunshine in which Margaret's new attachment could flower. She found herself once again a reluctant guest at Syon Abbey. The Dissolution of the Monasteries had swept away Dame Agnes Jourdain and her nuns, and the secularized Abbey was now a royal manor in the keepership of Sir John Gates. He received Lady Margaret rather as a guest than a prisoner, and her stay must have been all the more pleasant as she had the Lady Mary as her companion. They remained at Syon together while Henry VIII and Queen Katherine made their progress to the north, recently pacified after the Catholic uprising of the Pilgrimage of Grace. Henry's destination was York where a meeting was planned with James V. Henry hoped to woo James away from alliance with France and the papacy by pointing out the advantages of asserting his authority over the Church and seizing the clerical wealth of his country. But he had no opportunity to do so, for James reneged on the arrangement. Henry waited ten days, resenting James's non-appearance as an appalling snub, and began his return journey south festering with hostility towards his nephew.

Lady Margaret's gaffe in welcoming the advances of Sir Charles Howard had been Henry's principal reason for sequestering her at Syon, but a secondary reason may have been to ensure that she did not meet her half-brother King James. He would not have wished to provide an opportunity for a rapprochement between them, or for plotting, of which he was increasingly ready to suspect everyone. Whatever Margaret may have felt at being left behind when the court rode north, undoubtedly she would soon have been profoundly thankful to have been left.

At the beginning of November the King and Queen were at

Hampton Court, where Henry received a devastating series of revelations that Katherine Howard had been unchaste before their marriage, and unfaithful after it. In the face of this colossal drama the minor misdeeds of Lady Margaret Douglas seemed insignificant. Katherine Howard's tragedy, indeed, may have rescued her from further disfavour. By mid-November Syon Abbey was required as a prison for the unfortunate Queen. The Lady Mary was sent to join the household of Prince Edward, and Lady Margaret was sent to Kenninghall in Norfolk, with Mary Howard, Duchess of Richmond, as her companion and chaperone.[26] Before she left she had an unpleasant interview with Archbishop Cranmer. The Archbishop's instructions were 'to call apart my Lady Margaret Douglas, and declare to her how indiscreetly she hath demeaned herself, first with the Lord Thomas and secondly with Charles Howard . . . [and to] . . . charge her with over much lightness, and finally give her advice to beware the third time, and wholly apply herself to please the King's Majesty . . .'[27] With those chilling words in her ears she departed, perhaps doubting whether any 'third time' would present itself.

Katherine Howard was executed without trial under an act of attainder on 13 February 1542. But it was not until 12 July 1543 that Henry VIII married his sixth Queen, Katherine Parr.[28] Lady Margaret Douglas returned to court to act as one of the Queen's bridesmaids, which signified her recovery of royal favour. The next year brought the change in her fortunes which she had desired and despaired of: the King arranged her marriage, and his choice was more exalted than either of the men whom she had chosen for herself. Matthew Stuart, fourth Earl of Lennox, was an ally whose adherence Henry VIII valued sufficiently to secure it with marriage to his niece, and Margaret willingly accepted the customary destiny of royal ladies. Her acquiescence was rewarded by the acquisition of a devoted husband.

Matthew, Earl of Lennox was a great-great-grandson of King James II of Scotland (d. 1460), and considered himself the strongest claimant to the throne if the direct line should fail. This seemed likely, since both James IV and James V were unfortunate in the deaths of legitimate children, though their illegitimate families were contrastingly healthy. James II's daughter Princess Mary had married James, first Lord Hamilton, by whom she had a son and a daughter. The son was created first Earl of Arran, the daughter married the second Earl of Lennox. At this stage the position of the Hamiltons in the Scottish succession was the stronger, but Arran's matrimonial affairs were so confused that there was doubt as to his heir's legitimacy, whereas the Lennoxes were indisputably legitimate. Their counter-claims created a continuing feud, exacerbated by the murder of the third Earl of Lennox by a Hamilton after the Battle of Linlithgow in 1526.

Matthew was born on 21 September 1516 in Dumbarton Castle, which dominated the Clyde from its massive rock, and controlled the western approaches to Lowland Scotland. He had two younger brothers, John and Robert, and a sister, Helen. After the death of their father the family was divided. Robert and Helen remained with their mother in Scotland: Robert was educated for the Church, and became Bishop of Caithness; Helen married successively the Earls of Erroll and Sutherland. Matthew and John were sent to France, to be brought up in the household of their great-uncle, Robert Stuart d'Aubigny, Marshal of France.

A branch of the Stewart family had been established in France since 1429, when Sir John Stewart of Darnley fought for Charles VII in the Hundred Years' War, and was rewarded with the lordship of Aubigny-sur-Nère, from which the title derived. The French spelling 'Stuart' first appears in this Franco-Scottish family, which was not-able for military prowess, but plagued by lack of fertility. The Aubigny title had been kept in existence by the adoption of heirs from the Lennox family. Robert Stuart, Maréchal d'Aubigny, was the son of John, first Earl of Lennox, and had gained the title through marriage to the only daughter of Berault Stuart, third Sieur d'Aubigny.[29] Now he in turn was childless, though twice married. In taking charge of his orphaned nephews he was both acting as a good kinsman and looking for an heir. The two boys, who were ten and seven at the death of their father, received a military education, and accompanied their guardian on the French campaigns in Italy as soon as they were old enough to do so.

They were in France in 1536 when James V visited the French court to claim the bride promised him in the treaty negotiated by Albany during his childhood. On 1 January 1537 he married the Princess Madeleine, daughter of François Ier, in the Cathedral of Notre Dame in Paris. After the wedding Lennox and his brother

sought and received the permission of the King of Scots to be naturalized as French subjects. Dual nationality did not preclude the
Earl's right to his Scottish estates, to which he would return sooner
or later; but it enabled the Maréchal d'Aubigny to adopt John Stuart
as his heir, which had long been his intention. The Maréchal's wife,
Jacqueline de la Queulle, who was many years younger than he, had
a half-sister, Anne, who was younger than her husband's ward. A
marriage between John Stuart and Anne de la Queulle secured the
continuance of the Aubigny line. They had one son, Esmé Stuart
d'Aubigny, who would make a dramatic intervention in Scottish
politics many years later.[30]

Matthew, Earl of Lennox and John Stuart d'Aubigny, though their
lives diverged, remained united in their dedication to the aggrandizement of their family. Both were devious and ambitious, and Matthew
in particular was entirely devoid of principle in pursuit of advancement, as he soon demonstrated.

The marriage of James V and Madeleine of France was tragically
brief. Madeleine, who had been delicate all her life, died only six
weeks after her arrival in Scotland, in the early summer of 1537.
However, the Franco-Scottish alliance was soon renewed by a marriage between the widowed James and Marie de Guise, widow of the
Duc de Longueville, a marriage of political expediency and personal
consolation. Marie de Guise bore James two sons, who died within
a few days of each other in April 1541. This tragedy devastated
James, who was in poor health himself, and probably explained his
failure to meet Henry VIII at York later in the year. Henry's rancour
at this perceived insult revealed his latent enmity towards his nephew,
and confirmed James's determination to adhere to the auld alliance,
even though this once more brought Scotland and England into conflict. In the autumn the two countries were at war, and on 24 November the Scots suffered a humiliating defeat at Solway Moss. James
V was not present on the field of battle, for he was already seriously,
perhaps terminally, ill. His death shortly afterwards created the myth
that he had died of a broken heart as a result of the defeat. But his
last days were undoubtedly embittered by the news of the birth of
a daughter to Marie de Guise, on 8 December. His famous last words,
'Adieu, farewell – it cam wi' a lass, it will gang wi' a lass', expressed
his belief that his dynasty would not survive the minority of a baby

girl. The crown had come to the Stewarts through the marriage of Walter, High Steward of Scotland, to the daughter of Robert the Bruce. James supposed that it would fall to the Tudors through the marriage of his infant daughter to the son of Henry VIII, which was exactly what Henry intended.

The death of James V was followed by a power struggle between Cardinal Beaton, the late King's adviser, who had supported his Francophile and papalist policy, and James Hamilton, second Earl of Arran, who believed that he had a prescriptive right to be appointed Governor, as the infant Queen's nearest kinsman (just as Albany had been appointed Governor for James V). Arran triumphed, and the Cardinal was briefly imprisoned. The accession of Mary Queen of Scots at the age of one week inaugurated a minority of unprecedented length, and a period of religious confusion, as the crisis of the Reformation approached. The influence of Lutheranism had infiltrated Scotland during the reign of James V, but during the minority of Mary Genevan Calvinism steadily gained ground.

The Earl of Arran was a Protestant of some sort, and his name was rumoured to have headed a 'blacklist' of heretics which James V had kept as an instrument of terror. But both in religion and politics Arran was unstable and easily influenced by stronger personalities. His only constant principle was the advancement of his family, which he pursued resolutely. When he became Governor the recent defeat of Scottish arms left him vulnerable to English influence. Henry VIII was quick to seize his advantage. In mid-December he summoned the Earl of Angus and directed him to return to Scotland and resume his old task of guarding English interests. He also sent north a group of Scottish lords captured at Solway Moss, who were provided with English pensions and pledged to support alliance with England and marriage between Prince Edward and Mary Queen of Scots. In Scotland they were derisively known as 'the English Lords', and the nickname was well justified as some of them had promised to recognize Henry as King of Scots if Queen Mary should die young.

Arran received them on 25 January 1543, and began to negotiate with England under their influence. The resulting Treaties of Greenwich were completed on 1 July. The first was a treaty of peace, the second promised that Mary Queen of Scots should be betrothed to Prince Edward and sent to the English court when she had completed her tenth year, and after a proxy marriage had been solemnized. Henry VIII's long-term policy was the union of Scotland and England under English domination, although the independence of Scotland was theoretically guaranteed by the treaties. To advance unity of religion between the two countries Henry recommended to Arran that the Scottish Parliament should 'let slip the Bible', or authorize the import of vernacular translations of the scriptures into Scotland. Arran's Parliament did so, and the influence of the Bible proved more enduring in Scotland than any of the ephemeral political agreements of Mary's minority.

Meanwhile, France could not allow the auld alliance to collapse without interference, and the obvious candidate to rescue it was Matthew, Earl of Lennox. Encouraged by Cardinal Beaton, and well supplied with French gold, to counteract the effect of the English pensions, he arrived at Dumbarton on 31 March 1543. Cardinal Beaton saw Lennox as a useful ally in the overthrow of Arran. In Scotland, still a Catholic country, the Church pronounced on questions of legitimacy; if Beaton declared Arran illegitimate Lennox would take his place as heir presumptive. The declaration of Arran's bastardy would be Lennox's reward if he could unseat him. An effective way to do so would be by marrying the Queen-Dowager Marie de Guise, for his status as her husband would give him appropriate rank to be Governor, with the approval and support of France. Lennox threw himself into this ploy with gusto, but found that he had a rival in Patrick, Earl of Bothwell, who also aspired to marry Marie de Guise. The chronicler Lindsay of Pitscottie wrote an amusing account of their attempts to attract the Queen-Dowager:

These two earls daily frequented the court, striving in magnificence of apparel and in all courtly games the one to exceed the other, especially in the Queen's sight. But the Earl of Lennox, being well bred in the wars of France, surpassed the other, both in ability of body and dexterity of exercise. He was of a strong body, well proportionate, of a sweet and manly visage, straight in stature, and pleasant in behaviour. Bothwell was fair and whitely, something hanging shouldered and going forward [stooping], but of a gentle and humane countenance. These two being fed with fair words for a time, at length the Earl of Bothwell, having spent very much, was forced to retire.[31]

Marie de Guise had no intention of marrying either of them. Margaret Tudor's loss of influence and prestige through her marriages to the Earl of Angus and Lord Methven was perhaps a caution. Marie was content to dedicate herself to her daughter's interests. Lennox was doubly disillusioned: first the Queen-Dowager refused him, and then his erstwhile ally the Cardinal was reconciled to the Governor and received him back into the Church, so there would be no more talk of his illegitimacy in the foreseeable future. Arran had by now fallen under the influence of his genuinely illegitimate half-brother, John Hamilton, Abbot of Paisley, who was recognized as the brains of an exalted but not over-intelligent family. Arran's vacillating character was summed up in the derisive comment 'what the English Lords decide him to do one day the Abbot changes the next'.[32]

The Earl of Lennox, disgusted by his lack of success, withdrew to Dumbarton and put out feelers to his former enemies. He did not relinquish the idea of advancement through marriage, but he transferred his attentions to another possible bride. On 11 July 1543 the English ambassador in Scotland, Sir Ralph Sadler, reported to the English Privy Council, 'Your Lordships shall understand that this the Earl of Angus hath told me lately, that the Earl of Lennox would gladly make an alliance with him and marry his daughter, the Lady Margaret Douglas, whose marriage the said Earl of Angus saith he referreth wholly to the King's Majesty [Henry VIII]'.[33] The following month Sadler wrote directly to the King of England, describing how he had been visited by a servant of Lennox, who had brought him a letter from Lennox to Lady Margaret, to be delivered with Henry's approval. 'And for credence he told me that the Earl of Lennox, his master, had left the Governor and Cardinal's party, and being hitherto noted a good Frenchman, is now become a good Englishman, and will bear his heart and service to your Majesty, and very shortly intendeth to dispatch a servant of his to your Highness, and to the said Lady Margaret, with his full mind in all behalfs'.[34]

Lennox's value as an ally of England was greatly enhanced when Arran, under the influence of the Cardinal and the Abbot of Paisley, repudiated the Treaties of Greenwich, on the pretext that Henry VIII had not ratified them within the agreed time. Henry lost another ally when the Earl of Angus abandoned his long-standing attachment to England. He married the daughter of Lord Maxwell, and completely reintegrated himself and his family into the fabric of Scottish society. As a result of these defections, Henry found the adherence of Lennox not only desirable but necessary.

[33]

In an agreement made with English commissioners at Carlisle on 17 May 1544, in return for the hand of Lady Margaret in marriage, Lennox promised to recognize Henry VIII as Protector of Scotland, to arrange the marriage of Mary Queen of Scots to Prince Edward, and to place the Queen of Scots in English custody. He also promised to transfer several Scottish strongholds, including Dumbarton, to English possession and to permit the 'Word of God' – the vernacular scriptures – to circulate in Scotland. Lennox's brother Robert, Bishop of Caithness, became a hostage for the performance of these promises, which, if Lennox fulfilled them, would lead to his appointment as Governor of Scotland under the aegis of Henry VIII. If he could not gain his ambition through marriage to the French Queen-Dowager, he hoped to gain it through marriage to the English King's niece, as unromantic a motive for marriage as could be imagined.

The person who suffered most from Lennox's abandonment of the auld alliance was his brother John Stuart d'Aubigny. François Ier was understandably enraged by Lennox's betrayal of French interests, which he had been sent to Scotland to defend. As Lennox was out of reach of the French King's anger, his brother, who was mistakenly assumed to have abetted him, was imprisoned in the Bastille. As Lennox and his brother had corresponded after Lennox had returned to Scotland the case against John looked sinister, but in fact their contact was infrequent. In August 1543 Lennox had written to his brother, 'I her say at my Lord Obeneis wyf is wytht schild, the quhilkis I am rycht blytht of, and I pray God that scho fayr weal' (I hear say that my Lord Aubigny's wife is with child, which I am very glad of, and I pray God that she does well).[35] The interest of this letter, apart from its use of the Scots language between these Franco-Scottish brothers, is that Lennox was assuming 'my Lord Aubigny's wife' to be Jacqueline de la Queulle, who never bore a child. News of the pregnancy had outrun the news that the Maréchal d'Aubigny had died, and John inherited the title, so that the pregnant 'Lord Aubigny's wife' was Anne de la Queulle, about to give birth to Esmé Stuart. John's imprisonment left his wife and son unprotected, but fortunately the anger of François Ier did not extend to the forfeiture of the Aubigny estates. Anne and Esmé were permitted to remain at the Château of La Verrerie near Aubigny until the accession of François Ier's son Henri II in 1547 brought John Stuart's release.[36]

In June 1544 Lennox went to the English court to celebrate his marriage. The marriage contract, signed on 26 June, was one of the most insubstantial and insincere documents imaginable. It declared that as the Earl of Lennox had made humble suit to the King of England for marriage with his Highness's niece, Lady Margaret Douglas, it had pleased his Highness to grant his suit, for the good opinion which he had conceived of the Earl's constant loyalty towards him. Lennox promised to surrender to Henry his title to the throne of Scotland, to acknowledge him as supreme Lord and Governor of Scotland, and to support him in the assertion of his claim.[37] This was such high a price to pay for the possibility of becoming Governor with English support that it casts doubt on Lennox's sincerity. Lennox was still under thirty, whereas Henry was obviously nearing the end of his life. It seems likely that Lennox's excessive submissiveness was cynically offered. Equally insubstantial, though more sincerely intended, was the jointure that Lennox promised to Lady Margaret Douglas. This consisted of the lands of Glenrinnie, Balloch and Auchintorlies, in the earldom of Lennox and shire of Dumbarton; the baronies of Cruckisfew, Inchinnan and Craig of Nielston, in the lordship of Darnley and shire of Renfrew; and the lands of Erere in the shire of Perth.[38] Unfortunately Lennox's defection threatened him with forfeiture of his Scottish estates, so his ability to endow his wife with these lands depended on his success in fulfilling his promises to Henry VIII.

More substantial than the names of estates on the marriage contract were the jewels that the Lady Mary gave her cousin as wedding presents. These included a large balas ruby with a table-cut diamond set over it like a glass, ornamented with pendant pearls, and a 'George' (Saint George and the Dragon) set with diamonds, probably intended as a gift for Margaret to give to her husband. There were also several enamelled 'historiated' jewels, illustrating scenes from scripture: the 'History of Susanne' (Susannah and the Elders), the 'History of David', the 'History of Noah's Flood set round with many rubies and diamonds', and the 'History of Our Saviour healing the Man with the Palsy', which had a large table diamond in its gold surround.[39]

The marriage of Lady Margaret Douglas and Matthew, Earl of Lennox took place on 6 July 1544 in St James's Palace. Lennox was naturalized as an English subject before the marriage, presumably to ensure the English nationality of children born to the King of England's niece. At the wedding Henry announced that 'in case his own issue failed, he should be right glad if heirs of her body succeeded to the crown'.[40] He later changed his mind, but at that moment his declaration must have delighted both bride and bridegroom. Margaret's imprisonments had given her good cause to fear Henry's suspicion that everyone who possessed royal blood aimed at the throne; it must have amazed and gratified her to hear her place in the succession publicly acknowledged. Marriage to Lennox inspired Margaret to even greater ambition: their children would inherit the royal blood of both England and Scotland, their line might occupy the throne of the united kingdom which Henry VIII envisaged.

Margaret and Lennox made a political marriage, not a love match, but wisely prepared to see the best in each other. Margaret, having known love, still hoped to find it. Restored to favour after the second of her imprudent romances, she had had the temerity to ask King Henry's promise not to give her in marriage to a man she could not love, so evidently she had decided that it would be possible to love the attractive and accomplished Scottish earl, whose birth was equal to her own. Lennox married Margaret for her birth, but her appearance would not have disappointed him. If not beautiful, Margaret was certainly striking, with the fair complexion and red hair characteristic of the Tudors. She dressed with taste and elegance, and wore her magnificent jewels without vulgar profusion. Surviving portraits of the Earl and Countess of Lennox show them in later life, when their youthful good looks had faded. Perhaps it is the fault of second-rate artists that they appear rather alike, with regular features and expressionless, mask-like faces; perhaps their remote look conveys a truth about them – their remoteness from the rest of humanity in their pride of birth and secrecy of ambition. Shared ambition established an accord between them, which developed into a relationship of great mutual devotion. Quite unusually for their period they addressed each other by their Christian names. Lennox wrote to his wife as 'My sweet Madge' and signed himself 'Your own Matthiu, and most loving husband'. Lasting love was their good fortune, and their sustenance in the tragedies of their later lives.

Immediately after his marriage Lennox was compelled to act upon his promises to Henry VIII, who was determined that the Scots should repent of having repudiated the Treaties of Greenwich, and be forced to accept the English marriage for their Queen. Earlier in the summer the Earl of Hertford, brother of Queen Jane Seymour and uncle of Prince Edward, had invaded Scotland, to devastate the Borders and sack Edinburgh and St Andrews. This was the first move in the sequence of campaigns that the Scots, with black humour, called 'the Rough Wooing'. It was now Lennox's turn. He was appointed Lieutenant of Northern England and Southern Scotland, and provided with a flotilla of eighteen ships, carrying six hundred men, to seize Dumbarton Castle. He arrived at Dumbarton on 10 August, and was received into the castle by his own castellan, Sir George Stirling of Glorat; but when the castellan and garrison understood that he intended to transfer the castle into English possession, they mutinied, and forced him and his few companions to flee for their ships. One of Lennox's companions in arms later claimed to have suggested that he should seize a 'marrish pyke' (a Moorish pike) which was apparently conveniently to hand, and fight, but Lennox preferred to run away and live to fight another day. He exorcized his humiliation with some local destruction, and then sailed for Bristol.

Margaret, who had remained in London, in attendance on Queen Katherine Parr, soon discovered that she was pregnant. The first son of the Earl and Countess of Lennox was born in the Palace of Stepney, the London residence granted them by Henry VIII, in March 1545. He was Henry Stuart, Lord Darnley, not the subject of this book, but his short-lived elder brother, forgotten by history. The baby's birth was greeted with great rejoicing, and the Lady Mary, who loved children and longed for children of her own, noted a gift to him in her inventory of jewels: 'Given to my cousin Margaret Lennox's son, a lace of goldsmith's work set with little sparks of diamonds and rubies, and twenty-one pearls'.[41] This could have been a jewelled covering for the baby's caul or bonnet, a popular fashion of the period.

Lennox had little time to admire his son, as he was absent for much of the year. 1545 had begun badly for England when the Earl of Angus defeated an English force under Sir Ralph Eure, who was killed, at Ancrum Moor in Roxburghshire, on 27 February. Unfortunately for Scotland this was not a big enough victory to deter Henry VIII from his purpose – it only stung him to renewed efforts. Lennox was ordered to resume his operations in the west of Scotland, then he was directed to join the Earl of Hertford in his second 'Rough Wooing' which once again set the Borders ablaze. When Hertford retired to Newcastle in September, Lennox crossed over to Ireland, and on 17 November sailed from Dublin with a new expedition to capture Dumbarton Castle. Dumbarton was now strongly garrisoned by the Scottish government, and Lennox was ignominiously repulsed. To add to his humiliation he learnt that the previous month he had been declared guilty of treason by the Scottish Parliament, and his estates had been forfeited. His lands, including those he had promised to his wife, passed out of his possession for the next twenty years.

A greater sorrow awaited his discovery. During his absence his son had died in Stepney Palace, and been buried in the parish church of St Dunstan. The baby's grave was marked by a monumental brass with a simple and moving inscription:

> Here lieth Henry Stuart, Lord Darnley, of the age of three quarters of a year, late son and heir to Matthew, Earl of Lennox, and the Lady Margaret his wife, which Henry deceased the twenty-eight day of November, in the year of God 1545, whose soul Jesus pardon.[42]

Neither parent was with the baby when he died, for Margaret had travelled north to Temple Newsam, the Yorkshire property that Henry VIII had granted to Lennox as his Lieutenant in the North. She had left the baby in London, no doubt intending to send for him when she had settled into the house. Her absence when the baby died must have added to the sorrow of his loss. But grief was followed by joy. Margaret was pregnant with her second child, who must have been conceived almost immediately after the birth of the first, when she made the two-hundred-mile journey north. She gave birth to her second son, also named Henry Stuart, Lord Darnley, at Temple Newsam, on 7 December 1545.

Grief for their first son probably increased both parents' love for their second. As other children were born to them, and died, during the next few years, Henry's unique survival and robust health made him seem all the more precious and remarkable. He became the object of his parents' uncritical devotion, the embodiment of their hopes, the focus of their ambitions. They determined that he was to attain the highest destiny: he was to be a king.

2

DESTINED FOR KINGSHIP

> There is a certain noble lady called the Lady Margaret,
> a niece of Henry VIII . . . The crown, it is surmised, will
> descend to her son [Lord Darnley] . . . should anything
> unhappily happen to Elizabeth, which God forbid . . .
> There are, as is usually the case, various reports concern-
> ing him. The Queen of Scotland is, as you know, unmar-
> ried, so that a matrimonial alliance may possibly be
> formed between them.[1]

TEMPLE NEWSAM, which was to be Darnley's home throughout
his childhood, had been, as its name implies, a preceptory of the
Knights Templar, the military order subject to monastic rules formed
in 1119 to protect lay pilgrims to Jerusalem. The suppression of the
order in 1312, following sensational accusations of heresy, sodomy
and devil worship, delivered its vast possessions into the hands of
covetous temporal rulers (in England it was a blueprint for the Dissolution of the Monasteries two centuries later). In 1327 Temple Newsam was gifted by Edward III to Marie de St Pol, widow of a
much-honoured soldier and statesman, Aymer de Valence, Earl of
Pembroke, and foundress of Pembroke College, Cambridge. In 1337
Edward granted the reversion of Temple Newsam to John Darcy and
his heirs male, though it was not until the long-lived Marie de St Pol
died in 1377 that Sir Philip Darcy gained possession of it.[2] The
property remained in his family until 1537, when Thomas, Lord
Darcy was executed for his participation in the Pilgrimage of Grace.

Lord Darcy's Yorkshire properties of Temple Hurst, Temple New-sam, Silkstone and Beckay were confiscated by the Crown and regranted to Matthew, Earl of Lennox.[3] The properties were not secured to Margaret in the event of her widowhood; provision for her still depended on the notional jointure provided by her husband in the marriage contract.

The present Temple Newsam is not the house in which Darnley grew up. Part of the Tudor house remains embedded in the surviving structure, but the existing layout dates from the occupancy of the seventeenth-century financier Sir Arthur Ingram, who bought it from Ludovic Stuart, second Duke of Lennox, and rebuilt it extensively between 1622 and 1637. Ingram's house is built on three sides of a rectangle. The central part of the west front is Tudor, the rest of the house is Jacobean, with some Victorian alterations. The whole is united by a balustrade composed of lettering, which runs around the roof-line and forms the inscription ALL GLORY AND PRAISE BE GIVEN TO GOD THE FATHER THE SON AND HOLY GHOST ON HIGH PEACE ON EARTH GOOD WILL TOWARDS MEN HONOUR AND TRUE ALLEGIANCE TO OUR GRACIOUS KING LOVING AFFECTION AMONGST HIS SUBJECTS HEALTH AND PLENTY BE WITHIN THIS HOUSE. The king honoured in this loyal inscription was of course Darnley's son, James VI and I. The embracing effect of the lettered balustrade, the consciously antiquarian rebuilding by Sir Arthur Ingram, and the uniform mellowing of the pinkish-brown brick, have created a harmonious whole, suggesting greater antiquity.[4]

The house of which the Earl and Countess of Lennox took possession was modern in their eyes. Its brickwork would still have been a bright rose-pink, its construction still a little raw-edged, where one range of buildings remained unfinished. However, allowing for the necessity of adding finishing touches, the house formed a complete rectangle, enclosing its central courtyard. To its new owners its predominant characteristics would have been its modernity and its size. It was of palatial proportions, and had been planned for luxurious living, not for defence. Thomas Darcy, one of the greatest northern magnates, had come into his inheritance in 1488, three years after Bosworth, and assumed that he was going to live in peaceful times. He was raised to the peerage in 1505, and then began to envisage a house which would be the expression of his own greatness. The north was full of medieval fortresses, of which Middleham, Bolton, Raby, Alnwick, among others, are surviving examples. At the eastern and western extremities of the Border stood the walled towns of Berwick and Carlisle. If defence against the Scots were required again, it existed in strength and in depth. Lord Darcy planned a palace equal in opulence to any in southern England, and had almost completed it by the time of his fall. His house arose out of the wild surrounding countryside, as bright and elegant as the mythical 'House of Pride' in Spenser's *Faerie Queene*:

> A stately palace built of squared brick . . .
> Whose walls were high but nothing strong nor thick . . .
> High lifted up were many lofty towers . . .
> Full of fair windows and delightful bowers . . .[5]

The tall windows, with their small, glittering lead-set panes, looked out over the bleak distances around without the mediating vistas of the present landscaped park.[6]

The main entrance to the house was from the north, beneath a gatehouse that formed part of the northern range of buildings. This gave access to the courtyard. Opposite, in the southern range, was the doorway which gave admittance to the house itself. It led into the Screens Passage, a hallway which divided the domestic and social areas. The kitchens, and all the supply rooms, lay to the left of the entrance. The entering guest would turn right, through an arch in the Screens, and go into the Great Hall which occupied at least half the southern range of buildings, and was probably the full height of the house. The Great Hall was the principal public room of a great house of the period, in which members of the household, servants, tenants, messengers and passing travellers sat down to eat. A distinguished guest would be led through the Hall and out at the other end of it, up the stairs, and would turn right again into the western range of buildings, which contained the private apartments of the family.

Recent excavations at the south-west corner of the building have revealed polygonal foundations, suggesting the existence of a tower at this corner, which may have contained the stair. It was probably matched by a similar tower at each corner of the building. The first room in the western range was the Great Chamber, in which the Earl and Countess of Lennox would have dined before midday and supped in the early evening, and received guests whose status demanded higher honours than the general provision in the Great Hall. Beyond the Great Chamber, occupying the length of the western range, lay the private apartments, described in an inventory of the contents of the house compiled in 1565 as 'Lord Darnley's Chamber', 'The Chamber called the Ladies' Chamber', 'the Nursery', 'The Earl's Bedchamber', 'The Gentlewomens' Chamber', and 'The Closet'. Then came 'The Uttre [outer] Entry'. This probably completed the sequence of rooms in the western range, so that the 'entry' would imply the turn at the end of the building into the northern range. This contained the main storage room, 'The High Wardrobe', with further storage rooms on either side of it, and other chambers in which probably more members of the household slept. Those who were gentry would have had lodgings assigned to them; those of lower status bedded down all over the house for the night. The 'Gallery', 'The New Gallery' and 'The Chapel Chamber' may have been in the eastern range, incomplete when the Earl and Countess of Lennox took possession. The description 'New Gallery' suggests that it had been added during their occupation. There was also a 'Musicians' Chamber', probably close to the Chapel, where the musicians would have performed, and a 'Schoolmaster's Chamber', in which Darnley would have done his lessons.

'The Porter's Lodge' and 'The Warrener's Lodge' probably occupied the ground floor of the northern range, near the gatehouse. In the southern range, to the left of the courtyard entrance to the house, lay the Kitchen, Pantry, Buttery, Dry Larder, Brew House and Pateserie (patisserie). Possibly there was a subsidiary courtyard beyond this range of buildings, as there appear to be too many subdivisions of the kitchen quarters to be squeezed into the space remaining in the southern range. The ground floor of the western range, beneath the private apartments, may have been occupied by some of these domestic offices, or by wine cellars and storage rooms. Other ground-floor rooms all round the courtyard would have provided lodgings for guests and their attendants.[7]

The inventory compiled in 1565 was made when the Earl and Countess were no longer in residence, in circumstances to be described in the next chapter, which led to the contents of the house being in disarray. But the lists still suggest that it had been furnished with great splendour. The Great Chamber contained a picture collection amassed over the past twenty years – the portraits of royalties and relatives which typified the collections of the period. There were likenesses of Henry VIII, of Lady Lennox's mother Queen Margaret, of Lady Lennox herself, of John Stuart d'Aubigny and Lord Darnley, and of Queen

Mary I and her husband Philip of Spain. The Great Chamber also contained a 'tester of cloth of gold and silver with the arms of the earl and his wife embroidered [on it] and curtains of crimson damask', forming the Cloth of State beneath which the trestle table at which the Earl and Countess ate would have been placed.

The Earl and Countess had separate bedchambers. His contained a bed with 'a tester of cloth of gold and purple velvet with the arms of England embroidered [on it] and curtains of crimson damask'. This was the official marriage bed, and its heraldic embroidery bore silent witness to the fact that the children begotten in it were claimants to the English succession. The Countess's bedchamber was probably the one designated 'the Ladies' Chamber', next to 'Lord Darnley's Chamber'. The custom of royal and noble couples having separate bedchambers made it obvious when a king and queen or lord and lady were sleeping together and when they were not. Privacy existed only when the bed curtains were drawn and the occupants enclosed in fusty darkness. But privacy was little regarded, for all great persons went to bed with at least one attendant sleeping in the room on a truckle bed.

'Lord Darnley's Chamber', according to the inventory, contained tapestries of hunting and hawking, and 'one bedstead with gilt posts', apparently denuded of its hangings. Agnes Strickland stated that Darnley's bed hangings were embroidered with the Lennox and Douglas mottoes 'AVANT DARNLÉ – JAMAIS D'ARRIÈRE' [Forward Darnley, Never Behind], which profoundly influenced him. No such hangings were described in the inventory, though the mottoes and their message would have been familiar from many other sources. Family possessions of every kind, from books to weapons, were decorated with armorial bearings, crests and mottoes. These can be seen, correctly emblazoned, on the chimney breast of a room that a nineteenth-century owner of Temple Newsam mistakenly identified as 'Lord Darnley's Chamber', and decorated accordingly, but which was in fact one of the rooms built by Sir Arthur Ingram. Temple Newsam is indeed a palimpsest, and the best clue to reading it is the inventory of 1565.[8]

The life of a great house such as Temple Newsam was immensely formal, and the rituals differed little from one house to another. The household was a rigid hierarchy, a miniature court with its gentlemen, yeomen and simple domestics. It was under the direction of the Steward, who would be a knight or a gentleman of a leading family of the locality. His second-in-command was the Comptroller, who would take his place when the Steward's own affairs called him away. These functionaries ensured that everything was beautifully regulated, surrounding the lord of the house with rituals that defined his status, from dawn to dark.

Getting up and being dressed was a ritual, followed by Mass or Morning Prayer, according to the religion of the house. Temple Newsam was a Catholic household, and an increasingly devout one under the influence of Margaret Lennox. Her devotion to Catholicism was one of the ties which had bound her to the Lady Mary, who had suffered so much from her attempt to keep faith with her unfortunate mother, Queen Katherine of Aragon. Margaret had been obliged to bend to the will of Henry VIII and acknowledge the royal supremacy, but in later years her devotion to Catholicism became overt and notorious. In the early years of the reign of Elizabeth the Lennox household was a recognized centre of Catholic intrigue. The Earl of Lennox, brought up as a Catholic in Scotland and France, later changed his religion as politics dictated. Darnley was raised as a devout Catholic by his mother, but in later life followed the example of his father. They were all practising Catholics at home.

Their day would have begun with a procession to hear a sung Mass in the Chapel, or with a less formal procession to hear a low Mass in the Closet. While the family attended their devotions, preparations for dinner began. The early hour of dinner originated in the fact that at Mass the Holy Sacrament had to be received following a fast from the previous midnight. Most Catholics, other than the exceptionally pious, probably received it only on major feast days, but the habit of eating early remained.

After the 'levacion of high Mass' (the Elevation, about two-thirds of the way through the service), elaborate arrangements began in the Great Chamber. First the dining tables, composed of trestles and boards, were set up by the Grooms of the Chamber. The Earl's table was set beneath the Cloth of State, on a carpet. The knights' table, placed next to it, was for the Earl and Countess's personal attendants. Laying the tables was the duty of a higher rank of servants than the grooms. The Yeoman Usher of the Chamber and another yeoman spread the tablecloths, genuflecting to the Earl's place before doing so. A cupboard (sideboard) from which drink would be served was covered with a cloth by the Yeoman of the Cellar, and on ceremonial occasions an array of gold and silver plate was set out on it, some purely ornamental pieces, besides drinking cups. A procession headed by the Yeoman Usher bearing his rod of office next arrived to lay the table. Three bows were made to the Earl's place before it was laid. The Salt, a magnificent piece of silver, perhaps in the form of a 'nef' or ship, was set to the left of the Earl's place. His knife and spoon (forks were still rare) were placed under a fold in the cloth on the other side. The Yeoman of the Pantry set wine on the cupboard, and the Yeoman of the Buttery brought beer. It was then the turn of the Waiting Gentlemen, the Sewer, Carver and Cupbearer. They ceremonially washed their hands, and were 'armed' with their towels and napkins by the Yeoman of the Ewery, almost like priests being vested for Mass. The Carver took a slice from each loaf of bread provided for the Earl's table, and tasted it as a precaution against poison. Though poison was greatly feared, instances of deliberate poisoning were rare, or at least unsubstantiated; unintentional poisoning, resulting from contaminated food, was much commoner, and often imagined to have been deliberate, with resulting rumours and accusations. After the tasting of the loaves the Sewer, with an escort of gentlemen and yeomen, descended to the Great Hall, and through the Screens to the kitchen to collect the food. They returned with it in procession, to be met in the Hall on ceremonial occasions by the chief officers of the household, the Steward, Comptroller and Treasurer, who led the procession up to the Great Chamber. On ordinary days these three officers would stand in the Great Chamber to await the return of the procession. When the dishes were in place, the Carver again tasted each one.

Now the Earl and Countess would have returned from Mass to one of their bedchambers, and a Gentleman Usher would come to summon them to the table. The Earl and Countess, and their son as soon as he was old enough to do so, sat at the Earl's table. Tudor pictures show quite small children dining with their parents, when perfect manners would have been expected of them. Honoured guests were also seated at the Earl's table, and whether they were placed above or below the Salt was a matter of great social significance. The knights' table was for the Gentlemen Ushers and the 'Gentlewomen of Presence' – the Countess's attendant gentlewomen. The Earl's Cupbearer served him only, on bended knee. The Sewer and Carver served the family and the guests above the Salt; those below the Salt were served by another sewer 'unarmed' – not draped with the ritual towel and napkin – and by other yeomen. Once the Earl was in his place the Steward and Comptroller went down to the Great Hall to preside at the dinner of the household. Those who had waited at dinner in the Great Chamber and the Great Hall had their own dinner in Hall afterwards.

The distance from the kitchen to the Great Chamber at Temple Newsam and other great houses, and the elaborate ritual which preceded eating, make it obvious that no importance was attached to eating food while it was hot. Two courses were served, the second brought with as much ceremony as the first, set on the table with bows and genuflections, and tasted by the Carver before it was served. The courses were not different in character, as at a modern dinner. Each course consisted of a great variety of dishes: meat, poultry and game, 'potages' and sweets, which were sometimes fantastic sculptures of sugar or 'marchpane' (marzipan) in the shapes of castles, or heraldic animals or birds. On fast days the whole dinner would be equally rich and varied, but composed entirely of fish dishes.

Dinner ended, everyone rose from the tables and stood at the side of the room in rows, the most important in the front rank. The Earl alone remained seated while everything, including the table in front of him, was removed with as much ceremony as it had been brought. The Earl then rose and his hands were washed by two gentlemen, after which the hands of everyone else were washed in turn, with due regard for precedence. Grace was then said, and musicians were summoned to entertain the company or to accompany dancing. Dinner was the main meal of the day, but supper in the late afternoon or early evening was served with similar ceremony. When at last the Earl and Countess went to bed, they were provided with their 'All Night', a substantial snack of loaves of bread and jugs of wine and beer, in case they woke and felt hungry.

The 'Household Ordinances' on which this description is based prescribe the proper ritual for the service of an earl, but in Lennox's absences the Countess would have been the cynosure of all the ceremony.[9] He was absent in both 1547 and 1548, years that witnessed the culmination of the 'Rough Wooing' and the self-defeat of England's policy of violence towards Scotland.

Henry VIII died on 28 January 1547. His death had been preceded by a power struggle between the Earl of Hertford and the Howards.

But Henry did not intend Hertford to rule as Regent, and sought to limit his power by appointing a Regency Council. He also restored his daughters to the succession: should Edward die without issue, Mary was to succeed, and should Mary in turn do so, Elizabeth – as indeed happened. The problem of their legitimacy was passed over in silence.[10] The great surprise and injustice that the will contained was the exclusion from the succession of the descendants of Margaret Tudor. Should Elizabeth die without issue, Henry willed the crown to the descendants of his younger sister Mary, Queen-Duchess of Suffolk, whose daughter Frances had three daughters, the Ladies Jane, Katherine and Mary Grey. The exclusion of the Stewart line was obviously Henry's revenge for the enmity of his nephew James V and for Scotland's repudiation of the proposed marriage of Edward and Mary Queen of Scots. The exclusion of Mary might be justified, since she was an alien, but this did not apply to Lady Margaret Douglas, who had been born in England. And it cancelled Henry's pronouncement at her wedding 'that in case his own issue failed he should be right glad if heirs of her body succeeded to the Crown'.[11]

A hint of the cause of this sudden change of heart is provided by a memorial written by Thomas Bishop, who had been Lennox's companion in arms on the first Dumbarton expedition, to Elizabeth I's Secretary of State, Sir William Cecil, in 1562. Bishop refers to the 'breache with my Lady Levenax [the Latin form of Lennox] . . . a lytill affore the King's death'.[12] Bishop hated the Countess, who had called him a heretic, and destroyed his influence with her husband. In reminding Cecil that Lady Lennox had been in trouble at the end of Henry's reign, he was attempting to make trouble for her again. He did not state the cause of Henry's breach with her, but it is likely to have been religion. Someone, perhaps Bishop himself, had probably denounced her as a papalist to the King. The likely consequence would have been a return to the Tower for Lady Lennox, so the King's death would have been a relief to her. But her exclusion from the succession would have been a devastating blow, both to her and her husband. So long as the succession remained under discussion – from 1547 to 1603 – the will of Henry VIII was constantly invoked, and quoted as respectfully as Holy Writ. Yet it was set aside for the first time almost immediately the King was dead. Hertford swiftly asserted his authority over the Regency Council, and had himself appointed Protector of England and created Duke of Somerset.

Protector Somerset's ambition for his nephew Edward VI remained marriage to Mary Queen of Scots, with the ultimate goal of union between England and Scotland under English rule. He pursued it with the same blind faith in force as Henry VIII. In the late summer of 1547 Somerset invaded Scotland and inflicted a heavy defeat on the Scots, commanded by Governor Arran, on 10 September at Pinkie Cleugh, near Musselburgh. Two days before the battle Lennox and Lord Wharton invaded Scotland at the western end of the Border, to create a diversion and prevent reinforcements reaching Arran. They attacked and captured Castlemilk, burnt Annan, and blew up its church and steeple, to prevent their use for purposes of defence. The inhabitants of Annandale submitted to England, and took the oath of allegiance to Edward VI. After this minor success Lennox received Somerset's permission to rejoin his wife.

Early in 1548 Lennox and Wharton invaded Scotland again, intending to capture Lochmaben and Dumfries. They were promised support by the Master of Maxwell, who undertook to bring them a force of two thousand men, for which he gave hostages to Lord Wharton. However, Maxwell reneged on his agreement, and when Lennox arrived before Dumfries he found no local reinforcements. Meanwhile Wharton's force was attacked and defeated by the Earl of Angus. Wharton retreated to Carlisle, where he was joined by Lennox who, furious at Maxwell's treachery, urged the execution of the hostages. A court was convened to decide their fate, and of the ten hostages four were hanged and six reprieved. This was a ruthless act, but not by the standards of the time an atrocity. There is no reason to suppose that it so burdened Lennox's conscience that ever afterwards solitude was unendurable to him, a frequently repeated story. Lennox was later described by his wife as having 'a disease which solitariness is most against'. But the association of this psychological disorder with guilt for the execution of the hostages is the invention of Agnes Strickland, who wrote a colourful account of the episode.[13] Lennox's support of Somerset in the campaigns of 1547 and 1548 was rewarded by appointment as castellan of the castle of Wressil in east Yorkshire, and the grant of the manor of Hackney, then in the country outside London.

After his victory at Pinkie Cleugh, Somerset left English garrisons in southern Scotland, but a continuing English presence did not mask the failure of the 'Rough Wooing'. The immediate result of Somerset's victory was the revival of the auld alliance. Arran's loss of prestige through his defeat enabled the Queen-Dowager Marie de Guise to assert her influence. She appealed to the new King of France, Henri II, who agreed to send French troops to Scotland to help expel the English garrisons. In return for French assistance, Mary Queen of Scots was to be sent to France, where in due course she would marry Henri's eldest son the Dauphin, the future François II. There was little delay, for on 7 August 1548 Mary and her attendants sailed from Dumbarton *en route* for France. Marie de Guise had secured Arran's acquiesence by acquiring for him the French duchy of Châtelhérault and a large annual pension, while his illegitimate half-brother, John Hamilton, Abbot of Paisley, became Archbishop of St Andrews.

During the Anglo-Scottish hostilities several members of the Douglas family were captured, sent as prisoners to England and lodged in the Tower. The Earl of Angus wrote to his daughter to ask her help for them:

Derrest dochter,
    After my maist tender commendacionis and hertly blissing this salbe to advertise zou that . . . the hous of Dalkeith was distroyit, and takein furth of it oure cousing the Larde of Glenbervy, the Maister of Mortoune, George my sone [and others] . . . praying zou, with avise of zour housband, to se gif ze can get thame . . . put in frendis handis, and gentilly tretit thare. And specialy the Larde of Glenbervy, that is ane seikly tender mann and has ix motherles barnis [bairns] . . . And mak my hertly commendacionis to my lord zour housband . . . and God preserve you. Writtin at Edinburgh, the xxth day of June 1548.
    Zour ffather,

Ard [Archibald] Erl of Angus[14]

Angus's pleasant and humane letter was addressed to a daughter who was on the worst of terms with him. Throughout their years in England Margaret had remained devoted to her father. Their estrangement occurred after Angus's return to Scotland at the end of 1542, and was caused by his marriage to the daughter of Lord Maxwell. Margaret, like many daughters, resented her father's remarriage, and not only through natural jealousy at his involvement with a woman as young as herself: throughout her life Margaret had been her father's heiress, and had never imagined that her position could be threatened. But it was threatened by his remarriage, and by the birth of a son to his new wife. Margaret had assumed that her own son would succeed to the earldoms of both Lennox and Angus, but Angus's late-born son was the cuckoo that ousted her own nestling.

Despite her quarrel with her father Margaret had the strong Scottish sense of the obligations of kinship, and she persuaded her husband to arrange with Somerset for the prisoners to be entrusted to them, and permitted to live under their 'sure keeping' in Yorkshire.[15] Of the kinsmen mentioned in Angus's letter, the Laird of Glenbervy was one of the few Douglases who had not shared in the disgrace of the family under James V. He had received the grant of the barony of Glenbervy from the King, and had been his 'familiar servitour'. Frail health had not prevented him from marrying twice and begetting the large family that was such an anxiety when he was captured.[16] He plays no further part in this history. The Master of Morton was James Douglas, younger son of Angus's brother, Sir George Douglas of Pittendriech. He had married the daughter of the third Earl of Morton, who had no sons, and was to succeed to the earldom in right of his wife.[17] In the meantime he was known as Master of Morton, the title of a Scottish earl's eldest son. (Thus, in Scotland, Lennox's son would have been called 'Master of Lennox'; it was English usage which gave him the courtesy title 'Lord Darnley', ironically derived from one of his father's forfeited Scottish estates.) James Douglas had avoided exile with his father by remaining in Scotland under a false name. He was only in late boyhood at the time, but on reaching adulthood he worked as a 'grieve' or farm manager. His rough manner was probably part of his character, though enemies imputed it to his lack of courtly upbringing. His portrait, painted in later life, shows a bulky man with a florid face and a bushy red beard; from the picture it is not difficult to imagine a younger man with such an appearance in the making. The third prisoner, George Douglas, was Angus's son by Janet Stewart of Traquair. He was destined for a career in the Church, which was a

PLATE I: DARNLEY'S TUDOR ANCESTRY

Above right Henry Tudor, Earl of Richmond, later King Henry VII, by Jacques le Boucq.

Above Henry VIII as a young man.

Right Margaret, Countess of Lennox [née Lady Margaret Douglas], granddaughter of Henry VII, niece of Henry VIII and mother of Darnley.

Like as, the monumentes of auncient authors (most triumphant, most victorious, and most gratious Princesse) declare, how that a certaine excellent musician, named timotheus musicus, was woante with his sweete proporcioned and melodious armonye, to enflame Alexander the greate Conqueror and King of macedonia, to aduil warres, with a moste feruente desire: Euen so, I remember me with my self oftentymes how that ouer and besides, suche manifolde benefites, as your highnes heretofore haith bestowed on me it haith pleased your moste Excellent Maiestie laitlie to accepte a litle platte of my simple penning, which I termed Pomum Granatum for the which it being base, vile, and imaymed, your Maiestie haith gyuen me a riche cheine of goulde. The voyse I say of suche instrumentes, as I heire, now and then although their melody differ muche, from the sweete strokes and soundes of king Alexanders timotheus do not only, persuade and moue, yea pricke, and spurre me forwarde, to endeauoure my wittes daylie all vanities set aparte to vertuous lerning and study, being thereto thus encouraged so oftentymes, by your Maiesties manifolde benefites, giftes, and rewardes: Bat also I am enflamed and stirred, euen now, my tendre aige not withstanding, to be serding your grace, wishinge thing euery haire in my heade for to be a woarthy souldiour, of that same self herte, courage, and stomach that I am of. But when as I perceaue, that neither my witt, power, nor yeares ar at this present correspondinge unto this, my good will. This shall be therefore (moste gratious Princesse) moste humbly remaininge unto your Maiestie immortall thankes for your riche Cheine, and other your Higtnes syndrie giftes gyuen unto me, without anny my deseruinges, from tyme to tyme. Trustinge in God, one day of my tendre bounden dutie, to endeauour my self, with my faithfull hertie seruice, to remembre the same. And beinge afraid, with this my superflous woordes, to interlarde (God seruinge) your Highnes, who is Moste Excellent Maiestie is alwaies, and specialy now, occupied in moste weightie maters, thus I make an end. Praye God Almightie God, moste humbly, and faithfully, to preserue, keipe, and defende, your Maiestie laitly reigninge ouer vs, all your true, and faithfull subiettes, a moste victorious, and Triumphant Princesse, Amen. From Temple Newsome, the xxviij of marche. 1554.

Your Maiesties moste bounden, and obedient subiecte, and seruaunt.

Henry derrley.

PLATE II: DARNLEY AND MARY I OF ENGLAND

Left Darnley's letter to Mary I, written at the age of eight; a close look at the letter will reveal the guide lines ruled by Darnley's tutor, John Elder.

Inset Mary I of England, who showed friendship to the Earl and Countess of Lennox and favour to their son Darnley, but disappointed their hopes that she might recognize him as her heir.

PLATE III: PARENTAL AMBITION

Below Darnley at the age of nine, by Hans Eworth.

Right Mary Queen of Scots as Dauphiness of France.

Throughout his childhood Darnley's parents continued to hope that he might marry Mary Queen of Scots; her marriage to the Dauphin François was an obstacle removed by his early death.

PLATE IV: THE QUEEN'S SUITOR

Life-scale portrait of Darnley and his younger brother Lord
Charles Stuart, probably intended to be shown to Mary Queen of
Scots, to encourage her to favour her handsome cousin as a suitor.

Below Mary Queen of Scots wearing the *deuil blanc* [white mourning] which she wore for her father-in-law Henri II of France, for her first husband François II of France, and at her marriage with Darnley.

Right Coin of Mary Queen of Scots and François as King and Queen of Scots and Dauphin and Dauphiness of France. The Crown symbolized their joint sovereignty of Scotland, and is the 'Crown Matrimonial' which was later the object of Darnley's aspirations.

Below James Stewart, Earl of Moray, illegitimate son of James V, and Regent of Scotland after the downfall of Mary Queen of Scots.

Right Agnes Keith, Countess of Moray. Darnley claimed that Mary had urged him to seduce her.

PLATE VII: ELIZABETH AND LEICESTER

Above Queen Elizabeth I c.1565–68.

Left Lord Robert Dudley, created Earl of Leicester in 1564; favourite of Queen Elizabeth and reluctant suitor of Mary Queen of Scots.

My especiall good lorde yowre accustomed frendlines dewrynge my continuaunce in the courte, yea sence I fyrste knewe yowre L. can not thoughte I am nowe farre from yowe be forgotten of my parte, but the remembraunce therof constrainethe me in thess fewe lynes to geue yowre L. my humble thankes therfore, and to assuer yowre L. that dewrynge my lyfe I shall not be forgetfull of yowre great goodnes and good nature shewed sundry waies to me: but to my power shall euer be redy to gratefy yowre in any thynge I maye as assuredly as yowre owne brother. And thus withe my humble comendations to yowre good L. I wyshe yowre as well as yowre owne harte woulde. From Dunkel, the xxj. daye of february. 1564.

My lorde my father sendethe yowre L. his moste harty commendations.

Yowre L. assured to commaunde.

H. Darnley.

PLATE VIII: 'I SHALL NOT BE FORGETFUL OF YOUR GREAT GOODNESS . . .'

Letter from Darnley to the Earl of Leicester, probably intended to convey his gratitude for Leicester's assistance in gaining Queen Elizabeth's permission for Darnley to go to Scotland.

Inset Miniature of Darnley by an unknown artist.

convenient method of providing for royal and aristocratic bastards, and a contribution to the poor quality of the Scottish ecclesiastical hierarchy in the years preceding the Reformation. In 1546 George Douglas had been nominated to the abbacy of Arbroath, and while he awaited its reversion was known as 'The Postulate of Arbroath', or simply as 'The Postulate', for short. He eventually became Bishop of Moray, and was notorious for his scandalous life and theological ignorance.[18] So widely was he recognized as an unsavoury character that friendship with him was regarded as discreditable.

When Margaret Lennox's kinsmen arrived in Yorkshire she would have brought them to see her son, and expected them to admire the attractive little boy, not yet two. No doubt they dutifully did so, unaware that in visiting him they were taking the first step on a road that would lead to a sequence of deaths.

The little boy who was shown to his kinsmen in 1548 was just passing the threshold between babyhood and childhood. He would still have been dressed in skirts, as his younger brother Lord Charles Stuart (as yet unborn) is shown in the double portrait of the brothers attributed to Hans Eworth.

Putting a boy into breeches was a significant rite of passage. It signified transition from the care of nurse, governess and attendant ladies to that of tutors and gentlemen, from cossetting to lessons and sports. The Renaissance schoolroom was a forcing house in which the sons, and a few daughters, of kings and noblemen learned Latin vocabulary, grammar and syntax at an age when few modern children are even literate. It was accepted that a boy must learn Latin to join the international élite of educated people, who could read or write a Latin letter, converse with a foreigner whose vernacular was unknown, understand an allusion to a mythical god or hero, and cap a classical quotation. This was not to be learned as a Renaissance polymath understood it; but it was to be cultured, as the Renaissance prince or nobleman aspired to be. To dance, to play at least one musical instrument and to sing were accomplishments expected of any cultured person; to write a good hand, and to write verses, were abilities additionally admired.

While culture was the Renaissance ideal for a prince or nobleman, the medieval tradition that he should be a warrior continued. Darnley would have grown up with the knowledge that his father was a soldier, and so were his uncle Aubigny and his grandfather Angus. He was eager to follow in their footsteps and learn to handle weapons and practise the warlike sports that made a man feel like a warrior, even when there was no real warfare going on. Good horsemanship was the essential skill for war, and for sport and travel. For Darnley, as for most of his contemporaries, weapons and horses were favourite possessions, and hunting and hawking favourite recreations, almost to the point of obsession.[19]

Darnley had two tutors, John Elder and Arthur Lallart, and began his lessons with the former. Elder was a cleric, by his own account a native of Caithness, who had spent twelve years at the three Scottish universities of St Andrews, Aberdeen and Glasgow, and was a canon of the Collegiate Church of Dumbarton. He owed his recommendation as Darnley's tutor to Lennox's brother the Bishop of Caithness, who was also Provost of Dumbarton. Elder was an ambitious man whose efforts to thrust himself upon the attention of great persons did not bring him the rewards he hoped for, though they assured him a footnote in history, not entirely to his credit.

When Lennox transferred his allegiance to Henry VIII Elder took the opportunity to address to the English King a '*Proposal*' for the union of Scotland and England through the marriage of Prince Edward and Mary Queen of Scots, promising Henry the support of the Highlanders, amongst whom he counted himself.[20] Couched in an extravagantly humble style characterized by such sentences as 'it bicommes not me, a wretche destitude of all good lernynge and eloquence, to interturbe your noble Grace with theis my rude, barbarous and fessious [troublesome] letters', Elder's '*Proposal*' also contained much vituperation against the Scottish bishops as 'the Dewil's convocacion' and against 'David Beton ther cardinall, with Beelzebub's fles[h]mongers the abbotes . . .' Elder concluded with the hope that Henry would be able to 'hwnt, drwye and smoghe the forsaid fals papisticall foxis' out of the kingdom, 'at the which hwntinge, wold God that I and everye haire in my head . . . wer a man with your noble Grace . . .' And with typical Renaissance love of classical allusion, he wished that each of these imaginary warriors could have the strength of Hercules, the manhood of Hector, and the subtlety of Achilles. In 1546 Cardinal Beaton was murdered, a slaughter approved if not abetted by Henry VIII.

Elder wrote a beautiful hand, and his '*Proposal*' was submitted to Henry VIII in an elegant manuscript, with decorative little marginal notes introducing each new subject. Since Darnley was admired for his penmanship it has been assumed that Elder was his writing master, but if so, Elder taught him to write a different hand from his own. Darnley learnt the Italic hand which was just coming into fashion, and to modern eyes it is much more easily legible than Elder's writing, and its decorations do not interfere with its legibility. However, Elder was the overseer of his education, and undoubtedly composed the famous letter Darnley wrote to Queen Mary I, carefully copied between faint lines that his tutor had ruled for him:

Lyke as the Monumentes of auncient authors, most triumphaunte, moste victorious, and moste gratious Princesse, declare how that a certane excellent musician, Timotheus Musicus, was wounte with his swete proporcioned and melodious armonye to enflame Alexander the greate Quonquerour and King of Macedonia to civill warres, with a moste fervent desire; evenso, I remembring with my self oftentymes how that (over and besides suche manifolde benefites as your Highness hertofore haith bestoued on me) it haith pleased your moste excellente Majestie laitlie to accepte a little Plote of my simple penning, which I termed Vtopia Nova; for the which it being base, vile, and maymed, your Maiestie haith gyven me a riche cheane of golde. The noyse (I saye) of suche instrumentes, as I heire now and then, (although ther melody diffre muche from the swete strokes and sounds of King Alexanders Timotheus) do not only persuade and move, yea pricke and spurre me forwarde, to endevoure my wittes daylie, (all vanities set aparte) to vertuous lerning and study, being therto thus encouraged, so oftentymes by your Maiesties manifolde benefites, giftes and rewardes; but also I am enflamed and stirred, even now my tendre aige not withstanding, to be serving Your Grace, wishing every haire in my heade for to be a wourthy souldiour, of that same self hert, mynde, and stomake that I am of. But wher as I perceave that neither my wite, power, nor yeares ar at this present corresponding unto this, my good will: thes shall be therfore (moste gratious Princesse) most humbly rendring unto your Maiestie immortall thankes for your riche Cheane, and other your Highnes syndrie giftes, gyven unto me without anny my deservinges, from tyme to tyme. Trusting in God, one day, of my moste bounden duetie, to endevour my self with my faithfull hertie service, to remember the same. And being afraid, with thes my superflous woordes to interturbe (God forefende) Your Highnes, whois moste excellent Maiestie is alwaies, and specially now, occupied in most weightie maters, thus I make an end: Praing unto Almightie god, most humbly and faithfully to preserve, keipe, and defende your Maiestie, long reigning ouer us all, your true and faithfull subjectes, a most victorious and triumphant Princesse, Amen. From Temple Newsome, the xxviii of Marche, 1554.

Your Maiesties moste bounden and obedient

subjecte and seruaunt,

Henry Dernley.[21]

In the sixteenth century, which did not encourage childish self-expression, such pedantic displays of precocity were much admired. But Elder's authorship of the letter is indicated by the use of the unusual word 'interturbe' (disturb, interrupt), which had appeared in his *'Proposal'* addressed to Henry VIII, and by the repetition of the wish that every hair of the writer's head might become a soldier in the service of his sovereign. Elder evidently had been sufficiently pleased with this fancy to reuse it on Darnley's behalf. No doubt he had also composed the essay 'Utopia Nova' for Darnley to copy. Darnley's letter was intended to impress Queen Mary I, but it had additional significance in its political context.

On 6 July 1553 the sixteen-year-old King Edward VI had died. During the later years of his reign Somerset's authority had been superseded by that of John Dudley, Duke of Northumberland, a ruthless schemer who had sent his predecessor to the block. Northumberland aspired to transfer the succession to his own family, and persuaded the dying Edward VI to compose a 'Devise of the Succession', which excluded his half-sisters Mary and Elizabeth, and willed the crown to his cousin, Lady Jane Grey, recently married to Northumberland's fourth son, Lord Guildford Dudley. When Jane became Queen, Guildford would be King, allowing Northumberland, as he imagined, many years as the power behind the throne. The plot miscarried, in the face of overwhelming support for Mary. The nine days' reign of Queen Jane, from 9 to 18 July 1553, was a pitiful charade of which she was the tragic victim (though her refusal to make Guildford King without the consent of Parliament suggests that she may have been less biddable than Northumberland supposed). Northumberland was executed, but Jane and Guildford were imprisoned with the intention of sparing their lives. The radical Protestantism imposed on England by Edward VI's governments had not taken deep root, so Mary's Catholicism was no bar to her popularity. Nor was her restoration of Catholic worship as it had been practised at the end of Henry VIII's reign, though Parliament refused to rescind the royal supremacy, which was deeply repugnant to her. Her first unpopular decision was that she would marry Prince Philip of Spain, son of the Emperor Charles V who had been her only ally during her years of persecution. Her decision provoked the rebellion of Sir Thomas Wyatt, whose declared purpose was to secure the advancement of 'liberty and commonwealth . . . imperilled by the Queen's determinate pleasure to marry with a stranger'.[22] The rebellion was nationalist rather than religious, and its purpose was to substitute Elizabeth for Mary, with Edward Courtney as her husband, which would have linked one of the last Plantagenet descendants with the last Tudor heiress. The rebellion occurred at the beginning of 1554, and Mary's courage when London was attacked did much to ensure Wyatt's defeat. The participation of Lady Jane Grey's father in the rebellion sealed her fate and that of her husband. Both were executed on 12 February 1554. Wyatt himself was condemned to death on 15 March, to be executed on 11 April. Elizabeth was also in danger of death, for the Queen suspected her implication in the rebellion. On 18 March she was imprisoned in the Tower, her life in the balance.

When the nine-year-old Darnley carefully copied out his letter to Queen Mary she was indeed a 'most victorious and triumphant Princesse', and the weighty matters he did not wish to 'interturbe' were the impending execution of Wyatt and the preparations for her marriage with Philip of Spain. To Margaret Lennox the death of Edward VI had been excellent news, for it raised her friend and cousin Mary to the throne and restored the Catholic religion. The imprisonment of Elizabeth was also good news, and would be better were it followed by her execution, for this would bring Darnley a step nearer to the throne. As for the will of Henry VIII, it no longer looked so impressive. It had been flouted once by Somerset, and again by Edward VI at Northumberland's instigation. And Northumberland's plot had laid the stigma of treason on the Suffolk line, which Henry VIII had preferred to either the Stuart or Douglas descendants of his sister Margaret. Mary Queen of Scots was in France, promised to the Dauphin. At the moment the advantage was with Darnley. The purpose of the letter was to fix the attention of the Queen upon him, and to convince her that he was precocious, devoted, and in every way suitable to be recognized as her heir.

The Queen showed her affection for Margaret Lennox and her family with spectacular generosity. When they came to court they were given apartments in the Palace of Westminster, furnished at the Queen's expense with ten beds and twenty-one pieces of tapestry, enough to furnish a large suite of rooms for family and servants. The bed provided for Margaret herself was of purple velvet and cloth of gold 'with St George figured on it in sundry places'. The Earl of Lennox was appointed Master of the Hawks and given the best horse from the stable of Edward VI. Personal presents to the Countess included two gowns of gold tissue,[23] a gold girdle set with rubies and diamonds, and a large pointed diamond which had been repossessed from the Duchess of Somerset. Darnley was given several lutes[24] that had belonged to Edward VI, and three suits of his clothes. Edward had been small for his years, and Darnley was to grow unusually tall, but no doubt the clothes fitted him for a time. His hopeful mother may have seen them as a symbolic gift, and they may have been so intended; but symbolism stopped far short of the recognition she craved for him. Though the Queen favoured her young kinsman, she was hoping that marriage to the Prince of Spain would give her children of her own. Margaret, despite their friendship, could only hope that it would not.

Philip of Spain landed at Southampton on 20 July, and met the Queen three days later in the Bishop's Palace at Winchester. Mary was thirty-eight, and prematurely aged by ill-health and unhappiness. She could not fail to disappoint a bridegroom eleven years younger, who had already had a young wife. The wedding was celebrated with great splendour in Winchester Cathedral on 25 July, St James's Day. In preparation for the marriage the Emperor had created his son King of Naples, to give the royal pair parity of rank. But Philip's postition as King of England was in his view unsatisfactory. He became King in right of his wife, but her Council had resolutely refused him the Crown Matrimonial, which would have given him the right to continue as King of England should his wife predecease him. He regarded the refusal as an insult to him and a disparagement to his status.

Mary had the misfortune to fall in love with a husband who was unable to respond to her emotions. But Philip did his conjugal duty, and by the autumn the Queen believed herself pregnant. As the year ended she had another cause to rejoice, with the arrival of an ambassador from Pope Julius III, to reconcile England to the papacy. The Pope sent Cardinal Reginald Pole, great-nephew of Edward IV and son of the Countess of Salisbury, whose fate he would undoubtedly have shared if Henry VIII could have laid hands on him. Pole had lived in exile for twenty years and condemned Henry VIII's proceedings from the Continent. Queen Mary declared that when she met the Cardinal the child in her womb had leapt for joy, like the unborn John the Baptist when his mother was visited by the Virgin Mary. But the physical tremor of excitement was not the infant quickening, for excessive hope had produced a false pregnancy, a tragic humiliation which would be revealed the following year. Meanwhile, in unsuspecting joy, she prepared for the reconciliation of her country with the Holy See. On 28 November Cardinal Pole addressed both Houses of Parliament, and stressed the spiritual nature of his mission, reassuringly making no mention of papal jurisdiction or erstwhile Church property:

> I come to reconcile, not to condemn. I come not to compel but to call again. I am not come to call anything in question already done, but my commission is of grace and clemency to such as will receive it . . .

Two days later a delegation of both Houses, led by the Bishop of Winchester, petitioned the King and Queen 'as persons unsullied by heresy' to intercede with the Cardinal to end the schism. Cardinal Pole pronounced the papal absolution, and England was once more a Catholic country. At the end of 1554 none could have guessed how short-lived the 'return to obedience' would be.

At the beginning of 1555 John Elder, as a New Year's gift to his first patron, the Bishop of Caithness, sent him a detailed account of these momentous events. It is an important historical source for the marriage of Philip and Mary and the mission of Cardinal Pole, and an admirable piece of descriptive writing. Elder also had it printed as a small black-letter tract entitled 'The Copie of a Letter sent into Scotlande. . . to the ryght reverende. . . Lord Robert Stuarde, bishoppe of Cathenes'.[25] Its significance only becomes apparent when it is compared with Elder's 'Proposal' addressed to Henry VIII, which was the last thing Elder would have wanted, as the 'Proposal' contained views he had repudiated. But Elder had no fear that a private

attempt to curry favour with Henry would reappear to reproach him
– nor did it, until rediscovered by a nineteenth-century scholar. John
Elder, like an earlier Vicar of Bray, had now become a devout Catholic. His letter to the Bishop of Caithness contains reverential descriptions of Cardinal Pole as 'thys noble and vertuous prelate' and
references to 'the most holy Catholike fayth and true relygion of
Christ', which form a bizarre contrast to his vituperations against
Cardinal Beaton and those 'papisticall foxis' the Scottish clergy. Lest
the Bishop should think Elder was merely swimming with the tide,
he described his personal response to the reconversion of England:

> . . . although I was never (praysed be God) associated with any
> which wer erronious, or . . . defendours of hereticall and sinistrate
> opinions, but . . . during the last two kinges' procedinges, have
> kepte myself clere on every side, yet neverthelesse, as often as I
> . . . remember with myselfe how lasciviously I lived in Englande
> these xx yeres . . . I can no les doe, then lament and be sorye; yea,
> and with all my harte repente . . . purposinge (by God's grace) . . .
> to mend my most miserable and synfull lyfe, and so to continew to
> my lyves ende . . .

Having delivered himself of this humbug, Elder concluded with a
passage in praise of his pupil:

> I have also sent your lordship certain verses and adages written
> with the hande of the lorde Henry Stuarde, lord Dernley, your
> nephew, which he wrot this tyme twelvemoneth, I beinge with him
> then at Temple Newsome in Yorkshire. And what praise your
> lordship may thinke him worthie, for this his towardnes in
> wrighting, beinge not yet fully ix yeares of age, the like praise is
> he worthye (suerlye) in his towardnes in the Latin tounge, and the
> Frenche, and in sundrye other vertuous qualities; whome also God
> and nature hath endued a good wit, jentilnes, beutie, and favour.
> So yf it may please God to lend him long life, he shall prove a
> witty, vertuous, and an active, well learned gentle man, whose
> noble parentes are my singuler good patrons . . .[26]

John Elder, revealed to posterity, though not to the Bishop of
Caithness, as a sycophant and a hypocrite, may have been capable
of defining the qualities that constituted a 'vertuous' gentleman, but

he was scarcely qualified to instill them; the superficial polish and moral vacuity universally attributed to Darnley probably mirror the character of his tutor.

The verses and adages that Elder sent to the Bishop of Caithness were not included in the printed version of his letter. Later verses by Darnley show that he had some poetic talent, but there are no adages from any other source. Some twenty years later Peter Young, tutor to Darnley's son James VI, collected his pupil's sayings under the title 'Apophthegmata Regis', which illustrates the sort of remarks tutors considered promising: smart retorts, sententious utterances, jokes – feeble or otherwise – and bilingual puns were recorded by Young, and probably represent the type of 'adage' collected by Elder.[27]

There is no reason to doubt the 'towardnes' of Darnley in Latin and French. Bishop Montague in his preface to the Collected Works of King James VI and I (1616) reported that the King's father had translated the works of Valerius Maximus into English, and doubt has been cast on this by some historians, in view of Darnley's poor reputation. But there is nothing unlikely in Montague's claim. Valerius Maximus wrote and addressed to the Emperor Tiberius a handbook of illustrative examples for rhetoricians, 'Factorum ac Dicorum Memorabilium Libri IX' ('Nine Books of Memorable Deeds and Sayings'). The subject matter was grouped under useful headings for easy reference, such as 'Omens', 'Moderation', 'Gratitude', 'Chastity', 'Cruelty' – from which it would have been easy to select themes for translation. According to a critical scholar, 'The work is shallow, sententious and bombastic, full of the boldest metaphors and rhetorical artifices of the Silver Age, especially forced antitheses and far-fetched epigrams, only occasionally relieved by touches of poetic fancy or neat passages of narrative or dialogue'. Valerius Maximus's chief sources were Livy and Cicero, and some minor Roman and Greek authors, eclectically gathered. '... The variety and convenience of the compilation ensured some measure of success in antiquity and considerably more in the Middle Ages'.[28] In fact, it was exactly the type of book John Elder might have been expected to select: showy, not too difficult, suitable for providing his pupil with a veneer of classical knowledge without obliging him to read the works of the more serious classical authors in depth.

Darnley's tutor in French was probably Arthur Lallart, who on later evidence was the household's French language expert. But

Darnley would also have learnt French by informal means. Matthew, Earl of Lennox was bilingual in French and Scots, and had been speaking English since 1544. Margaret Lennox had spoken Scots in childhood, and may have learnt French during her father's exile in France, but English had been her daily tongue for many years. It is likely that Darnley was brought up to be familiar with all three languages. His parents' ambitions encompassed situations in which he might have to use all or any of them. Lennox envisaged the recovery of his Scottish estates, and Margaret the inheritance of her father's. Darnley, they hoped, would inherit both, so it behoved him to learn to speak and write like a true Scot. Though the Queen of Scots was to marry the Dauphin, the hope remained that this plan might miscarry. She might, after all, require an English or Scottish husband, and who better than the one who had claim to the crowns of both Scotland and England, especially if he had a veneer of the French culture to which she was accustomed. Besides, the Lennox family had French affiliations, so it was appropriate for Darnley to be educated in this tradition. Probably conversation with his parents ensured that he became fluent in Scots and French as well as English. That he could write both Scots and English with equal ease his later letters and verses testify, and there is a surviving example of a letter by him written in French.[29]

Other aspects of his education were not neglected. Queen Mary's gift of Edward VI's lutes was well chosen, for Darnley was later acknowledged as an expert lutenist and singer and an elegant dancer. He was strong and athletic, so that riding and martial sports came easily to him. He became a magnificent horseman, and his passion for hunting and hawking was matched by his knowledge and expertise in both. He was probably happiest out of doors, but as he progressed from childhood to adolescence he acquired with apparent ease all the accomplishments in which a prince or nobleman was expected to excel. He appeared to be everything his doting parents could have desired.

Apart from his formal and informal lessons, Darnley would have absorbed his parents' ambitions for him through the indoctrination of stories. Like any scion of a noble family he would have been told of its past glories. On his father's side there was the glory of the legitimate descent of the Earls of Lennox from King James II of Scotland, to be contrasted with the dubious descent of the Hamiltons, contempt for whom was an inevitable and dangerous lesson. On his mother's side there was the glory of descent from King Henry VII of England, whose success as a claimant to the throne was a triumph for Darnley to emulate. (Margaret Lennox may have envisaged for herself a role like that of Henry VII's mother Lady Margaret Beaufort, who had acted as the conduit of royal blood which enabled her son to claim the throne.)[30] The next Tudor success story relevant to Darnley's future was the marriage of Henry VII's daughter Margaret to King James IV, which enhanced Darnley's status as the grandson of a queen, though by her second marriage. He would have been told that the marriage of Queen Margaret to the Earl of Angus was more exalted than that of Mary Tudor 'The French Queen' to the Duke of Suffolk, for the Douglases were ancient nobility, whereas the dukedom of Suffolk was Henry VIII's creation. Darnley, royal on both sides of his family, would have been taught to believe that no one was his equal – neither the daughter of Henry VIII's 'concubine' Anne Boleyn nor the surviving sisters of the unfortunate Lady Jane Grey. The message of all the stories was that the throne of England ought to be his, and that the throne of Scotland was not beyond his reach.

Darnley's first portrait was painted when he was nine years old, by Hans Eworth. It shows him as a well-grown boy, mature for his years, proud and dignified in bearing. He is fair-skinned and grey-eyed with short blond hair and the open, ingenuous face of a child for whom life has always been pleasant. He is dressed in a black doublet and hose, with a black cloak hanging loosely from his shoulders. His doublet is fastened with gold buttons in the form of flowers, and sewn with parallel rows of gold 'aiglets' or ornamental tags. A dagger with a gold hilt is stuck into his belt, and the elaborate gold hilt of a sword, disproportionately large for him to wield, appears from beneath his cloak. His left hand, with a black enamelled ring on the fourth finger, clasps a pair of gloves. The boy's sombre costume is touched with white: a white plume in his black bonnet, narrow white ruffs at his throat and wrists, and an ostentatious white codpiece, suggesting a virility he did not yet possess. It is a typical sixteenth-century portrait of a young nobleman, intended as a likeness, but also as a portrayal of his status.

For the Earl and Countess of Lennox the happiest event of 1556 was the birth of their last child, Lord Charles Stuart, a healthy baby, following the two sons and three daughters who had died in infancy since the birth of Darnley.

The rejoicing was followed by a sequence of disappointments. Early in 1557 the Earl of Angus died at Tantallon, after prolonged sufferings from erysipelas. His death probably caused Margaret more chagrin than sorrow, for though she was his heir of line in Scottish law, he had entailed his estates to a male heir, the elder son of his brother, Sir George Douglas of Pittendriech. Angus's son by Lord Maxwell's daughter had died in the winter of 1548, shortly after which Margaret had heard the first rumours of his intention. She had written him an angry letter:

> My uncle George haithe said, as dyverse Skottesmen have tolde me, that thowe you had sones he wolde be eyre [heir] and make them all bastardis; butt, my Lorde, if God sende you moo [more] sons, and I Iyffe after you, he shall have leste [least] parte thereof, or elles many a man shall smarte for it . . .[31]

Angus was grieved by the quarrel, and hoped for a reconciliation with Margaret before his death, but he did not change his plan. Sir George Douglas indeed had 'leste parte thereof' as he had died in 1552, but Angus's title and estates went to Sir George's elder son David Douglas, who became seventh Earl of Angus, but died in 1557, to be succeeded by his young son Archibald. David's brother James, Earl of Morton became the boy's guardian. Margaret refused to accept these arrangements. She assumed her father's title and signed her letters 'Margaret Lennox and Angus'. She also appealed to Marie de Guise, who had been Queen-Regent of Scotland since 1554, to be admitted to pursue her claim to the estates in the Scottish Court of Chancery. Her request was initially granted, and then her right to do so was questioned again, since she was the wife of a forfeited traitor. In this unsatisfactory condition her case languished, but she did not abandon it.

More catastrophic was the extinction of her hope that Queen Mary I might recognize Darnley as her heir. Mary's accession to the throne, in overturning Edward VI's 'Devise', had restored Elizabeth to her place in the succession; and Mary, though suspecting her complicity in Wyatt's rebellion, had not removed her from it. Once Elizabeth had survived the crisis of imprisonment in the Tower, her position gradually grew stronger. She found an unexpected ally in King Philip, who wished her to marry his kinsman Emmanuel Philibert, Duke of Savoy. Already Philip envisaged the possibility of Elizabeth's succession, and wanted her securely bound to the Hapsburg interest. After Mary's false pregnancy of 1555, Philip concluded that his wife was incapable of childbearing, though Mary still clung pathetically to her hope of children. However, Philip's departure from England deferred the possibility. While Mary refused to face reality on the succession question, Philip opposed Darnley's claim; the Lennox Stuarts were too closely identified with France, his hereditary enemy.

Philip returned to England in 1557. He was now King of Spain, through the Emperor's voluntary demission of power. The imperial authority went to the Emperor's brother Ferdinand. Spain, the Netherlands and the Spanish conquests in the New World went to Philip. With this vast accession of power, England mattered less to him. He returned only to draw the country into his war with France, an unpopular policy which required his influence with the Queen. Philip's return gave Mary another chance to delude herself that she was pregnant. Not sharing her delusion, Philip again attempted to force Elizabeth to marry the Duke of Savoy – but Elizabeth began as she intended to continue, and evaded being pressurized into marriage. Discreetly, a strong party was preparing to support her accession, and soon it became obvious that she had only to wait, and the crown would be hers without the encumbrance of a foreign husband or an unpopular alliance.

The reign of Mary ended in a landslide of disasters: her burnings of heretics caused widespread revulsion against her religious policy; her involvement in Philip's French war brought war with Scotland, the ally of France, and the loss of Calais, the last vestige of England's medieval empire; finally, the Queen's apparent pregnancy proved to be caused by a malignant tumour, from which she died on 17 November 1558. Beyond her devoted household there was little pity for her tragic end. Elizabeth's accession was greeted with a surge of enthusiasm that revealed the hopes of other claimants as chimerical.

Earlier in the year, on 24 April, Mary Queen of Scots had married the Dauphin, who had been recognized as King of Scots, and granted the Crown Matrimonial. Thenceforward François and Mary were known in France as King-Dauphin and Queen-Dauphiness. On the death of Mary I, the French King Henri II had immediately caused them to quarter the arms of England with those of France on everything normally decorated with armorial bearings, from tilting armour to table silver. This was a visual assertion that Mary Stuart was the lawful successor to Mary Tudor, to the exclusion of the illegitimate Elizabeth. The implied threat had little substance (though the loss of Calais made it seem more serious than it appears in the perspective of history), but the insult was great, and its effect on the future relations of Mary Queen of Scots and Elizabeth of England was incalculably damaging.[32]

Margaret Lennox attended the exequies of Queen Mary I as chief mourner, and then retired to Yorkshire in great bitterness of spirit. The late Queen had disappointed her hopes, and it seemed that Darnley's royal destiny was thwarted. But hope revived, and with it ill-will to those who barred his advancement. Margaret had hoped for Elizabeth's death before, and could hope for it again. Though Elizabeth had not died in the Tower, she might be carried off by smallpox, or the sweating sickness, or the plague, as were hundreds of people from every stratum of society, every summer. An equally welcome misfortune might overcome the King-Dauphin, who was reported a sickly youth. If wishes could spread destruction, these two sovereigns would die. It was easy to hope for their deaths, but without the capacity to look into the future, to make contingent plans was impossible.

3

'YONDER LONG LAD'

> 'Yet', she said, 'you like better of yonder long lad',
> pointing towards my Lord Darnley, who, as nearest
> prince of the blood, did bear the sword of honour that
> day before her . . .'[1]

IN THE SUMMER OF 1559 the Earl and Countess of Lennox and their
sons were at Settrington, a house on the Yorkshire Wolds, where they
now spent more time than at Temple Newsam. It was nearer the coast,
within an easy day's ride of the little port of Bridlington, which traded
with Dieppe. By making use of the trading vessels it was possible for
Lennox and his wife to maintain secret contacts with France.

At Settrington they received news of the death of Henri II of
France, a bizarre misadventure rendered all the more sensational by
the accuracy with which it had been predicted by Nostradamus. In
1555 Michel de Nostredame, who like most Renaissance savants
latinized his name, had published his 'Centuries' (groups of one hundred) of arcane prophetic quatrains, which foretold coming events
from the near future to the far-distant twentieth century, and possibly
beyond. The book was an immediate success, although the language
was impenetrable and the sequence of the prophecies disordered. It
appeared at a time when prediction was taken extremely seriously,
and its very obscurity seemed authoritative and compelling. But interest in Nostradamus was replaced by awe-struck astonishment when
his prophecy of Henri II's death was fulfilled with hideous accuracy.
Nostradamus had written:

Le lyon jeune le vieux surmontera
En champ bellique par singulier duelle;
Dans cage d'or les yeux luy crevera
Deux classes une, puis mourir, mort cruelle.[2]

[The young lion shall overcome the old
In warlike field in single combat;
In a golden cage he will pierce his eyes
Two wounds one, then die a cruel death.]

In April 1559 the hostilities involving England, France and Spain ended with the peace of Cateau-Cambresis. The treaty was sealed in customary fashion with royal marriages. Madame Marguerite, sister of Henri II, married the Duke of Savoy, and Henri's daughter Elisabeth of France married the recently widowed Philip of Spain. The celebrations in Paris included a tournament held on 30 June, for which lists were laid out in the rue St Antoine beside the Hôtel des Tournelles. The King, an expert and enthusiastic jouster, participated in person. His opponents were the Duke of Ferrara, the Duc de Guise and the young Gabriel de Lorges, Comte de Montgomery, Captain of the King's Garde Ecossaise. The courses were run, and the King, who had been almost unseated by Montgomery, challenged him to joust again. Several people, including the Queen, Catherine de' Medici, and Montgomery himself, attempted to dissuade him, but the King peremptorily commanded Montgomery to joust with him again. The two opponents wheeled their horses and rode at each other once more. Montgomery's lance splintered against the King's helm, one sharp splinter entered between the gilded bars of the visor and pierced the King's right eye, while the jagged end of the broken lance pierced his throat – 'two wounds one'.

The King died in the Hôtel des Tournelles on 10 July, and the Parisian populace burnt an effigy of Nostradamus and clamoured for his death. But Catherine de' Medici protected him: she did not confuse prophetic power with malice, and resolved to consult him in the future.

With the death of Henri II, the King-Dauphin François and the Queen-Dauphiness Mary Queen of Scots became King and Queen of France.

Immediately on receiving the news the Earl and Countess of Len-

nox took the bold decision to send Darnley to France to congratulate
François and Mary on their accession. It was doubly bold because
in addition to the normal hardships and hazards of travel Darnley
would be going without a safe conduct (passport) from Queen Elizabeth. This was not requested because it would not have been granted,
but it meant that Darnley would be making the journey without
diplomatic protection, and would be arrested if he encountered any
agents of the English government. He travelled with John Elder, and
doubtless an additional escort of servants.

They found the French court at Chambord, in mourning for Henri
II. Though Darnley had been accustomed to splendour and formality
since the beginning of his conscious life, he could not fail to have
been impressed by the magnificence of the Château de Chambord
and the elegance of the court, even in its most sombre mood. He
was probably bemused by the sheer scale of it, the complexity of its
rituals, and the danger of its intricate web of friendships and enmities.
It was fortunate that his uncle John Stuart d'Aubigny was there to
act as his mentor and guide. D'Aubigny had been captured at the
Battle of St Quentin in 1557, and ransomed at the conclusion of the
peace. Lennox's substantial contribution to the ransom had placed
his brother under an obligation to him. As a kinsman of the new
Queen, d'Aubigny became a person of greater consequence at court.
He took Montgomery's place as Captain of the Garde Ecossaise,
probably owing this advancement to the friendship of the Queen's
uncle, the Duc de Guise, the eldest of Marie de Guise's six brothers,
who now headed the most powerful faction at court. He was able
to arrange a secret audience for Darnley with François and Mary.
Darnley was necessarily travelling incognito, and his identity was
successfully protected, for the English ambassador Sir Nicholas
Throckmorton reported only that 'a young gentleman, an Englishman or a Scottishman, who has no beard, was received with great
distinction by the King and Queen of France and Scotland'.[3]

The King and Queen were fifteen and sixteen respectively. François
Clouet's drawings of the King portray a boy who was not bad-
looking, though no one suggested that he had the makings of a
handsome man. He was small in stature and unhealthy in appearance. A cruel rumour circulated that he was sexually immature, and
unlikely to be capable of fathering a child. The black velvet mourning
costume that he wore for his father, and would wear at his coronation, probably lent him an unaccustomed dignity. There was a

poignant contrast between the King and his wife. The Queen possessed every quality her husband lacked: height and elegance, charm of manner and sexual attraction. Her long oval face, aquiline nose and delicately arched brows exemplified the style of beauty her contemporaries admired. She looked particularly captivating in her *deuil blanc*, the white mourning of a Queen of France. Over a plain black dress she wore a diaphanous white veil falling from a white hood which dipped low over her forehead and curved back from her temples, exposing her lightly frizzed auburn hair which almost matched the unusual golden brown of her eyes.

The first meeting of Mary and Darnley was entirely formal. No premonition suggested to the Queen of France that the tall blond boy with polished manners, who offered his congratulations and presented a letter from his father, was her future husband. The letter contained a request for the restoration of the Lennox estates, which she refused. But, impulsively generous, and not wishing to send her young kinsman away disappointed, she invited him to attend the coronation, and dismissed him with a present of one thousand crowns.

The coronation took place at Rheims on 18 September 1559. It was a sombre ceremony, shorn of celebrations. Mary Queen of Scots, a reigning sovereign crowned in infancy, required no coronation as a consort. She attended as a spectator, brilliantly dressed in her husband's honour, and resumed her mourning afterwards.

After the coronation John Stuart d'Aubigny invited Darnley to stay with his family. So Darnley travelled to Aubigny to be entertained by his aunt Anne de la Queulle and his slightly older cousin Esmé Stuart, who took him hunting in the forests that surrounded the little château of La Verrerie.[4] He returned home by way of Dieppe, to be welcomed back to Settrington, his secret journey safely accomplished.

Henceforward the activities of the Lennox family at Settrington were less secret than they supposed. Lennox's desire to recover his estates in Scotland and be cleared of the charge of treason gradually became an obsession. Since he and his wife were regarded with suspicion by Queen Elizabeth, the uncertainty of their prospects in England increased their desire to regain the Lennox and Angus patrimonies in Scotland. Towards the end of the year Lennox sent a confidential servant named Laurence Nisbet to Scotland to negotiate with the Queen-Regent Marie de Guise, and on his return sent him to London to contact the French ambassador, the Comte de Noailles. Nisbet was promptly arrested, imprisoned in the Tower and interrogated on the purpose of his mission. Fortunately for Lennox, Nisbet did not divulge anything treasonable to English interests. On 13 January 1560 Lennox wrote to Elizabeth's Secretary of State, Sir William Cecil, in a tone of injured innocence, requesting to know why his servant had been imprisoned, since Nisbet had only been ordered to 'travel concerning his rights in Scotland'. This letter crossed on the road with a sinister missive addressed to Lennox by the English Privy Council on 15 January, expressing regret that Nisbet's activities had been 'injurious to his Lordship's interests'. Lennox replied on 23 January that he was sorry offence had been given by his servant, who was only entrusted with matters concerning his affairs in Scotland, and requested Nisbet's release. Thereafter he changed his tactics and tried to persuade Cecil to induce Queen Elizabeth to assist his claim.[5]

Meanwhile the daily doings and sayings of the household at Settrington were being observed and recorded by one of its members, a man named William Forbes, who was also a spy in the pay of Lord Robert Dudley, the Queen's favourite. Lord Robert was the fifth son of the late Duke of Northumberland, and younger brother of Lord Guildford Dudley, the unfortunate husband of Lady Jane Grey. Northumberland's father, Edmund Dudley, a widely detested financial adviser to Henry VII, had been executed by Henry VIII at the beginning of his reign, so Lord Robert Dudley was the grandson, son and brother of convicted traitors. These were appalling antecedents for a queen's favourite, but as Lord Robert was a splendidly handsome man with whom the Queen was obviously enamoured, it was assumed that he was her lover; and as he was notoriously ambitious, it was also assumed that he aspired to marry her, if he could rid himself of the inconvenient encumbrance of a wife. The Queen was twenty-six at her accession, and it seemed unimaginable that she would not marry. That she might prefer Lord Robert Dudley to a suitable foreign prince terrified her ministers and scandalized foreign ambassadors. Lord Robert attempted to protect himself against his enemies by employing spies in influential households. William Forbes's report on the Lennox household was detailed and damaging. He reported that Lady Lennox kept a fool who was permitted 'to rail uncorrected on the Queen's Majesty and upon Lord Robert'. And when, later in the year, Lord Robert's wife, Amy

Robsart, was found dead at the foot of a staircase, Lady Lennox's comment was that he had obviously murdered her. This was a common opinion, but a dangerous one to utter. But Margaret Lennox had no inhibitions in her own house. Another of her reported speeches was 'that either Queen Mary [I] or the Queen's Majesty [Elizabeth] behoved to be a bastard. As for Queen Mary, all the world knew that she was lawful; and for herself, she desired nothing but her right, which she knew God would would send her one day'.[6]

Forbes went on to report that 'the schoolmaster', Arthur Lallart, 'had made a commentary on Nostradamus' Prognostications, to the pleasure of my Lady'. As the first English edition of Nostradamus was published in 1672,[7] the implication is that Darnley and John Elder had brought back from France a copy of the first edition, published in Lyons in 1555.[8] When they arrived in France the sensation caused by Nostradamus's prophecy of the death of Henri II was at its height, and since loose talk against Queen Elizabeth was permitted at Settrington, Elder would have recognized that a book which prophesied the death of sovereigns would be an acceptable offering to his patroness. Probably after a look at its Delphic lines she had handed it to Arthur Lallart, who was evidently regarded as the person most likely to make sense of it. Lady Lennox, said Forbes, was looking for a prophecy 'that the highest should have declined', and derisively commented that whereas Lallart imagined he had found a prophecy of the death of Elizabeth, it was really a verse referring to the collapse of the steeple of St Paul's Cathedral.[9] This remark suggests that Nostradamus's book had aroused great interest in the Settrington household, and that discussion had turned upon a particularly obscure quatrain[10]. Nostradamus in fact prophesied a long life and reign for Queen Elizabeth, though these lines were not decipherable until after her death in 1603; but in the meantime he was acknowledged to have made another accurate prophecy, of the death of François II.

> Premier fils vefve malheureux mariage
> Sans nuls enfans deux isles en discord
> Avant dix-huit incompetent age
> De l'autre pres plus bas sera l'accord.[11]

[The widow's eldest son in luckless marriage
A childless minor before eighteen shall die
Two island realms then in discord shall be
And the next son espoused at younger age.]

King François II's passion for hunting amounted almost to a mania. He was a good horseman who could overcome his physical limitations in the saddle, and could even forget his wretched health in the thrill of the chase. On 17 November 1560 when the court was at Orleans, the King returned from hunting on a bitterly cold afternoon suffering from earache. He developed an infection of the ear, and after days of agony, increased rather than alleviated by medical treatment, he died on 5 December.

Mary Queen of Scots was devastated with grief. No one doubted that she was devoted to François, though her attachment to the unprepossessing youth seemed inexplicable. Yet they had known each other since they were small children, and grown up accepting that they were destined for each other. Mary may have found in François amiable qualities unseen by anyone else; however, she did not write the touching poem of lament for him attributed to her and frequently quoted. There is strong evidence that it was written by Brantôme who fraudulently attributed it to her.[12] Without the evidence of its sentiments the nature of her grief becomes more elusive. But undoubtedly Mary was shattered by the consequences of her husband's death. Her future as Queen of France dissolved like a mirage, leaving her temporarily in despair.

A respite was provided by the convention that she should spend forty days of mourning in complete seclusion. Again dressed in *deuil blanc*, she retired to her black-draped mourning chamber. Mary's most recent biographer has criticized her for not thinking immediately of her obligations to Scotland, and preparing for a speedy return to her kingdom.[13] From the Scottish viewpoint this is a valid criticism. But Mary did not see things from the Scottish viewpoint. She had been absent from Scotland for so long that she did not instinctively think of it as either her homeland or her responsibility. Furthermore she had absorbed the condescending French view of Scotland as a poor and backward country. Her first thought when she emerged from the numbing shock of bereavement was that the death of her husband had reduced her status; her first determination was to recover it by remarriage.

The death of François also dramatically altered the status of Darnley. The Queen's widowhood made him a suitable candidate to become her second husband. Before the end of the year he arrived at Orleans to offer his parents' condolences on the death of the King of France. More hypocritical condolences could not have been offered; the Earl and Countess of Lennox must have rejoiced, if not gloated, over a death that revived their hopes for their beloved son. Though Darnley could do no more than deliver his parents' letters and return to them with the Queen's reply, he left her with a pleasant impression of himself, and with the satisfaction of having been and gone before the arrival of official condolences from Queen Elizabeth.[14] He also left Orleans with the assurance that his uncle d'Aubigny would ensure that the Queen did not forget him.

Darnley was now an official suitor, but Mary was not yet ready to take him seriously. Her ambition was to marry one of the European royalties. Her first choice was Don Carlos, son of Philip of Spain by his first wife, Maria of Portugal. As the heir of Spain and its vast possessions, Don Carlos was the greatest match in Europe, but little was known about him, and the discretion of Spanish diplomats was maintained for good reasons. Don Carlos was physically deformed and mentally abnormal, and within a few years he developed homicidal mania. Mary's desire to marry him might not have survived a true description of him, but her ambition was revealed by her eagerness to marry him as a complete unknown. Fortunately this aspiration was foiled by Catherine de' Medici, whose daughter Elisabeth had recently become Queen of Spain. Catherine would not permit her daughter to be outshone by Mary Stuart, a daughter-in-law for whom Catherine had no affection. Nor did she wish to see Mary's maternal relations in the House of Guise aggrandized by the Spanish marriage.

Failing Don Carlos, Mary was ready to marry her late husband's nine-year-old brother, who had become Charles IX of France. If a papal dispensation could be obtained, the marriage would make Mary Queen of France again, and preserve her from the need to return to Scotland. Charles had a great admiration for her, and was said to be eager to marry her, but the idea was highly distasteful to his mother. Queen Catherine had become regent for her son, and was determined to exercise her power. Nostradamus's prediction that her next son would be espoused when younger than his brother was fulfilled when he was affianced at the age of eleven to Elisabeth of Austria, whom he married in 1570.

Since both Mary's hopes for a European marriage had failed she was forced to face the daunting prospect of returning to a scarcely remembered kingdom, which had turned Protestant in her absence. The year 1559 had witnessed the Reformation rebellion against the Roman Church and the Francophile regency of Marie de Guise. It was led by a group of Protestant noblemen who called themselves the 'Lords of the Congregation', prominent amongst whom were Mary's half-brother Lord James Stewart, eldest illegitimate son of James V, and Archibald Campbell, fifth Earl of Argyll, who was married to James V's illegitimate daughter, Lady Jean Stewart. Mary Queen of Scots thus had a brother and a brother-in-law, two of the greatest magnates of Scotland, opposed to her politically if not personally, a dangerous situation in a period in which royal and noble families normally relied upon connections by blood and marriage for political support.

The regency of Marie de Guise was upheld by a standing army of French troops, which gave the forces of the Lords of the Congregation little chance of success without outside help. In February 1560 they gained the assistance of England, reluctantly granted by Elizabeth at the persuasion of Cecil. By the Treaty of Berwick, English soldiers arrived to reinforce the rebels. The Queen-Regent took refuge in Edinburgh Castle, where she died on 11 June. The main French force was besieged in Leith, cut off from further action in Scotland, while English ships in the Forth also cut their supply lines from France. English and French diplomats met to negotiate the Treaty of Edinburgh, concluded on 6 July, which provided that both English and French troops should leave Scotland, permitting the Scots to settle their own affairs. The French representatives, negotiating in the names of François and Mary, conceded that henceforward the King and Queen would cease to quarter the arms of England with their own, thus acknowledging Elizabeth's title to her throne, and Scotland's affairs should be settled by her own Parliament, thus ensuring the triumph of the Reformation. Scotland's Reformation Parliament met on 1 August 1560, sat for three weeks and passed three Acts: it abolished the authority and jurisdiction of the Pope in Scotland, forbade the celebration of Mass, and rescinded all Acts from the time of James I of Scotland 'not agreeing with God's holy word' (those that protected the Church of Rome). With this simple and comprehensive legislation, Scotland became officially a Protestant country. Mary Queen of Scots refused to ratify either the Treaty of Edinburgh or the Acts of the Reformation Parliament, but her refusal did not alter the situation. She could have reversed it only if she had returned to Scotland immediately, with sufficient force to impose her will, but she never believed it possible to do so. After the death of François II her marriage negotiations, by delaying her return, gave the new dispensation in Scotland the chance to establish itself.

In the spring of 1561 Mary was visited in France by two envoys from Scotland, one unofficial, the other representing the victorious rebels. The first was the Catholic John Leslie, later Bishop of Ross, who brought an offer from the Earl of Huntly to raise an army of Catholics and reconquer Edinburgh for Mary, if she would join him in the north. Mary refused, perhaps wisely, for had Huntly failed her she would never have reigned in Scotland; her position would have become comparable to that of James 'VIII' and Prince Charles Edward Stuart in the eighteenth century.

The rebels' envoy was Lord James Stewart, who recommended that Mary accept the religious metamorphosis of her kingdom, and return under guarantees that she could practise her religion privately and have Mass celebrated within her household. According to John Knox, Lord James 'was plainly premonished, that if he ever condescended that she should have mass publicly or privately within the realm of Scotland, then he betrayed the cause of God'. His reply was 'that she should have mass publicly . . . he should never consent; but to have it secretly in her chamber, who could stop her?'[15] It was a poor offer that placed her under such an abject disadvantage at the beginning of her personal rule, but it seemed the best that she could hope for, and she accepted.

It is only necessary to look at Hans Eworth's magnificent portrait of Lord James Stewart to understand his ascendancy over his sister and his influence upon his contemporaries. He closely resembled his father, though he was dark whereas James V had been red-haired, but he had his father's aquiline features, steely grey eyes and commanding presence. His portrait conveys the intimidating gaze which must have convinced his sister that there was no arguing with his terms. Mary had an exalted view of her honour and the reverence due to her as a sovereign, yet she had an instinctive inclination to turn to a strong man for guidance. Throughout her life in France she had relied on

the two eldest of her uncles, the Duc de Guise and the Cardinal of
Lorraine. When she returned to Scotland she transferred her reliance
to her brother, who was twelve years her senior. In consequence, she
never controlled her kingdom except through Lord James Stewart,
and when she forfeited his support she lost control of affairs and
thenceforward floundered from one crisis to the next. However, in
the spring of 1561 he seemed to provide the best guarantee that even
as a Catholic ruler she would be acceptable to her subjects.

She sailed from Calais on 14 August, to return to Scotland by sea,
since Elizabeth had refused her a safe conduct through England, as
a sign of her displeasure at Mary's refusal to ratify the Treaty of
Edinburgh. Mary's terrible reluctance to leave France was expressed
in her famous *cri du coeur*, as she sat in the stern of her ship, gazing
back at the receding French coastline: 'Adieu France . . . adieu donc
ma chère France . . . je pense ne vous revoir jamais plus.'[16]

Mary's flotilla reached Leith on 19 August. She disembarked in a
thick sea mist which John Knox interpreted as a sign of divine displeasure at her coming. But, he admitted, 'the most part' were blind
to the significance of the omen, and greeted her enthusiastically.

The Earl and Countess of Lennox would not risk sending Darnley
to Scotland to welcome her, for there would have been no chance
of keeping such a journey secret. Instead they sent Arthur Lallart,
ostensibly with messages to John Stuart d'Aubigny, but this proved
an inadequate cover story, as d'Aubigny had not come to Scotland
in the Queen's entourage. He had, however, sent a 'Book of
Emblems' as a present to Darnley. Emblems were immensely popular
throughout the sixteenth century, and were habitually adopted by
princes and noblemen as personal devices. Emblem books were the
sources of inspiration that provided the symbolic designs, each
accompanied by an appropriate Latin motto and an explanatory text.
The book sent to Darnley was probably 'Symbola Heroica' by Claude
Paradin, first published in 1557 in Lyons, which could have been
acquired easily by d'Aubigny.[17]

Though Lallart could no longer maintain the pretence that he had
only come to meet d'Aubigny he determined not to leave Scotland
without achieving his true purpose of speaking to the Queen. He
seized his opportunity at Stirling where he had followed the court
on the Queen's first progress of her reign, early in September. He

approached her as she was about to mount her horse to ride to Kincardine, *en route* to Perth.[18] Lallart, who was later arrested and forced to write an account of his doings for the English Privy Council, explained:

> I let her understand my Lord's mind regarding his estates, and also his request for his case being heard before Parliament [concerning the restoration of the Lennox estates]. The Queen replied that she was but newly returned into her realm, therefore she could not give me such an answer as she would; but all she might do for my Lord and my Lady her aunt, she would do at proper time, desiring my Lady to be always her good aunt, as she knew her for to be; with remembrances to them both.[19]

Lallart then took his leave and returned to Edinburgh, before beginning his long ride back to Settrington, bringing the most gracious and encouraging response the Earl and Countess had yet received.

Lallart's report to his patrons must have engendered a mood of cautious optimism, but soon disaster struck. All the recent intrigues and activities of the Lennox family, even their intimate conversations, had been reported to the English government: the treasonable study of Nostradamus, the jibes against the Queen and Lord Robert Dudley, the second journey of Darnley to France, and the mission of Lallart to Scotland, were all revealed. Shortly before Christmas royal messengers arrived at Settrington, arrested the family and their principal servants, and carried them off to London. The servants were lodged in the Gatehouse prison, the family confined in their own apartments in the Palace of Westminster. Suddenly it was noticed that Darnley was nowhere to be found. In the mêlée of their arrival, amidst the excitement caused by the sight of prominent people under guard, he had managed to disappear. He vanished so successfully that the government's search for him over the next few days proved fruitless.

The disappearance of Darnley was remarkable as he was already too tall and striking to disguise himself merely by donning nondescript clothes, and his upbringing had been too sheltered to have given him much chance of finding protection in London's underworld. Probably on the road between Settrington and London plans for his escape had been made and instructions given him of whom he should seek help. With his family's French connections these were probably people in the penumbra of contacts surrounding the French embassy, for Darnley was next heard of in France.[20]

The direct route to France was by the Dover road which ran from London Bridge along the south bank of the Thames to Gravesend, and thence by Rochester, Sittingbourne, Faversham, Canterbury, and over Barham Down to Dover, a seventy-mile ride, which normally took two days, though an official messenger using post horses could do it in one.[21] A favoured alternative was to go by boat from London to Gravesend, and take horse from there. England had few roads fit for fast travel, so the government could keep watch on those routes and the ports to which they led. Unless Darnley rode out of London before a watch was set for him, his whole journey was probably made by water. He did not risk visiting the French court, which might have led to a demand for his extradition; his most likely refuge would have been with his kinsfolk at Aubigny. He remained abroad for over a year.

His escape had unpleasant repercussions for his family. His father was sent to the Tower, his mother and brother placed in the custody of Sir Richard and Lady Sackville, at Sheen.[22] Margaret Lennox wrote a stream of letters to Sir William Cecil, whom she addressed as 'Good Master Sekretory', resolutely signing herself 'Margaret Lennox and Angus'. She requested an audience with Queen Elizabeth, which was refused, but continued to express fervent loyalty and devotion to the Queen, which contrasted unconvincingly with the revelations of William Forbes, of which she remained ignorant. She was informed that a Star Chamber enquiry was to be held into the question of her legitimacy. To the revival of this old threat to her status (and *ipso facto* that of her son) she replied with dignity:

> Even as God hath made me, so I am, lawful daughter to the Queen of Scots and the Earl of Angus, which none alive is able to make me otherwise, without doing wrong.[23]

The enquiry was eventually dropped, possibly because Elizabeth recognized the unwisdom of raising questions of legitimacy when her own position was so delicate.

Throughout 1562 Margaret's chief anxiety was for her husband who languished in the Tower in solitary confinement and in declining health. Her anxiety must have been increased by memories of the imprisonment and death of Lord Thomas Howard. On

22 July she wrote to Cecil, entreating him to relay her pleas to the Queen:

> ... beseeching her Majesty to have some consideration of me, her poor kinswoman, and of my husband ... who is in close prison without comfort, far unmeet to his nature, and ... not very healthful, having a disease which solitariness is most against ... beseeching her Highness, for the honour of God and for nature's sake, to mollify and appease her indignation against us ...[24]

This eloquent entreaty remained unanswered, while Lennox was several times interrogated, without being informed of the accusations against him. He stuck to the story that he had done nothing treasonable, and that his messengers to Scotland had dealt solely with his pursuit of the restoration of his estates. It was fortunate for him that Lallart told the same story, and that Forbes's revelations concerned his wife's indiscretions and not his own. However, he grew so desperate that the Lieutenant of the Tower wrote to Cecil, complaining of his prisoner's 'extreme passions' (rages).[25]

Margaret continued to plead for her husband, and when Queen Elizabeth fell ill with smallpox in October she renewed her entreaties to be allowed to see her. With fulsome hypocrisy she begged for the privilege of being permitted to nurse her. Surely such a dangerous request would convince the Queen of her loyalty![26] The Queen almost died, but the death that Margaret had hoped for the previous year would have been inopportune with Darnley abroad and his parents in prison. However, when the Queen recovered she felt more kindly towards her Lennox kindred: the spectre of a succession crisis had forced her to recognize that she preferred them to her father's chosen successors of the Suffolk line. In November Elizabeth released Lennox from the Tower and permitted him to join his wife at Sheen; they were both liberated in the spring of 1563, when the Queen declared 'that she had forgiven and forgotten their offence, yet she would not see them'. They returned to Settrington, comparatively impoverished, as Margaret complained, because while they had borne the costs of their own keep in prison, no one of sufficient authority had been left to manage their estates. They had even been forced to borrow from the Sackvilles.

Darnley rejoined his parents in 1563, and they found the money to commission, probably from Eworth, a life-size portrait of him with his little brother Lord Charles Stuart standing at his side. At the age of seventeen Darnley had reached his full height, and the portrait made the most of it. He passed six feet one inch, and may have been as tall as six foot four, which made him, in the opinion of a contemporary, 'almost the tallest man in the isle of Britain'.[27] With a man's average height at less than five and a half feet, Darnley was at least a head taller than most men, so it is not surprising that every description of him contains a reference to his height. As the portrait shows, he was well-proportioned, long-legged and graceful, and as he was an athlete his body was also well-muscled and co-ordinated. The plain black costume in which he was painted emphasizes his splendid silhouette and contrasts with his blond hair and fresh pink and white complexion. He rests an elegant long-fingered hand on the shoulder of his small brother, still in skirts, who stands beside him, scarcely reaching to his waist. The portrait was painted in the unusual medium of tempera on linen, so it could be rolled easily, and if necessary concealed, without damage. This suggests that it was intended for transportation, probably to show Mary Queen of Scots the latest likeness of her hopeful suitor.[28]

While Darnley was abroad and his parents were in prison, Mary was establishing her rule in Scotland, under the aegis of Lord James Stewart. There was a violent protest against Mary's Catholicism on the Sunday following her arrival, when the celebration of Mass in the Chapel Royal of Holyrood provoked a riot. Lord James fulfilled his bargain with Mary by defending the door of the Chapel with drawn sword, while two more of Mary's half-brothers protected the priest from rioters who shouted that 'the idolater priest should die the death'.[29] These three sons of James V were diverse characters: Lord James had an appearance of almost inhuman rectitude, Lord Robert had the reputation of a profligate, Lord John was an amiable young man who became Mary's favourite of the three.[30]

Mary endeavoured to reassure her Protestant subjects by issuing a proclamation forbidding any 'alteration or innovation of the state of religion . . . which her Majesty found public and universally standing at her Majesty's arrival in this her realm . . .';[31] she also permitted the prosecution of priests who celebrated Mass beyond the confines of the court, including Archbishop Hamilton, who was imprisoned for this offence. John Knox continued to thunder against Mary from the pulpit, and addressed disagreeable diatribes to her when she received him in audience, but he represented only a minority of irreconcilables. Under the guidance of Lord James Stewart, whom she created Earl of Moray, and of her astute Secretary of State, Sir William Maitland of Lethington, Mary reached an accommodation with the newly established Protestant Kirk. She agreed that two-thirds of the incomes of all benefices should be retained by their incumbents for life, while the other third should be divided between the Crown and the Kirk. In making provision, however ungenerously, for the ministers of the Kirk, Mary was granting it an official existence. Beyond insisting on her own right to practise her religion, she did nothing to defend Catholicism.

Disillusion with her may have inspired the rebellion of the Earl of Huntly in 1562, though he may have been more resentful of her gift of the earldom of Moray to her brother, since Huntly had been administering its lands and may have hoped to claim them. Huntly was defeated by the new Earl of Moray at the Battle of Corrichie on 28 October 1562, and died of a stroke immediately afterwards. His eldest son was imprisoned, and a younger son, Sir John Gordon, who was accused of plotting to abduct the Queen, was executed. This episode appeared to quell all disaffection with Mary's rule.

Less successful was the attempt of Moray and Lethington to reconcile the conflicting interests of Mary Queen of Scots and Queen Elizabeth, and establish a lasting 'Amity' between their two kingdoms. According to the Scottish diplomat and memoirist Sir James Melville of Halhill, '. . . my Lord Moray had great credit with my Lord Robert Dudley . . . and the secretary, Lethington, had great credit with the secretary, Cecil. So these four made a strict and sisterly friendship between the two Queens and their countries.'[32] However, it proved a fragile relationship.

Lethington's first mission to England took place shortly after Mary's arrival in Scotland. Without the French arms that Henri II might have considered employing on her behalf, Mary could not lay immediate claim to Elizabeth's kingdom, but as the legitimate claimant to the throne of an unmarried Queen she requested recognition as Elizabeth's successor. Elizabeth told Lethington that she was unwilling to commit herself on the succession, and renewed her demand that Mary should ratify the Treaty of Edinburgh. Mary's riposte was that she might ratify the treaty if Elizabeth would satisfy her on the succession. This compromise was the solution Lethington desired. Mary believed that it might be achieved by a personal meeting between herself and Elizabeth, which she proposed should take place in September 1562. Elizabeth agreed to meet her at Nottingham, but subsequently withdrew, suggesting a meeting for the following year. But the two queens never met, probably depriving history of an entertaining display of rivalry rather than an edifying show of friendship.

While the problem of the English succession remained unresolved, the question of Mary's marriage was of paramount importance. It was expedient that she should marry to secure the succession in Scotland, and if she produced an heir while Elizabeth continued unmarried, her claim to the English throne might seem increasingly attractive. Mary refused to marry the young Earl of Arran, son of the Duke of Châtelhérault, a match which would have benefitted the House of Hamilton, but had no advantages to offer her. The unfortunate Arran, who had always been mentally unstable, collapsed into insanity, and had to be kept in confinement for the rest of his life. Mary also refused to consider her uncle the Cardinal of Lorraine's favoured candidate, Archduke Charles of Styria, a younger son of the Emperor Ferdinand, for he could do nothing to assist her ambitions, which lay outside the sphere of his father's interests. Mary's thoughts returned to marriage with Don Carlos, which might bring her the resources to assert her claim to the English throne by force.

Moray and Lethington were prepared to support negotiations with Spain, less in the hope of bringing them to fruition than of using their implicit threat to coerce Elizabeth into naming Mary as her successor. Independently Moray may have calculated that if a Spanish marriage took place it would be more likely to take Mary to Spain than bring Spanish armies to Britain; then he might rule Scotland as Mary's viceroy, an attractive prospect to a man who enjoyed the exercise of power. Since Scotland had no direct diplomatic relations with Spain, Lethington approached Bishop Alvaro de la Quadra, the Spanish ambassador in London, and opened negotiations which, unknown to Mary or her advisers, were doomed from the outset. In the autumn of 1562 Don Carlos had fallen down a stone staircase and fractured his skull, an accident followed by paralysis and blindness. A trepanning operation by the great anatomist Vesalius restored his sight and movement, but left him subject to homicidal rages which included threats to kill his father. The tragedy was concealed by vague references to the Prince's poor health, and for years Philip II left his ambassadors to parry matrimonial diplomacy as best they might. By 1568 Don Carlos had become so maniacal that Philip was compelled to imprison him, and his death soon afterwards inevitably produced rumours that he had died at his father's orders. The truth about the wretched Prince was a starker tragedy than any romanticized version of it.[33]

Mary's Spanish negotiations failed to coerce Elizabeth. Her response to them was to declare that if Mary married Don Carlos or any other foreign prince she would regard her as an enemy, whereas if she married with Elizabeth's approval she might win the coveted recognition. To do so seemed at least worth consideration. But when Elizabeth was asked to name her approved candidate, after much prevarication she made the extraordinary suggestion of Lord Robert Dudley. Whether or not Elizabeth intended the nomination seriously, the man himself was scarcely acceptable, with his lack of royal blood and the taint of treason in his family, besides the gossip concerning his relations with Queen Elizabeth and the unsavoury business of his wife's mysterious death. Yet Mary, still allured by the mirage of recognition, did not reject him outright. He provided the central figure in protracted and ultimately fruitless negotiations, keeping Mary still unmarried, which may have been Elizabeth's only intention.

Meanwhile the fortunes of the Lennox family had been repaired. Queen Elizabeth's change of heart towards them dated from the 'great terror and dreadful warning' of her near death from smallpox in 1562.[34] When her death was expected her council had shown a preference for the Suffolk line, and the same message was delivered by the Parliament which met in January 1563. Elizabeth was reverently but insistently entreated either to marry or to nominate a successor. The Queen was relentlessly opposed to public discussion of the succession, and infuriated by the publication of a pamphlet by a court official, John Hales, entitled 'A Declaration of the Succession to the Imperial Crown of England', which disseminated the views of radically Protestant members of Parliament on the superiority of the Suffolk claim.[35]

The Suffolk line was now represented by Lady Katherine Grey, who had offended Elizabeth in 1560 by secretly marrying Edward Seymour, Earl of Hertford, son of Protector Somerset, an offence compounded by the birth of a son. Elizabeth had no greater liking than her father for secret liaisons among her kindred. Hertford and his wife were imprisoned in the Tower, where clandestine meetings resulted in the birth of a second son. Their success in extending the Suffolk line angered Elizabeth even more than their secret marriage. While Elizabeth refused to name Mary Queen of Scots as her successor, and opposed the claim of Lady Katherine, she indicated a preference for the English descendants of Margaret Tudor. Though she had no intention of nominating any successor, she allowed a gleam of favour to illuminate Margaret Lennox and her son, which also indicated to Mary another danger in contracting a foreign marriage. According to Quadra:

> Many people think that if the Queen of Scots does marry a person unacceptable to this Queen [Elizabeth], the latter will declare as her successor the son of Lady Margaret, whom she now keeps in the palace and shows such favour to as to make this appear probable.[36]

Elizabeth also decided to support Lennox's plea for restoration to his Scottish estates, and wrote to Mary that 'having been sundry times requested by her dear cousin the Lady Margaret and her husband the Earl of Lennox to recommend their several suits which have long continued in Scotland . . .' she now desired Mary to 'give their causes such consideration as in honour and reason they shall merit'.[37] And while the tortuous negotiations for Mary's possible marriage to Lord Robert Dudley continued without showing signs of progress, Elizabeth also continued to show favour to Darnley and his mother.

In June 1564 Queen Elizabeth and the Countess of Lennox were godmothers to the infant daughter of Sir William Cecil, a shared honour which implied that Margaret was the second lady in the kingdom. In July Darnley was sent to welcome the new Spanish ambassador, Don Diego Guzman de Silva, on his arrival in London, and conduct him to his first audience with the Queen.[38] He came to replace Quadra, who had died of the plague.

At about the same time Elizabeth won Mary's agreement that Lennox should be permitted to return to Scotland, and she granted a 'license' to Margaret to accompany him. Then suddenly she changed her mind, and wrote to Mary to cancel their departure.

Silva thought that this was because they 'asked leave to take with them a son of theirs, who is an amiable youth, but the Queen was angry at this, and revoked the license she had given them'.[39] Mary, who had stressed that she was receiving Lennox at Elizabeth's request, was exasperated, and responded with an angry letter; but in the meantime Elizabeth had decided to release Lennox after all, on condition that he went to Scotland alone.

In September 1564 Mary sent Sir James Melville to the English court, partly to repair the damage to diplomatic relations caused by her impulsive letter, partly to discuss a proposed conference to be held at Berwick to discuss Mary's marriage to Lord Robert Dudley and her claim to the succession. As Melville rode south the Earl of Lennox was riding north, but they did not meet; possibly Lennox left the direct route to visit Temple Newsam, which was not far from it. After his long exile Lennox returned to Scotland with a display of splendour. According to an anonymous Scottish diarist who witnessed his arrival in Edinburgh on 23 September, 'The said Matthew, Earl of Lennox . . . had riding before [him] twelve gentlemen clothed in velvet coats, with chains about their necks, upon fair horses, and behind him thirty other gentlemen and servants riding upon good horses, clothed all in grey livery coats.' He was received by the Queen 'in presence of the most part of the nobility of the realm', and on 9 October he was 'restored to his lands, heritage and good name, by open proclamation at the Mercat Cross of the burgh of Edinburgh'.[40] His restoration was followed by the rumour that soon he would be joined by his wife and son, and thenceforward the possibility of Mary's marriage to Darnley was openly discussed.

When Melville reached the English court he found Darnley and his mother still in high favour, despite the recent ructions between Elizabeth and Mary. Elizabeth received Melville graciously and permitted him to smooth over the matter of Mary's letter. He then presented his proposals for the conference:

'The Queen my mistress [he said] . . . is minded to send for her part my Lord of Moray and the secretary Lethington, and hopes that your Majesty will send my Lord of Bedford [the Governor of Berwick] and my Lord Robert Dudley'. She answered that it appeared that I made but little account of my Lord Robert, seeing that I named the Earl of Bedford before him; but ere long she would make him a far greater Earl, and that I should see it before my returning home . . .[41]

Melville witnessed the creation of Lord Robert Dudley as Earl of Leicester, ostensibly to give him appropriate status to become the husband of the Queen of Scots, on 29 September.

[It] was done at Westminster with great solemnity, the Queen herself helping to put on his ceremonial, he sitting upon his knees before her, keeping a great gravity and discreet behaviour. But she could not refrain from putting her hand in his neck to tickle him smilingly, the French ambassador and I standing by.

The gesture which obviously shocked Melville was perhaps less an impulse of affection than a humiliating reminder to a proud and ambitious man that his status was wholly dependent on her favour. To underline the message, with Leicester still on his knees, the Queen turned to Melville:

Then she asked me how I liked him. I answered that as he was a worthy subject, so he was happy who had a princess who could discern and reward good services. 'Yet' she said 'you like better of yonder long lad', pointing towards my Lord Darnley, who, as nearest prince of the blood, did bear the sword of honour that day before her. My answer was that no woman of spirit would make choice of such a man; for he was very lusty [lovely] beardless and lady-faced. And I had no will that she should think that I liked him, albeit I had a secret charge to deal with his mother, my Lady Lennox, to procure liberty for him to go to Scotland . . . that he might see the country and convey the Earl his father back again to England.[42]

This famous scene, in which Melville's dismissive comment on Darnley fixes his image for posterity, also reveals that Elizabeth suspected a plot to marry Darnley to Mary, and that Mary herself, who had given Melville the 'secret charge', desired him to come to Scotland.

The conference at Berwick which opened on 18 November 1564 foundered on the determination of Moray and Lethington that Mary's marriage to Robert Dudley, Earl of Leicester, must be conditional upon her recognition as Elizabeth's successor, with that recognition ratified by Parliament. The English refusal to grant this condition could only be seen by the Scots as bad faith, for without it Mary's marriage to Leicester would bring her no advantage whatsoever. But the failure of the conference was not regarded as the end of the affair, though Cecil warned Moray and Lethington not to permit their negotiations to be 'converted to a matter of bargain and purchase . . . to compass at my sovereign's hands a kingdom and a crown, for it may be sooner lost than gotten; and not being craved for, may be as soon offered as reason can require.'[43] Despite such obfuscation, Moray and Lethington continued to negotiate, because the 'Amity' with England and the recognition of Mary remained their aims, and if they failed to achieve them, their policy was bankrupt.

Elizabeth now seemed to be in the position of a patron who could give or withhold favours, and while she refused the demands of Mary and her advisers, she listened to the supplications of the Countess of Lennox. While Margaret continued to entreat Elizabeth to allow Darnley to join his father in Scotland, Lennox requested his son's presence for legal reasons: following the restitution of his estates he wished his son to be enfeoffed with him, to ensure that in future Darnley's inheritance should be unchallenged.[44]

The pleas of the Earl and Countess of Lennox for the release of Darnley were supported by the Earl of Leicester. Throughout the negotiations for his marriage to Mary Queen of Scots he played a passive role, and before the departure of Sir James Melville from London, Leicester told him that he had no aspiration to marry her:

> . . . he began to purge himself of so proud a pretence as to marry so great a queen, esteeming himself not worthy to wipe her shoes; declaring that the invention of that proposition of marriage proceeded from Mr Cecil, his secret enemy. 'For if I' says he, 'should have appeared desirous of that marriage, I should have lost the favour of both the queens . . .'[45]

Behind this façade of humility, Leicester had not relinquished the hope that Elizabeth might marry him, and did not do so for some years to come. The author of a famous study of the relationship of Elizabeth and Leicester believed that 'for a great many years the prime object of his life was to marry her, an important element in hers to keep him from doing so without finally refusing him'. If this is correct it makes sense of Elizabeth's dealings with Mary: her intention was not to marry her to Leicester, but to keep her unmarried as long as possible. It also explains Leicester's support of the pleas for the release of Darnley: if Darnley went to Scotland and married Mary it would extricate Leicester from the embarrassment he had revealed to Melville.

Less explicable is why Elizabeth suddenly decided to let Darnley go. Possibly she imagined that she could control both Lennox and Darnley by the threat of confiscating Lennox's English possessions, and by keeping the Countess of Lennox at the English court as a hostage for their obedience.

In January 1565 Elizabeth finally agreed to let Darnley go, ostensibly to fulfil his father's legal requirements, and with permission to remain in Scotland only for three months. But with all these provisos, once the 'long lad' had left England he passed out of Queen Elizabeth's control.

4

'HENRICUS ET MARIA'

My hope is yow for to obtaine
Let not my hope be lost in vaine . . .
But now receave by your industrye and art
Your humble servant Hary Stuart.[1]

'Henricus et Maria D Gra R & R Scotorum'
(Henry and Mary by the Grace of God King and Queen
of Scots).[2]

THE WINTER OF 1564 discouraged travel. In the words of Stow's
Chronicle 'the one and twentieth of December began a frost which
continued so extremely, that on New Year's even people went over
and along the Thames on the ice from London Bridge to Westminster
. . . as if they had been on the dry land.' Then 'on the third day of
January at night it began to thaw, and on the fifth day there was no
ice to be seen . . . which caused great floods and high waters . . .
and drowned many people in England, especially in Yorkshire . . .'[3]
   Defying the weather, Darnley left London at the first opportunity.
'The third day of February,' said Stow, 'Henry Stuart, Lord Darnley
. . . having obtained licence of the Queen's Majesty, took his journey
toward Scotland, accompanied with five of his father's men . . .',[4]
and on 12 February he was reported in Edinburgh. This was fast
travelling, especially in the depths of winter. The Great North Road
in the sixteenth century linked towns that lie far from the modern

route. Darnley rode by way of Royston, Huntingdon, Stamford, Grantham, York, Darlington, Durham, Newcastle and Alnwick, to the frontier at Berwick-on-Tweed, and thence by way of Dunbar and Haddington to Edinburgh. For most travellers the journey took a fortnight, though a messenger riding post horses could do it in five days.[5] Darnley made good speed and reached the border on 10 February. He was entertained by the Earl of Bedford at Berwick, and he stayed the next night at Dunbar, then stopped again at Seton Palace, just beyond Haddington, to be entertained by Lord Seton, his father's friend and ally. His arrival in Edinburgh was reported by the English ambassador, Thomas Randolph, who had been instructed by both Cecil and Leicester to receive him honourably. Randolph reported that Darnley arrived with a cold, which had better not be mentioned to Lady Lennox, who was an anxious parent.[6]

As Darnley rode through the sodden and sometimes dangerously flooded countryside, he had opportunity for thought. He had travelled abroad three times, twice under parental instructions and surveillance, once as a fugitive, on a journey which had given him a taste of independence. His journey to Scotland was the first occasion that offered him initiative. If he had drawn any conclusions from the cycle of hopes and disappointments that had dominated his childhood – as on the evidence of his later actions he had – his conclusions were that hopeful inaction was futile, and that ambition had to be pursued as resolutely as any beast of the chase. He may also have concluded, more dangerously, that if people obstructed his ambition, there were surer ways of removing them than looking for prophecies of their death.

When Darnley reached Edinburgh, ahead of his attendants and without spare horses, he paused to await letters from his father. He was entertained at Holyrood by Lord Robert Stewart, and visited by his cousin the Earl of Morton, the Earl of Glencairn, and 'other gentlemen'. According to Thomas Randolph he made an excellent impression: 'his courteous dealing with all men deserves great praise and is well spoken of'.[7] He learnt that the court was in Fife, where he would find Mary at the castle of Weymess. He borrowed horses from the obliging Randolph and crossed the Forth by the Queen's Ferry, to pay his respects to the Queen of Scots before riding north to Dunkeld, where his father was staying with their kinsman the Earl of Atholl.

Darnley's third meeting with Mary took place at Weymess on 17 February 1565, and made a far greater impression on her than their brief encounters at the court of France. According to Sir James Melville:

Her Majesty took well with him, and said that he was the lustiest
and best proportioned long man that she had seen; for he was of
a high stature, long and small [slender], even and erect . . .[8]

He had grown from a youth into a man since Mary had last seen
him, and now she was admiring him as a man, and perhaps for the
first time considering him as a suitor. As her words to Melville suggest, his height had an immediate attraction for her. Mary was six
feet tall, and probably had never met a man who was taller. As a
young girl at the court of France she had been criticized for stooping,
perhaps in an attempt not to tower over François. To be the one
who looked up was a novel experience.

Darnley stayed the night at Weymess and the next day continued
his journey to Dunkeld, whence he wrote to the Earl of Leicester:

> My especial good Lord,
> Your accustomed friendliness during my continuance in the
> court, yea, since I first knew your Lordship, cannot, though I am
> now far from you, be forgotten of my part: but the remembrance
> thereof constraineth me in these few lines to give your Lordship
> my humble thanks therefore, and to assure your Lordship that,
> during my life, I shall not be forgetful of your great goodness and
> good nature showed sundry ways to me; but to my power shall
> ever be ready to gratify you in anything I may, as assuredly as
> your own brother. And thus with my humble commendations to
> your good Lordship, I wish you as well as your own heart would.
> Your Lordship's assured to command,
> H. Darnley
> My L. my father sendeth your Lordship his most hearty commen-
> dations.[9]

This is a fulsome letter of thanks for unspecified favours, and no
doubt Leicester was to understand it as thanks for securing Darnley's
permission to go to Scotland. It is also the earliest example of Darnley's literary style, and a pleasant contrast to the tortuous concoction
which John Elder had produced for him to address to Queen Mary
I. It probably reflects the lessons of Arthur Lallart, who used language
with clarity and elegance, both qualities which characterize Darnley's
surviving letters and reported speech.

After a brief stay at Dunkeld Darnley rejoined the court on its way back to Edinburgh, recrossed the Forth with the Queen, and returned with her to Holyrood.[10] The following day, Sunday, 25 February, he accompanied the Earl of Moray to Kirk, 'heard Mr Knox preach', and afterwards dined with Moray and Randolph. In the evening there was dancing at court, and Darnley watched the Queen dancing with her ladies, and at Moray's suggestion danced a galliard with her.[11] Possibly Moray imagined that Darnley had been sent to Scotland by Elizabeth as an alternative suitor to Leicester, and since the negotiations with Leicester were so discouraging, was prepared to favour him. Possibly he also imagined that the courteous young man would be a biddable consort who would permit his ascendancy to continue, but if so this was a fleeting impression, of which he was soon disabused.

Henceforward Darnley was constantly in the Queen's company, and he continued to create a good impression, though not everyone thought him an appropriate suitor for the Queen. 'A great number wish him well,' wrote Randolph, 'others doubt him, and deeplier consider what is fit for the state of their country than (as they call him) a fair jolly young man'.[12] But Mary, who for so long had thought of marriage solely in terms of political advantage, was susceptible to the charms of just such a man, especially when marriage with him would not lack political advantage. Though Darnley had neither the wealth nor power of a foreign prince, he shared her descent from Henry VII, and a match with him would be a merger of their claims. Darnley began his courtship with this advantage to assist the attraction of his person, in his determination to captivate the Queen.

The court of Mary Queen of Scots was a civilized milieu into which Darnley fitted easily, and in which he could shine. Mary had a cosmopolitan and polyglot entourage, based on her household, which was funded by the income from her French jointure as *reine douairière de France*. Before returning to Scotland she had agreed that Frenchmen should not hold public office in Scotland (a grievance during the regency of Marie de Guise), but this did not affect her private appointments. The Comptroller of her household was a Frenchman, Bartholomew de Villemore, who had served her mother in the same capacity. The Master of her Wardrobe was another Frenchman, Servais de Condé. The Lady Governess was a Frenchwoman, Madame de Briante. The male household servants, the *valets de chambre*, included Frenchmen and Italians. Among the latter was the ill-fated David Rizzio who had arrived in the suite of the ambassador of Savoy in 1561, and had been appointed to her household as a singer. From being the bass in a quartet that performed the courtly four-part songs which provided musical settings for many contemporary poems, he was advanced to the position of Mary's secretary for French correspondence. However, Mary's own compatriots were not neglected. Scottish courtly poets, or 'makars', of whom the unofficial laureate was Alexander Scott, addressed poems to Mary, some of which were set to music. Scott wrote the elegant salutation 'Welcum, illustrat Ladye and our Quene', in which he expressed the hope that she would soon 'get a Gudeman' (a husband), and Sir Richard Maitland of Lethington, the father of her Secretary of State, wrote a similarly loyal if less distinguished poem which expressed the same hope.[13] Another Scot, George Buchanan, a humanist scholar and Latin poet of international reputation, wrote Latin '*Pompae*' or masques for court festivities, including the Queen's marriage to Darnley. Mary, who had learnt Latin, besides Italian and French in childhood, appreciated these entertainments, and also employed Buchanan to read Latin with her, an unexpectedly serious occupation of her leisure hours.

Darnley could share these pleasures with her, converse with her in French or Scots, and dance, sing and make music with her. His father later claimed that the Queen 'was stricken by the dart of love, by the comeliness of his sweet behaviour, personage, wit and virtuous qualities . . . as also in the art of music, dancing and playing.'[14] He also wooed her with verses. Probably the first he addressed to her, of which a copy exists exquisitely written in his own hand, is this simple plea to her to accept his suit:

> My hope is yow for to obtaine,
> Let not my hope be lost in vaine.
> Forget not my paines manifoulde,
> Nor my meanynge to yow untoulde.
> And eke withe dedes I did yowe crave,
> Withe swete woordes yow for to have.
>
>
> To my hape and hope condescend,
> Let not Cupido in vaine his bowe to bende,

Nor us two lovers, faithfull, trewe,
Lyke a bowe made of bowynge yewe.
But nowe receave by your industrye and art,
Your humble servant Hary Stuart.[15]

This poem could have been presented to the Queen as a manuscript, or performed for her as a part-song. Darnley and his father
had musicians in their service who could have written and performed
the music, and they may have introduced to court the musical
Hudson family, a father and four sons who played the viol. They
were a Yorkshire family who had probably belonged to the Lennox
household at Temple Newsam and Settrington, and followed the
rising star of Darnley to the Scottish court, where their establishment
is confirmed by the provision of liveries for them at the marriage of
Darnley and the Queen.[16]
A second poem, equally suitable to be read or sung, is a more
sophisticated example in Scots, in which Darnley represents himself
as a disappointed lover, who is obliged to find perverse pleasure in
the pangs of despised love:

Gife langour makis men licht
or dolour thame decoir,
in erth thair is no wicht
may me compair in gloir:
gif cairfull thochtis restoir
my havy hairt frome sorrow,
I am for evirmoir
in joy both evin and morrow.

Gif plesour be to pance,
I plaint me nocht opprest,
or absence micht avance,
my hairt is haill possest:
gif want of quiet rest
frome cairis micht me convoy,
my mind is nocht mollest
bot evirmoir in joy.

Thocht that I pance in pane
in passing to and fro,
I laubor all in vane,
for so hes mony mo
that hes nocht servit so
in suting of thair sweit —
the nar the fire I go
the grittar is my heit.

The turtour for hir maik
mair dule may nocht indure
nor I do for hir saik,
evin hir, quha hes in cure
my hart, quhilk salbe sure
in service to the deid
unto that lady pure,
the well of womanheid.

Schaw, schedull, to that sweit
my pairt so permanent
that no mirth quhill we meit
sall caus me be content,
bot still my hairt lament
in sorrowfull siching soir
till time scho be present.
Fairwell. I say no moir.[17]

[If anguish lifts men's hearts
or sorrow gives them grace,
there's no one on this earth
can match me in solace;
if sombre thoughts can raise
my heavy heart from sorrow,
I'm joyous all my days,
each evening and each morrow.

If painful thoughts can please
I'll say I'm not oppressed,
if absence leads to ease
my heart is self-possessed;
if lack of quiet rest
can take my cares away
no grief may me molest
I'm joyful every day.

If thinking gives me pain
as I go to and fro,
I labour all in vain
and many more do so –
many who do not go
courting their lover sweet –
the nearer the fire I go
the more I feel the heat.

The mourning turtle-dove
such sorrow cannot bear
as I do for my love
who holds within her care
my heart, which shall be there
to serve her until death,
vowed to that lady pure,
the well of womanliness.

My message, tell my sweet
my part so permanent:
no pleasure till we meet
shall make me feel content.
My heart shall still lament
in sorrowful sighing sore
till once more she's present.
Farewell. I'll say no more.*]

* English version by CB.

This poem appears, attributed to Darnley, in the Bannatyne Manuscript. George Bannatyne's great collection of medieval and Renaissance Scottish poetry was probably begun as an anthology of courtly verse in the reign of Mary Queen of Scots,[18] and the inclusion of Darnley's poem suggests that it was current at court even if its theme suggests that Darnley's courtship was not prospering. It was probably composed when his courting received a temporary setback, as reported by Sir James Melville:

> After he had haunted court some time, he proposed
> marriage to Her Majesty, which she took in an evil
> part at first, as that same day she herself told me,
> and that she had refused a ring which he then
> offered unto her. I took occasion . . . to speak in
> his favour, that their marriage would put out of
> doubt their title to the [English] succession . . .
> She took ever the longer the better liking
> of him, and at length determined to marry him.[19]

A lover's complaint that delicately blended ardour with irony may have played its part in repairing the error of a presumptuous or premature proposal. Mary scarcely needed Melville to remind her of the chief advantage of marriage to Darnley, and after a brief show of displeasure had denied him her presence, he was restored to favour, and her 'liking' of him soon ripened into love.

The restoration of Lennox and the success of his son at court destabilized Scottish politics by causing a recrudescence of factions. Mary, aware of the danger of a revived Lennox–Hamilton feud, arranged a formal reconciliation between the Earl of Lennox and the Duke of Châtelhérault; but this was unlikely to hold if the Hamiltons saw their claims threatened by the advancement of a member of the Lennox family to kingship.

The Earl of Moray, after his initial affability to Darnley, soon grew suspicious of his ambition. An unfortunate episode turned suspicion into enmity. Darnley, looking at a map of Scotland, was shown by Lord Robert Stewart where Moray's estates lay, and Darnley remarked that the extent of them was 'too much'. Moray, hearing about it probably from his brother Lord Robert, was incensed, and Mary persuaded or ordered Darnley to apologize. But the damage was done, and thenceforward the two men were enemies. Accusations were exchanged: Darnley was plotting to murder Moray; Moray was plotting to kidnap Darnley and his father and send them back to England. In the summer, in a mysterious incident called 'the Raid of Beith', Mary and Darnley, in a headlong early morning ride, claimed to have escaped an ambush laid for Darnley, which may or may not have been imaginary.

In an atmosphere so charged with suspicion, new factions were formed. Lennox and Darnley were supported by the Earl of Atholl. Margaret Lennox won the support of the Douglases for her son by yielding her claim to the earldom of Angus to her father's great-nephew, the Earl of Morton's ward.[20] Thenceforward Darnley could rely on the support of Morton, James Douglas the 'Postulate of Arbroath', Lords Lindsay and Ruthven whose wives were Douglases, and lesser members of a large and powerful connection. The Earl of Moray, whose control of affairs was slipping, had a powerful friend in the Protestant Earl of Argyll. He was also supported by Sir William Kirkaldy of Grange, a soldier of great reputation, whose friendship with the Earl of Bedford, Governor of Berwick, to whom he wrote accounts of Scottish events, was ceasing to be compatible with his duty to the Queen of Scots.

Thomas Randolph viewed these developments with alarm, and reported them with displeasure. He was strongly in favour of the marriage of Mary Queen of Scots to Leicester, to which he believed Elizabeth and Cecil were genuinely committed. He was highly critical of Leicester's passivity, as he complained to Leicester's brother-in-law, Sir Henry Sidney:

> ... he whom I go about to make as happy as ever was any, to put him in possession of a kingdom, to make him prince of a mighty people, to lay in his naked arms a most fair and worthy lady, either nothing regards the good that shall ensue unto him thereby, the honour that shall be to his name and race, the profit that shall redound unto his country – but so uncertainly dealeth that I know not where to find him, nor what to speak or promise, that I shall not be forced to alter or call back again [contradict].[21]

Leicester's inaction was understood by Sir James Melville, and what he aptly described as the English Council's 'shifting and drifting' was brought to an abrupt end in March when Queen Elizabeth announced that she would make no pronouncement on the succession until she herself had either married or resolved never to marry. On receiving this pronouncement Mary 'wept her fill' at the realization of how humiliatingly she had been duped in her negotiations with Elizabeth. If she had kept Darnley at arm's length in case Elizabeth should suddenly decide to grant her recognition if she married Leicester, she had reason to do so no longer.

At this dramatic moment in his life, with success in sight, Darnley fell ill. On 5 April, struck with a feverish cold, he retired to bed to sweat it out. But soon 'mesels came out on him marvellous thick',[22] as Randolph reported, and he remained confined to bed for weeks. It might have seemed a disastrous stroke of bad luck for an ardent suitor to go down with a complaint that temporarily marred his looks and took him out of circulation. But it proved to be a fortunate misfortune, for Darnley's illness made Mary realize how much he meant to her. She sent Lethington to the English court to inform Queen Elizabeth that she had resolved to marry Lord Darnley, and to request the Queen's approval.

While she awaited the result of Lethington's embassy Mary spent much of her time at Darnley's bedside. Many of her biographers have said that she 'nursed' him, which would not have been consonant with her dignity. But she cossetted him with kindly attentions, which can do much in laying the foundations of love. Probably, as she sat beside him, chatting and gossiping in relative privacy, their intimacy advanced far more rapidly than it would have done in the formal circumstances of the court. It may have been the time of their lives when they most enjoyed each other's company, and the fact that it caused scandal probably added spice to the pleasure of it.

Elizabeth's reaction to Lethington's news was predictable: she was furiously angry, and far from approving Mary's marriage to Darnley she determined to put a stop to it. She sent Sir Nicholas Throckmorton to Scotland to forbid the match, and to order Lennox and Darnley on their allegiance to return at once to England. Mary could choose any other nobleman 'either in this realm, or isle or in any other place' – but only if she married Leicester would her claim to the English succession be enquired into, judged or published. With this message, which had now lost its power to move the Queen of

Scots, Throckmorton rode north, shortly followed by the returning Lethington.

Near Grantham Lethington met a Scottish envoy, John Beaton, riding south with a letter from Mary Queen of Scots to Queen Elizabeth. Beaton had been instructed to intercept Lethington and give him the letter, telling him to return to Elizabeth and deliver it. Lethington read it and discovered that in it Mary declared she would no longer be fed with 'yea and nay', but would make her own choice in marriage – in other words she was withdrawing her request for Elizabeth's approval and announcing her intention in defiant words. Determined to protect the tottering 'Amity', Lethington pocketed the letter and continued his journey to Scotland. At Alnwick he caught up with Throckmorton and told him all this. Never, said Throckmorton, had he seen Lethington in such a passion.[23]

Lethington had acted with outrageous presumption, and Mary was justly furious when she heard of it. But Lethington also had cause for anger, since his sovereign had acted on a passionate impulse and expected him to deliver a letter that would destroy his diplomacy. Inevitably their relationship, hitherto confidential, was undermined. Lethington remained out of favour until necessity caused the Queen to turn to him again.

When the envoys reached Scotland the Queen was at Stirling with Darnley, and Throckmorton was denied audience until she had so far committed herself to her intended marriage that his instructions could not affect the issue. On 15 May Darnley rose from his sickbed to be created knight, baron, and Lord of Ardmanoch, 'Lord of our Sovereign Lady's Parliament', and Earl of Ross, a title previously bestowed on younger sons of the Kings of Scots. He swore allegiance to Mary as a knight and as an earl, the words of the latter oath being

'I shall be true and leel [loyal] to my Sovereign Lady, Queen of Scotland, maintain and defend Her Highness' body, realm, lieges, and laws, at the uttermost of my power. So help me God, the Holy Evangel, by my own hand, and by God Himself.'[24]

By this solemn oath Darnley abjured his allegiance to Queen Elizabeth, and became the subject of the Queen who was soon to raise him to equality with herself. Darnley was then permitted to create fourteen knights, who were to be his personal supporters. Four of

them were Stewarts and one a Douglas. Prominent among the rest
was Sir William Murray of Tullibardine, who later became
Comptroller of the Queen's Household.[25] After this ceremony Darnley retired to his sickroom again. When the Queen received Throckmorton his arguments with her were predictably fruitless, and he
concluded that her determination to marry Darnley was 'irrevocable,
and no place left to dissolve the same by persuasion or any reasonable
means, otherwise than by violence'.[26] By way of retaliation he recommended to Elizabeth the 'harder sequestration' of Lady Lennox, who
had already been placed under house arrest, and in response to his
recommendation was sent to the Tower. Lennox's English estates
were confiscated, after which the Temple Newsam 'Inventory', previously quoted, was compiled.[27] These misfortunes could be endured
with equanimity now that triumph was in sight.

Darnley's illness was unusually protracted for measles, and besides
revealing Mary's attachment to him, it also revealed unattractive
aspects of his character. He had a violent temper, which in his early
wooing of the Queen he had managed to conceal, both from her and
from others, so that he had appeared simply as a 'fair, jolly young
man'. But the frustration of being confined to a sickroom soon made
his violence explode.

Randolph, once he had realized that Darnley was a threat to the
Leicester marriage, no longer had a good word for him, and posi-
tively enjoyed describing, and possibly exaggerating, his tantrums.
'The passions and furies I hear say he will sometimes be in are strange
to believe',[28] he told Leicester, in a description reminiscent of the
'extreme passions' of which his father had been accused when he
was a prisoner in the Tower. The comparable frustrations of a sickroom and a prison had similar effects on the father and the son.

Randolph also reported that Darnley gave vent to threats and futile
gestures of actual violence: 'My young Lord, being sick in bed, has
already boasted [threatened] the Duke [of Châtelhérault] to knock
his pate when he is whole',[29] and 'He spares not to let some blows
fly where he knows they will be taken [not returned]'.[30] Randolph
even said that 'With his dagger he would have struck the Justice
Clerk that brought him word that the creation of his being Duke
was deferred for a time',[31] this outburst resulting from his expec-

tation that the Queen would create him Duke of Albany, without the interim advancement to the earldom of Ross.

The Queen intended to deny him nothing, but his anger, impatience and frustration spilled over in arrogant behaviour even to her. This suggests that so long as Darnley was wooing the Queen he was 'your humble servant Hary Stuart', and if he overstepped the bounds of humility he quickly recovered himself and became a languishing suitor again. But, once he was sure of her, he was less concerned to conceal the natural arrogance and ill-temper which his illness exacerbated, and he became 'almost forgetful of his duty to her already, that has adventured so much for his sake'.[32] Since Mary could see no fault in a man whose unpleasant traits were all too obvious to everyone else, 'the saying is that surely she is bewitched'[33]: but the only enchantment was the natural magic of infatuation. That Darnley was ever touched by the same magic seems unlikely. His English poem suggests that he loved her as a prize to be won, and his Scots poem displays more artificial grace than depth of feeling; his behaviour suggests that his strongest emotion was triumph, agreeably enhanced by lust.

Darnley's slow recovery from his sickness occasioned no surprise at the time, but the history of his later ill-health raises the possibility that his supposed attack of measles may have been an early manifestation of syphilis. This disease had appeared in Europe in the late fifteenth century in an extremely virulent form, and throughout the sixteenth century it was a scourge all the more terrifying because of the variety of its forms. A preliminary skin eruption, followed by an apparent though temporary recovery, was a typical, though not initially obvious, manifestation.[34] Darnley could have contracted syphilis on his third journey to France, when, free of the surveillance of his tutors and the vigilance of his virtuous parents, he would have been most likely to seize the opportunity for sexual adventures. However, by the end of May 1565 he appeared to have recovered from a much less serious illness, which left his face unmarked, and cast no shadow on his future.

When Sir Nicholas Throckmorton left Scotland the only concession he had extracted from Mary Queen of Scots was a promise that her marriage to Darnley would not take place for three months. The Queen probably did not regard this as a concession, because it was about the length of time she expected to wait for the arrival of the papal dispensation for the marriage, which was required under canon law since she and Darnley were cousins.

Mary had entrusted the application for the dispensation to her uncle the Cardinal of Lorraine. As a high-ranking and influential churchman he was the obvious choice (in 1561 he had even been confident that he could obtain a dispensation for Mary to marry her young brother-in-law, Charles IX). But the Cardinal was disappointed in his niece's choice, which brought no advantage to the House of Guise, and he condescendingly referred to Darnley as merely *'un gentil hutaudeau'* – 'a pleasant young cock' – a man of the world's judgement of the youth he had glimpsed years before at the court of France.[35] Chagrined that Mary had done no better for herself, the Cardinal delayed applying for the dispensation. His envoy, Monsignor Musotti, did not reach Rome until 20 July, though Mary assumed that her request had arrived long before.[36]

As early as May she became aware of mounting opposition within Scotland to her intended marriage. Most ominous was Moray's withdrawal from her Council. Mary, with characteristic impetuosity, mishandled the situation by summoning Moray to Darnley's bedside and demanding her brother's approval of their marriage. She insisted that he sign a paper declaring his approval. Moray refused to sign on the grounds of religion, saying 'he would be loth to consent to the marriage of any such one of whom there was so little hope that he would be a favourer or setter forth of Christ's true religion . . . who hitherto had showed himself rather an enemy than a preferrer of the same.'[37] A 'great altercation' ensued, in which Moray skilfully identified his objection to Darnley as religious and not personal, though it was at least as much the latter as the former.

Mary realized the importance of creating a party to support her marriage. The first step, which took place a few days later, was Darnley's creation of fourteen knights, following his elevation to the earldom of Ross. The next, reported by Randolph on 3 June, was the summoning of a Convention of Estates, to meet at Perth on 10 June, 'to persuade those present to allow her marriage with Lord Darnley . . . They begin now to count their friends, Atholl, Caithness, Erroll, Montrose, Fleming, Cassillis, Montgomerie, Home, Lindsay . . . Ruthven and the Lord Robert [Stewart]. These they are assured of . . .'[38]

Though Mary collected an impressive body of supporters, Moray gathered Argyll, Glencairn, Rothes, Kirkaldy of Grange and Lord Ochiltree, the father-in-law of John Knox (the elderly reformer had recently married Ochiltree's teenage daughter Margaret Stewart, which incensed the Queen, who resented Knox's marriage to one who bore the royal surname). It was inevitable that Moray's objection to Darnley would also attract the Duke of Châtelhérault and the Hamilton connection. The division into factions was not strictly along religious lines, though Moray did his best to create the impression that opposition to Darnley was a religious issue.

Mary's situation was dangerous, and Randolph expressed pity for her, little as he sympathized with her attachment to Darnley:

> I know not how to utter what I conceive of the pitiful and lamentable estate of this poor Queen [he wrote to Leicester], whom ever before I esteemed so worthy, so wise, so honourable in all her doings; and at this present do find so altered with affection towards the Lord Darnley that she hath brought her honour in question, her estate in hazard, her country to be torn in pieces! I see also the amity between the countries like to be dissolved, and great mischiefs like to ensue . . . Woe worth the time (and so shall both England and Scotland say) that ever the Lord Darnley did set his foot in this country![39]

On 18 June Queen Elizabeth wrote Mary a peremptory letter in which she 'expressly commanded' Lennox and Darnley, as her subjects, to return to England, and 'required' Mary to issue a safe conduct to them. To a woman as proud as Mary such a letter could only be a provocation. Its effect, and that of the opposition within her kingdom, was to make her hasten preparations for her marriage. To buttress her against Elizabeth's enmity she sought the approval of both Philip II and Charles IX, to whom Darnley also wrote, promising his future services. To neutralize the effect of Moray's propaganda she issued a proclamation that she intended no alteration of the religion practised in Scotland.

On 16 July Randolph reported to Elizabeth that on the ninth of the month 'this Queen was secretly married in her own Palace to the Lord Darnley, not above seven persons present, and then went that night to their bed at the Lord Seton's house . . . if true, your Majesty sees how her promise [to wait three months] is kept . . .'[40] Randolph seemed uncertain of his information, though evidently some private ceremony had taken place. Probably it was an espousal *per verba de praesenti*, which would have permitted Mary and Darnley to consummate their union. The whiff of scandal arose from the secrecy of the event and the sudden departure for Seton. In a more detailed letter to Cecil, Randolph wrote:

> Two nights she tarried there, and the next day came to dinner to the castle of Edinburgh . . . that afternoon she and my Lord Darnley walked up and down the town disguised until supper time, and returned thither again, but lay that night in the Abbey [Holyrood] . . .[41]

This incognito stroll in the streets of Edinburgh, in which Mary's disguise was said to have been male costume, was one of the few informal occasions she and Darnley were permitted to enjoy, even though their disguises did not prevent their recognition.

Preparations for the wedding now progressed apace. On 20 July Darnley was created Duke of Albany, a title exclusively identified with Scottish royalty.[42] On the 21st the banns of marriage were published in the Kirk of the Canongate by its minister, John Brand, 'to proclaime Harie Duk of Albaynye . . . upon the one part . . . and Marie, be the Grace of God Quene soverane of this realme on the uthair . . . with invocation of the name of God.'[43] This was a gesture of appeasement to the Protestant Kirk, which also entered the marriage in its register, although the ceremony itself was to take place by Catholic rites. Late in the evening of 28 July, the night before the wedding, Mary issued a proclamation read at the Mercat Cross of Edinburgh:

> Forasmekill as we intend . . . to solemnizat and compleit the band of matrimonie in face of Hallie Kirk with the rycht nobill and illuster Prince Henry Duke of Albany: in respect of the whilk marriage . . . we will, ordane, and consentis, that he be namit and stylit King of this our Kingdom, and that all our letters . . . be in the names of the said illuster Prince our future husband and us as King and Queen of Scotland conjunctlie.[44]

An interesting comment on this proclamation was made by Adam Zwetkovitch, the Imperial ambassador to England, who told the Emperor that, as he heard, Mary had created Darnley King before she married him, saying 'she had previously been married to one of the greatest Kings in Christendom and therefore intended to wed no-one unless he were a King'.[45] This would have been consonant with her pride, but it was not the limit of her desire to exalt Darnley. A new coin was issued to commemorate the marriage, a silver 'ryal' which bore the heads of Mary and her husband in profile facing each other, surrounded by the inscription 'Henricus et Maria D. Gra R & R Scotorum' (Henry and Mary by the Grace of God King and Queen of Scots). The proclamation gave Darnley equality with the Queen; the inscription on the coin gave him precedence.

On the eve of the wedding the papal dispensation had not arrived. It was not until 1 September that the Pope addressed the Vatican Consistory and announced his intention to grant the dispensation, as otherwise the Queen of Scots might marry without it, and the Catholic religion in Scotland be endangered. He issued it about a fortnight later, and dispatched it on 25 September; but he had liberally backdated it 'viii kal. Junii' (25 May) so that the marriage would be valid had it been celebrated in the interim. Mary had received a letter from the Pope in mid-July, which was generally believed to be the dispensation, and this she did not deny, since she had resolved to marry without it, trusting that it would follow.[46]

On the morning of 29 July, before six o'clock, Mary entered her private chapel in the Palace of Holyrood, escorted by the Earls of Lennox and Atholl. She was dressed in mourning, the custom of Catholic widows making a second marriage. It was not the unrelieved black so frequently imagined, but the *deuil blanc* she had worn for her father-in-law Henri II and for François II, the black gown, white hood and filmy white veil falling to her waist. In this simple and beautiful costume Mary was left alone to await her bridegroom. Then Lennox and Atholl returned, leading Darnley 'clad in splendid garb and glittering gems'. The banns of marriage were called for the third time, and the marriage service was performed by the Dean of Restalrig. The Catholic ceremony was very brief: the priest placed the right hand of the bride in the right hand of the groom, who said 'I take thee to my wedded wife', and the bride replied 'I take thee to my wedded husband'. Then both said in unison 'In the name of the Father and the Son and the Holy Spirit'.[47] To symbolize the Trinity, Darnley placed three rings on Mary's finger, the middle one being a fine diamond in a red enamelled setting. 'They knelt together, and many prayers were said over them . . . He taketh a kiss and leaveth her there and went to her chamber . . .'[48]

Mary remained in the chapel to hear the nuptial Mass alone. Since Darnley's departure did not distress or surprise her it seems obvious that it had been prearranged, probably as a further appeasement of Protestant opinion. When the Mass was concluded Mary followed her husband to her chamber

and there being required according to the solemnity, to . . . lay aside those sorrowful garments . . . after some pretty refusal, more I believe for manner sake than grief of heart, she suffereth them that stood by, every man that could approach, to take out a pin, and so being committed to her ladies changed her garments.[49]

Sixteenth-century clothes were made of separate component parts, usually joined by 'points' or laces. On this occasion the sleeves, bodice and skirts of Mary's dress had evidently been pinned together for ease of changing. Unfortunately Randolph, who described the ritual, did not describe the clothes into which she changed, but Mary's wardrobe contained dresses of cloth of gold and silver, and bright satins – white, orange, blue and green. Probably gold or silver would have been her choice for this occasion of triumph and rejoicing.

Randolph, who wrote his description of the wedding for the Earl of Leicester, stressed that Mary and her husband did not immediately go to bed, 'to signify unto the world that it was no lust moved them to marry'. Evidently he had concluded that the rumour that they had slept together at Seton had been untrue: 'I would not your Lordship should so believe; the likelihoods are so great[ly] to the contrary that if it were possible to see such an act done, I would not believe it'.[50]

The day passed in celebrations. There was dancing throughout the morning. Then to the sound of trumpets a largesse was cried, and 'money thrown about the house in great abundance to such as were happy to get any part'. The King and Queen then went to dine, escorted by a procession of nobles. They ate alone, seated side by side at the table. The Queen was served by three Earls – Atholl as Sewer, Morton as Carver, and Crawford as Cupbearer;

the King was similarly served by the Earls of Cassillis, Eglinton and Glencairn.

> After dinner they dance awhile [Randolph's account concluded], and retire themselves till the hour of supper, and as they dine so do they sup. Some dancing there was, and so they go to bed.[51]

This was the consummation of Darnley's triumph as well as of his marriage, and if the rumour concerning François II was true, he would have found his widowed bride a virgin.[52]

5
THE QUEST FOR
THE CROWN MATRIMONIAL

He is of an insolent temper, and thinks that he is never
sufficiently honoured. The Queen does everything to
oblige him, though he cannot be prevailed upon to yield
the smallest thing to please her. He claims the Crown
Matrimonial and will have it immediately. The Queen
tells him that it must be delayed till he be of age, and done
by consent of Parliament, which does not satisfy him.[1]

AT NOON ON THE DAY after the wedding three heralds appeared at
the Mercat Cross in Edinburgh and, after a flourish of trumpets, 'King
Henry' was proclaimed for the second time. But on this occasion the
proclamation had a significant difference: it was signed by 'Thair
Majesties . . . the penult day of Jully, and of our reignes the first and
twenty-third years.'[2] By public declaration the new-made King was
given precedence over the hereditary sovereign, and the proclamation
bore the first instance of his signature as King. The assembled nobility
heard it in silence, and the silence of the nation's leaders probably
inhibited the response of the populace. At last a lone voice shouted
'God save His Grace!' – it was the voice of the King's father.

Despite this ominous lack of public enthusiasm, the celebrations
at court continued, and John Knox wrote that 'during the space
of three or four days there was nothing but balling, dancing and
banquetting'.[3] But, though Knox's censorious judgement recorded
only frivolity, the celebrations provided sophisticated entertainment.

Each day a masque was performed on an aspect of the triumph of love. The first was George Buchanan's Latin 'Pompa Deorum' (Masque of Gods), in which the maiden goddess Diana complained to the assembled Olympian gods and goddesses that one of her bright band of Maries had been stolen from her by the powers of love and marriage: the goddess's band were Mary Queen of Scots and her four ladies-in-waiting, Mary Seton, Mary Beaton, Mary Livingstone and Mary Fleming. The Olympians gave their answers, and finally Jupiter dismissed the complaint. The second of Buchanan's Latin 'Pompae' was an equestrian masque in which processions of exotically costumed knights arrived to offer praises, and the knights of Pallas and Cupid exchanged challenges. In a third masque by Buchanan the four 'Queen's Maries' offered oblations to the Goddess of Health for the future of the royal pair.[4] Yet another Latin entertainment was an 'Epithalamium' by the young lawyer and poet Sir Thomas Craig of Riccarton (later a distinguished jurist), addressed to the King and Queen:

> Thy Henry at thy side, by Heaven's decree
> His prime of manhood consecrate to thee;
> Thou first, thou last, wakest in him love's pure blaze,
> Ah, how may I th'accomplished hero praise
> Whose worth's excess my humble strain o'erlays? . . .
> Th'observed of all observers on our stage,
> Yet other eyes shall Albany engage,
> Model and boast of many a coming age! . . .

After this fulsome adulation the King was left in no doubt that his marriage had given him not only position but power and responsibility:

> Thou chiefly, Henry, placed at Scotia's helm
> On whom suspended hangs a powerful realm,
> Thou from those cares thyself canst never free;
> The law which binds on us our loyalty
> Thee too constrains – that none unscathed may dare
> To trample on our rights whilst thou art there . . .[5]

The Queen herself could not do enough to assure him that she had made him not only a titular king, but a sovereign:

All honour that may be attributed to any man by a wife, he hath
it wholly and fully . . . all dignities that she can endow him with
are already given and granted [this was Randolph's opinion] . . .
She hath given over unto her whole will, to be ruled and guided
as himself best thinketh . . .[6]

The only portrait of Mary and Darnley (as he shall continue to be
called, for familiarity and convenience) as King and Queen of Scots
is a double portrait that shows them at three-quarters length, standing side by side against a patterned background, perhaps a wall-
hanging of stamped leather. Darnley, his colouring brighter than in
other portraits, is pink-cheeked and blue-eyed; his golden-blond hair
is half concealed by a black velvet bonnet banded with jewels. He
wears a doublet and hose of rose-pink satin, patterned with slashes
to display a lining of darker pink. He stands in an arrogant attitude,
with one hand on hip, the other on the hilt of his sword. Mary,
darker in colouring than her husband, is more sombrely dressed,
though with equal richness. She too wears a black velvet bonnet,
embroidered and banded with pearls, and a black velvet gown
embroidered with gold spots, over a kirtle of gold and brown tissue,
with sleeves of the same material. One hand, holding a fan of white
ostrich feathers set in a jewelled and enamelled handle, rests on her
husband's arm; in the other hand she holds a pair of gloves and a
lace kerchief. Whether the portrait was painted from life or composed
at a later date from existing likenesses, it captures the brief period
of Darnley's triumph, when Mary 'did him great honour herself, and
desired everyone who would deserve her favour to do the like . . .'[7]

Unfortunately, Darnley remained dissatisfied. He did not consider
that he had received all the dignities due to him. A medal issued to
commemorate the royal marriage showed the crowned heads of
Henry and Mary, and this represented the final acknowledgement of
his sovereignty, which he both desired and expected – his coronation
with the Crown Matrimonial.

Ambition led him to desire it, but he also believed that he had the
right to expect it. Just as a woman who married a king became
queen, so a man who married a queen regnant expected to become
king. Philip of Spain had become King of England on marrying
Queen Mary I, and Queen Jane (Lady Jane Grey) had nonplussed
her father-in-law the Duke of Northumberland by refusing to allow

Lord Guildford Dudley to become King without the consent of
Parliament – this was contrary to expectation. But Mary Queen of
Scots had stressed that Darnley's position was different by creating
him King before their marriage, a gesture that implied recognition
of his royal status, as did the proclamation's naming him 'Prince
Henry'. Whether or not this premature exaltation of him was beyond
her legal powers, as some argued, it convinced him that his status
was superior to that of a king consort. Besides, the Queen's first
husband had received the Crown Matrimonial – and if King François
had worn it, then so should King Henry.

This may have been Mary Queen of Scots' intention, as the issue
of the medal bearing their crowned heads suggests. But the Crown
Matrimonial was more than a symbol of status; it conveyed future
powers. It signified that if the King's wife predeceased him he would
continue as sovereign. Furthermore, if his wife died childless, or died
having borne him a daughter, and he then remarried and begot a
son, the son of his second marriage would succeed. Thus the Crown
Matrimonial gave the Queen's husband the power to bring about a
change of dynasty.

For this reason the English Council and Parliament had refused
the Crown Matrimonial to Philip of Spain; for this reason the Parliament of Scotland, with less control over the situation, had reluctantly
granted it to François, and had been thankful that his early death
had saved Scotland from its potential problems. For this reason,
too, Mary Queen of Scots was aware that bestowing the Crown
Matrimonial on Darnley was beyond her personal power, and would
require the consent of Parliament, which no doubt, in the early days
of their marriage, she intended to obtain, as she promised him.

Darnley's desire would have been intensified by the mission of an
English envoy, John Tamworth, who arrived in Scotland soon after
the marriage, to state Queen Elizabeth's objections to Mary's marriage with one whom Elizabeth continued to regard as a disobedient
subject. Tamworth was instructed not to recognize or address Mary's
husband as King of Scots, but to use the title 'the Lord Darnley'.
Mary defended his status with dignity and determination. However,
when Tamworth left Scotland he refused to accept a safe conduct
bearing the signature 'Henry R'. Randolph otiosely explained to
Mary that the envoy could not accept it as that would be to acknowledge Darnley as a king. 'Well,' she replied, 'he is now a king.'[8]
Tamworth left without the safe conduct, and was arrested and

imprisoned before he reached the Border. In due course, to regain his freedom, he was instructed to accept the offending document.[9] This unpleasant diplomatic incident, in which the Scottish victory was probably dearly bought, would have increased Darnley's conviction that coronation would put his status beyond doubt. His impatient demands for it, and Mary's cautious response, would soon bring them into conflict. But in the meantime more urgent matters demanded attention.

The Earl of Moray's disapproval of the Queen's marriage led him in the course of the summer from disaffection to rebellion. In a man of such consummate political ability as Moray, this is the one anomalous episode of his career./He rebelled too late to prevent the Queen's marriage, and without a convincing rallying cry if he intended her overthrow. If that was his intention, he did not state it clearly, though Randolph reported that the Queen once said 'he would set the crown on his own head'. That was indeed the only aim which would have made sense of his rebellion.[10] His propaganda appealed to the 'danger to religion' represented by the Queen's marriage; but Mary's appeasement of Protestant opinion did much to disarm his arguments. His appeals for English assistance suggest that he may have hoped to replicate the conditions of 1560, to bring English arms and money to overthrow a Catholic ruler. But the situation was not the same. Marie de Guise had been a foreign regent (albeit the widow of the King of Scots) maintaining her rule with the assistance of foreign troops; Mary Queen of Scots was a hereditary sovereign ruling with the support of a majority of her subjects, as events were to prove. Queen Elizabeth had been reluctant to support the 'Lords of the Congregation', though she had finally done so to ensure the success of the Reformation Rebellion; but she refused to support a rebellion against a legitimate sovereign when the Reformation in Scotland was not under immediate threat. Besides which, she was well aware of the risk of supporting rebellion against legitimate authority; it was a dangerous precedent which might encourage similar action against herself. If Moray had overthrown his sister without her help she would have offered him alliance, as she did in 1567, after the fall of Mary Queen of Scots. But in 1565, apart from sending secret financial support on a minimal scale, she left Moray and his supporters to their own devices.

Nonetheless, the rebellion was dangerous, for Moray's support within Scotland was formidable, and Mary's marriage was not popular. Few of the nobles who had agreed to support it at Perth were men who customarily played much part in public affairs, whereas Moray's supporters included two of the most powerful magnates of the realm, Châtelhérault, the premier nobleman of Scotland and the only duke (though his title was French) before the creation of Darnley as Duke of Albany, and Argyll, whose power was paramount in the west.

The Queen's response to the threat of rebellion was courageous. Immediately after her wedding, Moray was summoned to appear before her to explain his opposition. But, despite her promise of safe conduct for himself and eighty of his followers, he did not come. Accordingly, on 6 August Moray was 'put to the horn' as an outlaw (the sentence of outlawry was publicly pronounced after three blasts of the horn), and Châtelhérault and Argyll were informed that they too would be outlawed if they continued to support him. On 14 August the properties of Moray himself and two more of his supporters, the Earl of Rothes and Kirkaldy of Grange, were seized by the crown.[11]

On Sunday, 19 August, as part of the continuing appeasement of Protestant opinion, the King attended divine service in St Giles, where a throne had been placed for him, and heard John Knox preach. As an exercise in public relations this misfired badly. Knox preached on a text of Isaiah: 'O Lord our God, other lords than thou have ruled over us.' Making a transparent comparison between Henry and Mary and Ahab and Jezebel, Knox demanded of his hearers:

Did he remove his idolatry? Did he correct his idolatrous wife? No, we find no such thing; but the one and the other we find to have continued and increased in their impieties. But what was the end thereof? The last visitation of God was that dogs licked the blood of the one and did eat the flesh of the other.[12]

There was a great deal more offensive matter, including a thinly veiled comparison between Darnley and Julian the Apostate, and a concluding prayer that 'we may see . . . what punishment he [God] hath appointed for the cruel tyrants . . .'[13] Knox continued preaching 'an hour and more longer than the time appointed', and Darnley, not surprisingly, 'was so moved at this sermon, that he would not dine; and being troubled with great fury he passed in the afternoon to the hawking'.[14] He may have cooled his temper, but he returned determined to silence the preacher.

Knox was summoned before the Council, informed that 'the King's majesty was offended', and ordered to abstain from preaching for fifteen or twenty days 'and let Mr Craig supply the place'[15] – John Knox was minister of the High Kirk of St Giles, John Craig the assistant minister. It is worth remarking that when Mary Queen of Scots received Knox in audience early in her reign and attempted a religio-political discussion with him, by his own account he reduced her to tears. Darnley's method of dealing with him was more effective.

Meanwhile, the forces of the rebels had gathered at Ayr. On 22 August Mary Queen of Scots ordered a muster, and pledged her jewels for her soldiers' pay. In the ensuing military operations the forces of the Queen and the rebels never met in battle, which gave the rebellion its descriptive name – 'The Chaseabout Raid'. On 26 August the royal forces left Edinburgh, and marched by way of Linlithgow and Stirling to Glasgow, presumably collecting reinforcements as they went. Lennox was in command of the vanguard, Morton of the 'middle battle', the King and Queen of the rearguard, where Darnley was conspicuous in a suit of gilded armour. The Queen herself wore a steel cap and had a pistol at her saddle-bow. The day after they reached Glasgow the rebels encamped at Paisley, and 'on the morrow they came to Hamilton, keeping the high passage from Paisley hard by Glasgow, where the King and Queen easily might behold them . . .'[16], which suggests there was a genuine reluctance to fight.

The rebels were expecting Argyll, who had not arrived when the royal forces appeared. Fearing to wait longer, they marched for Edinburgh, with the hope of gathering reinforcements there, but 'none or few resorted unto them'.[17] The King and Queen set out in pursuit

> . . . but there arose such a vehement tempest of wind and rain . . .
> so that . . . the raging storm being in their face, with great difficulty
> they went forward: and although the most part waxed weary, yet
> the Queen's courage increased manlike so much that she was ever
> with the foremost . . .[18]

The Keeper of Edinburgh Castle was the Earl of Mar, a supporter of the Queen, and it was presently commanded by his brother, Sir

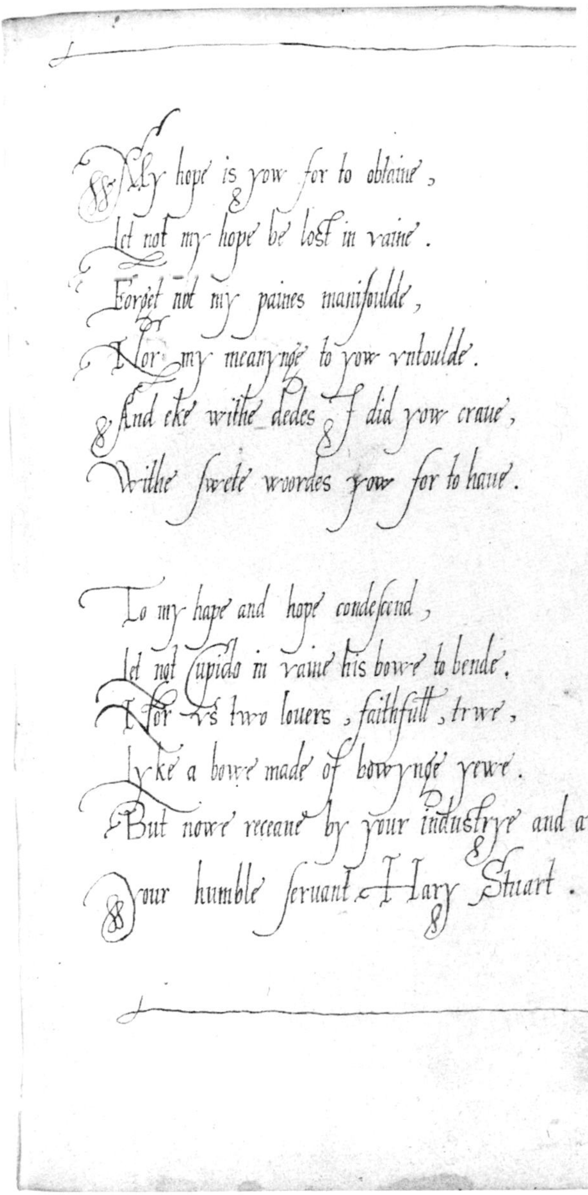

My hope is yow for to obtaine,
let not my hope be lost in vaine.
Forget not my paines manifoulde,
Nor my meanynge to yow vntoulde.
And eke withe dedes I did yow craue,
Withe swete woordes yow for to haue.

To my hape and hope condescend,
let not Cupido in vaine his bowe to bende.
Nor vs two louers, faithfull, trwe,
lyke a bowe made of bowynge yewe.
But nowe receane by your industrye and art,
Your humble seruant Hary Stuart.

PLATE IX: 'MY HOPE IS YOU FOR TO OBTAIN . . .'

Holograph manuscript by Darnley, in his much admired 'Roman hand', of a poem addressed to Mary Queen of Scots.

Inset Mary Queen of Scots, c.1565.

PLATES X AND XI: KING AND QUEEN OF SCOTS

Henry and Mary, King and Queen of Scots.

Opposite page: top Medal struck in honour of the marriage of Mary and Darnley, showing them both crowned, and therefore probably signifying the Queen's intention to grant her consort the Crown Matrimonial.

Centre Silver ryal issued in honour of the marriage, inscribed 'Henricus et Maria D. Gra. R & R Scotorum' [Henry and Mary by the Grace of God King and Queen of Scots].

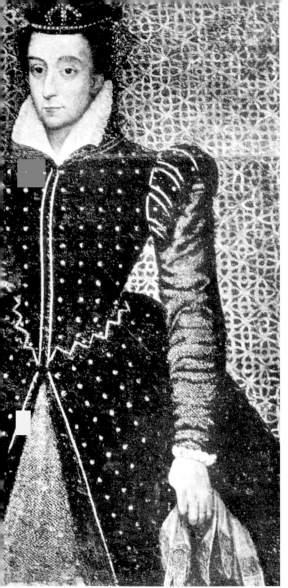

Right Silver ryal with the inscription reversed to read 'Maria et Henricus'. The reversal of the order of names was reported by the English ambassador as indicative of the Queen's growing disillusionment with Darnley. The 'Henricus et Maria' coin was recalled, and only two examples of it are known to have survived.

The inscription on the engraving reads:

OBIIT 1566 · ILLUSTR · PRIN · HEN

STEWARD · DOMIN

DARNLEY · DUX AL BANIÆ

The
Pourtraicture of the right Excellent Prince.
HENRY Lo: Darnley, Duke of Albany, Father to
our Soueraigne lord Iames of Greate Brittaine France,
and Ireland King, Knight of the noble order of S*Michael.

PLATE XII: DARNLEY RECEIVES AN HONOUR

Engraving of Darnley wearing the insignia and robes of the Order of St
Michael, presented to him by Charles IX of France. The inscription identifies
him as 'The Illustrious Prince Henry Stewart, Lord Darnley, Duke of Albany',
but not as King of Scots.

Monsieur mon bon frere. Jay receu par le sieur de Mammiffere, cette lettre que par luy vous a pleu m'escrire, et entendu le credit d'icelle qui ne m'a donné peu de fascherie pour apperceuoir par icelluy combien a tort le bruit m'a rendu coulpable d'un faul lequel j'aborre tant. Mais d'autre part esperant que mon Innocence entendue par le susdit sieur de Mammiffere auquel j'ay esclaré la verité de tout, ne permettra que j'imprimez autre que bonne opinion de moy. Je suis hors de ceste peyne, me confiant en sa suffisance pour ne faire tort a laquelle je finiray la presente. Priant le createur vous donner Monsieur mon bon frere en bonne sante tresheureuse et treslongue vie. De Edenburg ce vj Jour de May 1566.

Vostre affectioné bon frere

Henry

PLATE XIII: DARNLEY PROTESTS HIS INNOCENCE

Darnley's letter to Charles IX of France, in which he protests that he has been unjustly rumoured to have been guilty of Rizzio's death, a crime which he abhors. The text of the letter is in the hand of a secretary, the concluding greeting and signature written by Darnley.

Left A Dutch engraving of Darnley in the robes and insignia of the Order of St Michael; the inscription on this engraving gives him the style 'Coninck van Schotlant' [King of Scotland].

Darnley's eagerness to exonerate himself in the eyes of Charles IX would have been increased by his anxiety not to be obliged to return the Order of St Michael, which was an obligation upon anyone who disgraced the Order by committing a crime.

Henrie Steuart Duke of Albanye and Marie Quem of Scotland 1566

PLATE XIV: 'THE QUEEN BADE GIVE HIM ONLY HIS DUE . . .'

'Henrie Steuart Duke of Albanye and Marie Quene of Scotland, 1566', an illumination from the Seton Armorial, which may illustrate the armorial bearings which the Queen had come to consider were 'his due'.

Inset Silver testoon of 1560–65, with profile portrait of Mary Queen of Scots, showing the derivation of the likeness in the Seton Armorial.

PLATE XV: MORTON AND BOTHWELL

James Douglas, Earl of Morton, cousin of Darnley's mother, and Regent of Scotland for Darnley's son James VI; Darnley's accomplice in the murder of Rizzio, and later executed after admitting foreknowledge and concealment of the murder of Darnley.

Inset James Hepburn, fourth Earl of Bothwell, third husband of Mary Queen of Scots; generally believed to have planned the murder of Darnley, if not personally to have murdered him.

PLATE XVI: JEWELS ASSOCIATED WITH
MARY QUEEN OF SCOTS AND DARNLEY

Left A jewelled and enamelled pendant
mounted with a cameo of Mary Queen
of Scots.

Below Two views of the Lennox or
Darnley Jewel, commissioned by
Margaret, Countess of Lennox. Its
mysterious symbolism may
commemorate the murder of Darnley,
and express the hope that the heir of
the Lennox Stuarts will inherit the
thrones of Scotland and England. This
was the message of its inscription
QUHA HOPIS STIL CONSTANTLY VITH
PATIENCE SAL OBTEIN VICTORIE IN YAIR
PRETENCE [Who continues to hope
constantly with patience shall obtain
victory in their claim], which was
fulfilled by the succession of Darnley's
son as James VI of Scotland and I of
England.

Alexander Erskine of Gogar. The King and Queen with their forces had arrived at Callendar 'well wet', when they received a messenger from Sir Alexander asking if he should use the artillery of the castle against the rebels, and thereby endanger 'a multitude of innocent persons' in the city. According to Knox, the messenger returned with Mary's command to do so, and 'six or seven shot of cannon' dislodged the rebels from the city on 1 September.[19] The rebels retreated by way of Lanark, to Dumfries. Knox, who had shown imprudent sympathy with them, also fled. This was in effect the end of the rebellion, though the royal forces reoccupied the capital and the Queen ordered a larger force to assemble at Glasgow, to pursue the rebels over the Border. They advanced as far as Dumfries, but further action proved unnecessary, though it was not until 6 October that Moray and most of his confederates acknowledged defeat and fled south to claim asylum in England.

Although he was instructed to remain in the north of England, Moray went to London, and presented himself at the English court, where he was subjected to a public humiliation. Queen Elizabeth received him in the presence of the French ambassador, and berated him for rebelling against his lawful sovereign. Thus Elizabeth publicly washed her hands of the taint of association with a failed rebellion; but the Spanish ambassador Guzman de Silva believed that the scene had been rehearsed the previous evening. Moray returned to Newcastle to await a turn of events that would permit his return to Scotland. He was not without friends, even among those who had not supported the rebellion.

The brief visit of Mary and Darnley to the west of Scotland in the course of the Chaseabout Raid provides the only occasion when they could have visited Crookston Castle, which a later legend made a scene of their courtship.[20] They may have wished to see it since it was one of the properties recently granted to Darnley, but they would not have stayed there as it was uninhabited, perhaps already ruinous. But near it grew an already ancient yew tree, and a brief pause beneath its branches may have been enough to give rise to the legend that it had been their trysting tree. According to a descriptive poem entitled 'Clyde' written in 1764:

By Crookston castle waves the still-green yew
The first that met the royal Mary's view
When, bright in charms, the youthful princess led
The graceful Darnley to her throne and bed.[21]

In 1820 Sir Walter Scott introduced the 'Tree of Crookstone' into
his novel *The Abbot*, in which Mary Queen of Scots stands beneath
it to await the outcome of the Battle of Langside (1568) and recalls
its happier associations:

> The Queen . . . fixed her eyes upon the spreading yew, 'Ay, fair
> and stately tree', she said . . . 'there thou standest, gay and goodly
> as ever, though thou hearest the sounds of war instead of the vows
> of love. All is gone since last I greeted thee – love and lover –
> vows and vower – king and kingdom . . .'[22]

As a result of Scott's popularity the legend outlasted the original
tree (which was destroyed by souvenir hunters) and produced some
curious by-products. On 22 December 1565 a new coin known
as the 'Mary ryal' was commissioned, to bear on the obverse an
emblem of a crowned palm tree being climbed by a tortoise
(described in the Register of the Privy Council as a 'schell padoke'
or shelled toad).[23] This emblem was later interpreted as a representation of the ascent of Darnley (the tortoise) to kingship by climbing
the palm tree (Mary),[24] and nineteenth-century numismatists, dening
the ocular evidence of a very clear design, decided that the palm tree
represented the famous yew, and designated the coin the 'Crookston
Dollar'. The whole edifice of legend was demolished by later scholars.

Shortly after this coin was commissioned, Randolph reported that
the 'Henricus et Maria' ryal had been recalled from circulation.[25] It
was reissued in identical form except that the inscription now read
'Maria et Henricus'. The original issue may have been very small
and not widely circulated, for the recall was so successful that only
two examples of the 'Henricus et Maria' coin are known to exist,
one in the British Museum, the other the property of an anonymous
collector.[26]

Probably the reversal of names on the coin reflects Mary's second
thoughts on her husband's status. During and after the Chaseabout
Raid they had several disagreements, in which Mary discovered that

Darnley expected to use the authority she had given him, and even to assert it over hers when they clashed. This was not surprising, because it was the orthodoxy of the age that the husband held authority over the wife; but it surprised Mary, who had bestowed authority on Darnley in the first flush of affection, but did not expect him to presume upon it.

In quest of active supporters against Moray and his confederates, Mary pardoned Lord Gordon, son of the late Earl of Huntly, who had been imprisoned since his father's defeat and death in 1562, and restored him to the earldom. She also recalled from exile the Earl of Bothwell, son of the earl who had been Lennox's rival as suitor of Marie de Guise. James Hepburn, fourth Earl of Bothwell, had succeeded his father in 1556, and loyally served Marie de Guise until her death. Although he was a Protestant he had intercepted one of the subsidies sent by Elizabeth to the 'Lords of the Congregation' and delivered it to the Queen-Regent. As an enemy of Moray he was out of favour after the return of Mary Queen of Scots, and was imprisoned and then exiled when Châtelhérault's son the Earl of Arran accused him of suggesting a plot for the abduction of the Queen. Throckmorton described him as 'a glorious [vainglorious], rash and hazardous young man', and Randolph as 'a blasphemer and irreverent speaker both of his own sovereign and the Queen my mistress'.[27]

Mary decided to overlook the abduction plot and the lewd remarks about herself (which Randolph had reported to her), and summon Bothwell home to take command of her forces. Darnley wished his father to command them, which in effect he had done on the march to Glasgow and on the returning pursuit of the rebels, by commanding the van of the army. But Mary wanted to give Bothwell supreme command 'by reason he bears an evil will against Moray'. In her bitterness against her brother she had told Randolph that she would sooner lose her crown than fail to be revenged on him. Darnley apparently resisted Mary's will successfully, for when Bothwell arrived in Scotland in mid-September he was not given supreme command, but was merely appointed to join the noblemen in attendance on the King in command of the army.[28] But in future Mary turned increasingly to Bothwell for military support. Once re-established in his earldom, Bothwell was the most powerful magnate in the Borders, where his anti-English sentiments could be relied upon if the frontier required defending, and he proved effective in reducing the disorder endemic in the area. He also held the office of hereditary Lord High Admiral of Scotland.

The dispute over Bothwell was an ill omen for the future. Quarrels with the Queen reduced Darnley's chances of securing the Crown Matrimonial, but not his desire for it.

At his best Darnley could be impressive, as the French ambassador to Scotland, Castelnau de Mauvissière, acknowledged when he wrote: 'As to the King of Scotland, it is not possible to see a more beautiful Prince, and he is accomplished in all courtly exercises. He wishes much . . . that he might go and see the King of France [Charles IX] . . . and professes a sincere desire to render any service in his power to his Majesty, and in all things to follow the example of the Kings of Scotland his predecessors'.[29] Here, it appeared, was a young man who deserved all the honours to which he aspired. Perhaps his well-known poem of advice to the Queen, 'Be Governor both Good and Gracious', should be read in the context of his attempt to persuade Mary to grant him the Crown Matrimonial. He wrote:

> Be gouvernor baith guid and gratious
> Be leill and luifand to thy leigis all
> Be large of fredome and no thing desyrous
> Be iust to pure for ony thing may fall
> Be ferme of faith and constant as ane wall
> Be reddye evir to stanche evill and discord
> Be cheretabill and sickerlye thow sall
> Be bowsum ay to knaw thy God and lord . . .

> Be weill awysit of quhome thow counsale tais
> Be sever of thame that thai be leill and trew
> Be think thee als quhidder thai be freindis or fais
> Be to thy saull thair sawis or thow persew
> Be nevir o'r haistye to wirk and syne to rew
> Be noct thair friend that makis the fals record
> Be reddie evir all guid works to renew
> Be bowsum ay to knaw thy God and lord . . .

Be to rebellis strong as lyoun eke
Be ferce to follow thame quhairevir thai found
Be to thy liege men bayth soft and meik
Be thair succor and help thame haill and sound
Be knaw thy cure and caus quhy thow was cround
Be besye evir that iustice be nocht smord
Be blyith in hart thir wordis oft expound
Be bowsum ay to knaw thy God and lord . . . [30]

[Be governor both good and gracious
Be loyal and loving to thy lieges all
Be free of largesse and nowise covetous
Be just to the poor whatever may befall
Be firm in faith and constant as a wall
Be ever ready to stay evil and discord
Be charitable and certainly thou shall
Be ever humble to know thy God and lord . . .

Be well advised for counsel to whom thou goes
Be sure of them that they be loyal and true
Bethink thee whether they be friends or foes
Be certain of wise advice that thou pursue
Be not too hasty to act and then to rue
Be friend to none that keeps a false record
Be ever ready all good works to renew
Be ever humble to know thy God and lord . . .

Be against rebels strong as a lion eke [also]
Be fierce to follow wherever they be found
Be to thy liegemen both soft and meek
Be their succour and keep them safe and sound
Be conscious of the cause why thou was crowned*

---

* Cause why thou was crowned, i.e. to be responsible to God for her people; 'cure'
in the original line has the same meaning as in 'cure of souls'.

Be ever busy lest justice be ignored*
Be light of heart and these words oft expound
Be ever humble to know thy God and lord . . .†]

If Darnley had been capable of following his own advice, all might have been well with him. But unfortunately his polished presentation of conventional wisdom grew increasingly remote from his personal behaviour. Perhaps it was unrealistic to expect that a spoilt and ambitious young man, who in his own estimation had triumphed over the opposition of Elizabeth and her ministers, overcome the combined animosity of Moray, the Hamiltons and other Scottish enemies, and silenced John Knox, who having compared him to Ahab had now fled from Edinburgh, should have patience when he was denied immediate coronation. He was deaf to Mary's explanation that the bestowal of the Crown Matrimonial required the consent of Parliament; it appeared to him that if she could proclaim him King she could command his coronation. Nor could he accept that the grant of the Crown Matrimonial should await his coming of age; he could reply that it had been granted to François as the fifteen-year-old Dauphin of France. If Mary's arguments for delaying it were reasonable, Darnley's arguments in demanding it seemed to him equally reasonable. The dispute reached an impasse, and he could not see that the cause was his own conduct.

At first he refused to accept any limitations on his authority. According to the memoirs of Lord Herries:

The King had done some things and signed papers without knowledge of the Queen . . . which she took not well. She thought although she had made her husband partner in the Government, she had not given the power absolutely into his hands . . . She thought nothing should be done by him, in relation to affairs of state, without her concurrence and knowledge . . . and then, lest the King should be persuaded to pass gifts or any such thing privately by himself, she appointed all things in that kind should be sealed with a seal, which she gave to her secretary David Rizius

* lit. 'That justice be not smothered'.
† English version by CB.

[Rizzio] in keeping, with express orders not to put the seal to any papers unless it be first signed with her own hand.[31]

This 'seal' was a stamp of Darnley's signature, which is usually said to have been made for use in his absence, because he was unwilling to attend to affairs of state; but by Herries's account it appears to have been made in the first instance not to supply his absence but to control his independence of action. A more insulting form of control could not have been devised, and the proud youth's response was to absent himself. Just as his anger at Knox's preaching had driven him to absent himself from dinner and to spend the afternoon 'at the hawking', so anger at his wife's determination to control him drove him to absent himself from court, not for an afternoon, but on hunting expeditions which took him to Fife or to the country around Peebles for days at a time. When the Queen fell ill during the autumn he did not sit at her bedside as she had sat at his, but continued 'at his passtime'. His companions were 'gentlemen willing to satisfy his will and affections',[32] who sycophantically listened to his grievances and led him astray, drinking and 'vagabondizing' in disreputable parts of Edinburgh, to which he accompanied them with alacrity.

By the end of the year Randolph reported, 'A while [ago] there was nothing but "King and Queen, his majesty and hers"; but now the "Queen's husband" is more common . . . There are also private disorders among themselves, but may be but *Amantium Irae* [lovers' quarrels] . . .'[33] But the increasingly frequent quarrels only revealed that there was not enough love to provide a basis for understanding and reconciliation.

The Queen faced larger problems than those caused by her husband's misconduct, but these in turn became focused upon him.

Moray's protestations that his opposition to the Queen's marriage and later rebellion were in defence of 'religion' enabled Mary in turn to represent herself to the Catholic powers of Europe as an embattled Catholic sovereign acting in defence of her faith. Having secured Philip II's approval of her marriage to Darnley, she was well placed to appeal for Spanish support. Her emissary was Francis Yaxley, a

Catholic who had made a career in the shadowy milieu between diplomacy and espionage, and who had recently become Darnley's secretary.[34] Yaxley obtained from the King of Spain a grant of 20,000 crowns, in the form of a letter of credit to be cashed in Antwerp. With this very considerable sum in gold Yaxley sailed for Scotland, but was shipwrecked on the English coast and drowned. The wreck was salvaged and the gold was claimed by the Earl of Northumberland as 'Lord of the Foreshore' and by the English crown, as treasure trove. Not a coin of it reached Scotland. Mary's appeal to the Pope for money was entrusted to the Bishop of Dunblane, and elicited promises of assistance and a fulsome letter from the newly elected Pope Pius V, applauding her 'brilliant proof of your zeal by restoring the due worship of God throughout your whole realm', which was far more than she had even imagined achieving. The French ambassador, Castelnau de Mauvissière, who had written so admiringly of Darnley, had come to Scotland to inform Mary that she could expect no help from France, where the Wars of Religion were already straining the military and financial resources of the government to the uttermost.

Without foreign help on a large scale Mary could not adopt a Catholic policy. Personal popularity had enabled her to defeat rebellion, but thereafter even a feeble show of favour for Catholicism alienated Protestant supporters who had been unconvinced by Moray's propaganda.

Mary's pro-Catholic gestures were tentative. Archbishop Hamilton, imprisoned earlier in the reign, was now set free. The Protestant Provost of Edinburgh, Douglas of Kilspindie, was replaced by a Catholic, Preston of Craigmillar. Wishart of Pitarrow, the administrator of the 'thirds of benefices', a zealous Protestant, was replaced by Murray of Tullibardine, also a Protestant, but 'more complaisant to the demands of the Crown',[35] who soon caused complaints that ministers' stipends could not be paid out of the proportion of the 'thirds' which now reached the Kirk. These pro-Catholic gestures, with the Queen's expressed intention to take Parliamentary action on behalf of the 'auld religion', merely served to 'antagonize and alarm the Protestants, while failing to satisfy the Catholics'. By the end of 1565 all Mary had achieved was to give Moray's propaganda retrospective credibility.

In consequence, support for Mary's government by the Scottish nobility became dangerously narrow. Only four earls regularly appeared at court: Lennox, who supported his son's demand for the

Crown Matrimonial, and his kinsman Atholl, Bothwell, who was a man of action rather than a statesman, and Huntly, who was young and inexperienced. This exiguous attendance advertised decreased prestige, for a sovereign's greatness was demonstrated by the number of great persons attendant at court. It was also dangerous, for keeping territorial magnates within the orbit of the court controlled their actions. The exiles and the absentees together formed a dangerously large proportion of Scotland's nobility beyond the Queen's control, but Mary seemed oblivious of the threat.

Throughout her reign she had spent most of her days within her predominantly foreign household, leaving the guidance of affairs to Moray and Lethington, and seldom attending meetings of her Council. After the Chaseabout Raid Mary did not change her habit of reliance, but since Darnley failed to be reliable in the way that she required, she turned to a member of her household whose influence had been growing quietly for some time.

David Rizzio had manoeuvred to make himself indispensable. He had ingratiated himself with Darnley, and assured the Queen of his support for their marriage when others opposed it. He had found her appreciative of both his advice and his company, for he was amusing, cosmopolitan, deferential and useful. Above all, unlike territorial magnates with local responsibilities, he did not disappear, but was always available when he was needed. Rizzio is said to have been ugly and even deformed, but this is not necessarily true. Politicians have not yet outgrown the tradition of ridiculing the looks of their opponents, and this childish form of mockery was more effective and could be more extreme when everyone's face and form was not universally familiar. But if Rizzio was unimpressive-looking it mattered little to the Queen, who was interested in his reliability, not his appearance.[36]

Rizzio was not the Queen's only new confidant, but he was the one who attracted enmity, as a foreigner, a Catholic and an upstart. Inevitably he was imagined to be a papal agent, though there is no evidence that he was one. According to another rumour Mary intended to appoint him Secretary of State, or even Chancellor in place of Darnley's cousin the Earl of Morton, but the Queen did not break her agreement not to appoint foreigners to public office. Rizzio's position was informal but influential, and as a typical royal favourite he made a tactless parade of his good fortune by dressing with ostentatious splendour and assuming arrogant manners. He became universally disliked, but the person to whom he was most objectionable was his former patron the King, who saw Rizzio first as undermining his influence, but soon imagined him as alienating the affections of his wife.

During the autumn of 1565 Mary Queen of Scots was in poor health. She was never strong, though she could display great vigour and energy in times of crisis, as she did during the Chaseabout Raid, but such efforts were often followed by physical prostration and sometimes by nervous collapse. Mary's ill-health presents a challenge to the notorious difficulty of historical diagnosis. Hypothetical diagnoses have been porphyria, a disorder of the spleen, gastric ulcers and neurotic hypochondria, but a conclusive diagnosis is impossible.[37]

In November she was confined to bed with a pain in her side which was described as an 'old malady'; but reports of a chronic ailment were superseded by excited rumours that she was pregnant. Her sufferings were probably enhanced by the symptoms of early pregnancy, which can be discomforts to some women and miseries to others. Early in December she journeyed from Edinburgh to Linlithgow in a horse-litter, to meet Darnley who had been hunting in Fife. Normally Mary rode everywhere, so her decision to travel in a litter was regarded as a public acknowledgement of her pregnancy.

It was already public knowledge that she was no longer on good terms with her husband, so their rendezvous at Linlithgow was assumed to be a meeting for discussion, not a happy reunion. If she had summoned the King to meet her to inform him of her pregnancy, it was not good news for him, for his desire for the Crown Matrimonial far outweighed his pride in paternity. Indeed, it was a bitter blow to his hopes. If, as he could imagine, the Queen gave birth to a healthy son, and being sickly herself died in childbed, the child would be King of Scots, and himself only the King's father. This was not the purpose for which he had wooed and won the Queen: he had done so for his own ambition, not for the sake of his posterity.

6

THE KING AS MURDERER

> He is an ambitious and inconstant youth, and would like
> to rule the realm, which was the subject of the plot he
> hatched . . . when he made the . . . rebels come secretly
> to the court with the purpose of getting himself crowned
> King, and . . . it was he who got the said rebels to murder
> poor David Rizzio, the Queen's Piedmontese secretary.[1]

ON CHRISTMAS EVE 1565 Mary Queen of Scots sat up all night playing cards, while Darnley went ostentatiously to his devotions. Mary
went to bed at daybreak, but Darnley 'was at Mass and Matins before
day, and heard the High Mass devoutly upon his knees'.[2] Probably he
made a display of piety merely to highlight the Queen's neglect of her
religious duties, though possibly he was one of those not uncommon
people who veer between bouts of profligacy and religiosity. His public
displays of drunkenness were growing more frequent, but Christmas
would have been a likely occasion for a reaction.

Immediately after Christmas he went to Peebles on an extended
hunting trip and was absent from court until mid-January. The Earl
of Lennox had spent Christmas in Glasgow, and then planned to
meet his son, to whom he wrote:

Sir,
I have received by my servant Nisbet your natural and kind
letter, for the which I humbly thank your Majesty, and as to the
contents thereof, I will not trouble you therein, but refer the same

till I wait upon your Majesty at Peebles, which shall be so soon as I may hear the certainty of your going thither. And for that [because] the extremity of this stormy weather causes me to doubt of your setting forward so soon in your journey, therefore I stay till I hear further from your Majesty, which I shall humbly beseech you I may, and I shall not fail to wait upon you accordingly. Thus committing your Majesty to the blessing and governance of Almighty God, who preserve you in health, long life and most happy reign. From Glasgow this 26th day of December.

Your Majesty's humble subject and father,

Mathew Levenax.[3]

This was a properly formal letter to a king, though extravagantly reverential from a father to a son. It would have served to heighten Darnley's dissatisfaction with his anomalous position, which no doubt Lennox intended, for he was determined that his son should have the Crown Matrimonial. Some reference to this was no doubt the 'contents' of Darnley's previous communication, which Lennox intended to discuss with him when they met at Peebles. Darnley's dissatisfaction was reaching the point where he would cease attempting to persuade or bully the Queen into granting his desire, and would begin plotting to obtain it in spite of her. His quest for the Crown Matrimonial was about to become a treasonable and criminal enterprise.

While Mary Queen of Scots was preoccupied with her ill-health and disillusioned with her marriage, she was under continuous pressure to pardon the Earl of Moray and his confederates. Queen Elizabeth, despite her public castigation of Moray, interceded for him, and to Mary's surprise and displeasure, so did the King of France. It was probably in response to French intervention that Mary pardoned the Duke of Châtelhérault, on condition that he lived in France for the next five years. Mary's partial forgiveness of Châtelhérault was symptomatic of her disillusionment with Darnley and consequent disfavour to the Lennox claim. But Mary remained adamant in her resolve not to pardon Moray and the rest of the rebels. She was particularly bitter towards Moray because she saw his rebellion as unpardonable treachery and ingratitude, after the confidence she had shown him and the rewards she had heaped on him. It was one of Mary's many misapprehensions that she expected gratitude from men who merely accepted her rewards as their just deserts, and still thought them insufficient. This was the dissatisfaction that brought the divergent interests of Darnley and Moray together. Mary's initial injustice to her husband in withholding the Crown Matrimonial appeared increasingly justified by his misconduct, and her refusal to pardon her brother appeared to need no justification, but she could not afford to be so inflexible when her attitude caused irreconcilable interests to coalesce.

The link between Darnley and Moray was the Earl of Morton. His basic sympathy was with Moray, his coreligionist and ally in the crisis of the Reformation; but family interest also bound him to Darnley, especially since Margaret Lennox had yielded her claim to the Angus title and estates to Morton's nephew and ward. Furthermore, since Darnley was 'mother's kin' to the Douglases, his elevation to the Crown Matrimonial would be to their greater glory. Morton could serve both interests by reconciling them.

According to the Queen's apologist, Adam Blackwood:

> Morton cometh to the young Prince . . . he putteth into his head to take the sole government upon him, excluding the Queen from all authority . . . it being a thing against nature that the hen should crow before the cock; yea, against the commandment of the eternal God, that a man should be subject to his wife, the man being the image of God, and woman the image of man.[4]

This was the orthodoxy of the period, which Darnley fully accepted, but to have it presented to him in forceful terms by Morton confirmed his dissatisfaction. Morton's next step was to offer the remedy:

> He promised him the Queen of England's assistance, with Moray's his own, and all the rest of their faction, to stand sure his [be his adherents], and do the best they could for him . . . if it would please him to pardon their former facts [deeds] and restore them to their estates . . .[5]

It was an attractive prospect that the very men who had rebelled against his marriage to the Queen should now conspire to give him the honour that the Queen withheld.

*   *   *

At the beginning of February Darnley made as great a display of Catholic devotion as he had done at Christmas. He swore that he would have a Mass celebrated in St Giles, which, said Randolph was moved in Council, but 'I believe rather to tempt men's minds [test opinion] than intended in deed'.[6] Darnley also tried to persuade several lords to accompany him to Mass, and when they refused 'gave them all very evil words'; the Queen was equally unsuccessful in persuading others, and was offended that her request was refused by Bothwell, but he, though a notorious 'evil liver', was a firm Protestant. However, on Candlemas, 2 February, a High Mass was held in Holyrood Chapel, with a procession in which candles were carried by the King and Queen, Lennox, Atholl, and other Catholic courtiers. Though the ceremonies took place within the confines of the court, it appeared that Catholicism was stronger than it had been at the beginning of the reign, when the first Mass celebrated for the Queen had caused a riot.

On 4 February a French ambassador, the Sieur de Rambouillet, arrived to invest Darnley with the Order of St Michael, bestowed on him by Charles IX. Rambouillet had been first to the court of England to present the Order to the Duke of Norfolk and the Earl of Leicester. Darnley's investiture took place in the chapel of Holyrood on Sunday 10 February, after Mass, and he wore a robe of crimson satin 'guarded' (bordered or banded) with black satin and black velvet, and sewn with gold aglets.[7] At the conclusion of the ceremony Darnley swore an oath to be loyal to the sovereign of the Order in so far as it was compatible with his loyalty to the Queen, and if ('which God forbid') he should commit a fault which disgraced the Order, to surrender the collar to the sovereign 'without ever wearing it again'.[8] Several who heard him must have known that he was already forsworn.

After the investiture the ambassador wished to know what arms should be given to the King – presumably to be emblazoned in the armorial of the Order. This was discussed in Council. 'Some thought he should have the arms of Scotland; some others said, seeing it was not concluded in Parliament that he should have the Crown Matrimonial, that he should have arms ... as Duke of Rothesay [should be Albany], Earl of Ross etc. The Queen bade give him only his due; whereby it was perceived her love waxed cold towards him'.[9] The Queen's response was ambiguous, and the outcome uncertain, but the discussion would have been sufficiently humiliating to the

King to confirm his determination to pursue the Crown Matrimonial by the means Morton had suggested.

There are two engravings of Darnley in the robes and insignia of the Order of St Michael, each showing his portrait bust surrounded by a cartouche bearing his titles: on one he is described as 'illustr: Prin: Hen: Steward: Domin: Darnley Dux Albaniae' (The Illustrious Prince Henry Stewart Lord Darnley Duke of Albany), and above the portrait are three shields, bearing the arms of Scotland, Albany and France respectively; on the other, produced in the Netherlands, he is described as 'Henricus Dominus de Arnley [sic] Rex Scotorum' on the cartouche and below the portrait as 'Henrick Heere van Arnley, Coninck van Schotlant'. The Scottish Seton Armorial, though not connected with this investiture, may show what Mary considered 'his due': it shows Mary and Darnley standing side by side, the Queen wearing a heraldic kirtle embroidered with the royal lion rampant, Darnley in full armour with a shield bearing the arms of Albany and Lennox. Above the figures is an inscription: 'Henrie Steuart Duke of Albanye and Marie Quene of Scotland, 1566'.

Despite the Queen's coldness towards Darnley, his investiture with the Order of St Michael was magnificently celebrated. On Sunday evening there was a banquet for Rambouillet and his suite at which the Scottish lords performed a masque after supper; and on Monday evening there was a second banquet after which the Queen and her ladies performed: 'the Quenis Grace and all her Maries and Ladies wer all cled in men's apperell; and everie ane of thame presentit ane quhinger [dagger] bravelie and maiste artificiallie made and embroiderit with gold, to the said Ambassatour and his gentilmen, everie ane of thame according to his estate'.[10] On Tuesday the Lords of Council entertained the Frenchmen, and again there was a masque, in which the performers were the King and Queen, Rizzio and seven others. On Wednesday the Earl of Mar gave a dinner for the Ambassador in Edinburgh Castle, which was attended by the King and Queen, and when they left the artillery of the castle fired a salute. In the evening a farewell entertainment was given at Holyrood, which was marred by Darnley's making some of the ambassador's suite hopelessly drunk. They left Scotland the following day, and reached Berwick on 15 February. Next day Sir William Drury, Captain of Berwick Castle, wrote to Sir William Cecil:

M. de la Roc Paussay and his brother arrived here yesterday. He is sick, my Lord Darnley having made him drink *acqua composita* [whisky]. All people say that Darnley is too much addicted to drinking . . . There was some jar betwixt the Queen and him in a Merchant's house in Edinburgh, she only dissuading him from drinking too much himself, and enticing others; in both which he proceeded, and gave her such words that she left the place with tears . . .[11]

Drury added that according to people who saw Mary and Darnley frequently such a scene was nothing unusual. They quarrelled repeatedly over the Crown Matrimonial, the recall of the 'Henricus et Maria' coin,[12] and the Queen's conditional pardon of Châtelhérault, which had infuriated both Darnley and his father. Drury concluded his letter with the story that Darnley had recently gone to the Isle of Inchkeith in the Firth of Forth with Lord Robert Stewart, Lord Fleming and others, and there done something so disgusting that Drury could not bring himself to describe it, although 'too many were witnesses'. The English diplomats were inclined to heighten the effect of their gossip with such innuendoes, but whatever Darnley's misconduct at Inchkeith, it can only have been insignificant compared with what he planned.

The plans co-ordinated by Morton reached the point at which they could be formulated in bonds, or binding agreements, between the participants. The well-informed Randolph knew of the bonds as early as 25 February, and was able to send full details of them to Cecil on 6 March. The bond given to Darnley contained seven articles promised by or on behalf of Moray, Argyll, Glencairn, Rothes, Boyd, Ochiltree 'and their complices'. They bound themselves 'as true subjects' to support Darnley in his 'just and lawful' actions; at the next Parliament to consent to his receiving the Crown Matrimonial; to maintain his just title to the Crown 'failing the succession of our Sovereign Lady'; to maintain the religion established by the Queen at her arrival 'by the help of the said noble Prince' (Darnley); as his true subjects to 'spare neither life nor death in setting forward his honour'; to 'labour' with the Queen of England for the liberation of his mother and brother; and to procure the Queen of England's support for him against all foreign princes.[13] Darnley's bond, in which he was described as 'Our most high and mighty Prince Henry, King of Scotland', contained his promise 'of his mere mercy and clemency' to obtain the rebels' remission, to prevent their forfeiture, to support them in the exercise of the reformed religion, and to maintain them as a good master should. It was signed 'Henry R'.[14]

It was an extraordinary agreement, in which Darnley promised to protect the reformed religion within days of having made an ostentatious display of his Catholicism, and the lords who had rebelled against Darnley's marriage to the Queen promised to assist him to the Crown Matrimonial. Darnley, with his immense egotism and arrogance, does not seem to have asked himself what obedience he could expect from such turbulent men when the coup had been carried out. The only aspect of the agreement which displays any decent feelings in Darnley was his requiring the lords to 'labour' for the liberation of his mother and young brother. Darnley had written letters to his mother that she had not been permitted to receive, which had distressed him, and both he and the Queen had repeatedly requested her liberation. Indeed, Mary's most recent request had been written on 12 February, protesting that Lady Lennox had not deserved imprisonment 'for merely wishing well to her son'.[15]

Remarkably, the Queen of Scots received no hint of a conspiracy that involved so many people. However, she discovered that Randolph had been arranging for funds, supplied by the Countess of Moray, to be sent to the rebels; for this Mary ordered him to leave Scotland, and wrote to inform Elizabeth of his expulsion on 20 February.[16] Randolph was still in Edinburgh five days later, and when forced to leave he went only as far as Berwick, where he continued to receive detailed information on events in Scotland. After dealing with Randolph, Mary had pleasanter matters to occupy her attention. On 24 February Bothwell married Huntly's sister, Lady Jean Gordon. Mary was delighted by a wedding that sealed an alliance between two of her most powerful adherents. She gave Lady Jean seven ells of cloth of silver for her wedding dress.[17] While the court celebrated, doubtless with the usual round of masques and banquets, the coup was approaching fruition.

Before his departure, Randolph had discovered that the coup would include the destruction of David Rizzio. As early as 13 February he had told Leicester, 'I know that . . . David with the consent of the King, shall have his throat cut within these ten days'.[18] Rizzio lived slightly longer than Randolph anticipated, but the date of his death was decided by the date of the Parliament at which the Queen of Scots had resolved to enact the attainder and forfeiture of Moray and his confederates.

On 7 March 'the Queen came from the Palace of Holyroodhouse to the town in wonderous gorgeous apparel, albeit the number of lords and train was not very great',[19] to open Parliament. Darnley refused to accompany her, as a protest that he was not to receive the Crown Matrimonial. 'With seven or eight horse he went to Leith to pass his time there',[20] suggesting that his displeasure was to be shown in his customary fashion by absenting himself. Parliament, at the Queen's demand, reluctantly agreed to enact the attainder of Moray and his confederates on 12 March. The coup, therefore, had to take place before that date.

The removal of Rizzio had not been mentioned in the bonds exchanged by Darnley and the rebels. As an object of general animosity, obviously Rizzio would be removed from the court, but as a man of no importance he might have been killed in a casual affray, or even ordered to leave the country. The rumour Randolph had heard was of a more sinister plan, which originated in Darnley's personal hatred for the Queen's secretary.

Darnley's resentment of Rizzio had grown with the secretary's encroachment into the Queen's confidence, and no doubt had been exacerbated by the humiliating matter of the stamp of the King's signature which had been entrusted to Rizzio's keeping. When the Queen's anger with her husband and the discomforts of her pregnancy had alike made her avoid his bed, she had done so by playing cards with Rizzio, and interposing the secretary's company between her husband and herself. Any young man who desired his wife would have leapt from resentment of the situation to jealousy of the man whose company she so obviously preferred. It probably did not require Morton to suggest that Rizzio was both advising the Queen to withhold the Crown Matrimonial from her husband and cuckolding him to inspire Darnley with murderous hatred of the secretary. Adam Blackwood's suggestion that 'the poor Prince' was the victim of his own advisers was the most charitable interpretation of Darnley's determination that the secretary must die;[21] but it was Darnley's desire that he should be done to death with the maximum brutality and in the Queen's presence.

Sir James Melville also blamed Darnley's confidants:

The Earl of Morton had a crafty head, and had a cousin called George Douglas, natural son to the Earl of Angus [George Douglas, the Postulate of Arbroath] . . . The said George was continually about the King, as his mother's brother, and put in his head such suspicion against Rizzio that the King was won to give his consent over easily to the slaughter of Signor David. This the Lords of Morton, Lindsay, Ruthven and others had devised, to become that way masters of the Court . . .[22]

As Morton and George Douglas were Darnley's close kinsmen, and Lords Lindsay and Ruthven were married to ladies of the Douglas family, the intended coup could be seen as a plot for family aggrandizement.[23] Probably they all encouraged Darnley's suspicions of Rizzio and were desirous to get rid of him, but so long as Rizzio went it mattered little to them how he went, dead or alive. As ruthless men they were ready to kill Rizzio if Darnley wished it, but it was Darnley alone who desired to kill him in the Queen's presence. His hope was that the shock of the event might make her miscarry, for he did not want the child that she was carrying to be born. The signatories to the bond had promised Darnley 'to maintain his just title to the Crown failing the succession of our Sovereign Lady', and Darnley desired her succession to fail, and his own to be established. Whether he believed the child to be his own or Rizzio's, he still wished it to die. He might even have preferred that the Queen herself did not survive the coup, as ensuing events suggested. His desire for the Crown possessed him to the exclusion of every other emotion.

Darnley's first confidants were George Douglas and Lord Ruthven. Both had unsavoury reputations, and Ruthven was rumoured to be a warlock. Neither discouraged Darnley's plan, though Ruthven raised objections which were not moral but prudential. He pointed out that if Rizzio were murdered in the Queen's presence 'sundry great persons' who would be with her might try to prevent the enterprise, and that some of these and the conspirators might kill one another, and then blood feuds would be obligatory on their families. The question was discussed by the conspirators. Darnley pressed his wish, 'which the said Earl [Morton] and Lords were very loth to grant, and gave many reasons . . . that it was better to have been done out of her presence . . . Notwithstanding no reason might avail, but the King would have him [Rizzio] taken in her Majesty's presence, and devised the manner himself . . .'[24]

This was Lord Ruthven's version, which obviously sought to lay as much blame as possible upon Darnley, and some historians have doubted that he was as entirely responsible as Ruthven claimed. But it was chiefly in Darnley's interest that the murder was committed as Ruthven claimed that he demanded, and Ruthven produced conclusive evidence in the form of a bond signed by Darnley in which he assumed responsibility for the crime and promised to protect the participants or indemnify their heirs or successors, if any of them were killed and feuds resulted. He signed this on 1 March 1566, apparently without realizing that whether the coup succeeded or failed, he had mortgaged his reputation to his confederates.[25]

There was a curious story that one John Damiot, described as 'a priest and sorcerer', recommended Rizzio to take the fortune he had amassed and leave Scotland, but Rizzio brushed this advice aside, saying that his enemies might talk against him but would do nothing, whereupon Damiot told him at least to 'beware of the bastard'. Rizzio, assuming that Damiot meant the Earl of Moray, replied that he would take good care that the bastard never returned to Scotland. Damiot's advice was later seen as a typical oracular ambiguity, for one of Rizzio's murderers was another bastard, George Douglas, Postulate of Arbroath.[26]

Sir James Melville independently warned Mary Queen of Scots that if she did not show clemency to Moray and his confederates they might be tempted to plot some desperate action. Mary replied contemptuously 'that our countrymen were talkative'. Melville then tried to warn Rizzio, 'for then he and I were under great friendship. But he disdained all danger, and despised counsel'.[27] It sounds as though Rizzio and the Queen had convinced each other of the mistaken view that Scottish conspirators were more talkative than active.

Despite these rumours and warnings, the conspiracy continued undiscovered, even though the conspirators recruited a large body of helpers, of whom Randolph was able to supply the English Council with a full list.[28] Lennox knew of the plot to restore the rebels and crown his son, though not of the plans to murder Rizzio. Lethington knew of both, though he played no part in the murder.

The slaughter of Rizzio is so famous as a historical drama that it is difficult to recapture its horror as a contemporary event. But there were contemporary accounts, by Mary Queen of Scots herself, by

Lord Ruthven, who had a gift for dramatic narrative, and by Thomas Randolph and the Earl of Bedford, who wrote a joint report to the English Council, having talked to Ruthven and sent their own representative to Edinburgh to speak to the Queen, Darnley, and other witnesses.[29] John Knox and the anonymous author of the 'Diurnal of Occurrents' were both in Edinburgh on the night of the murder, but were not witnesses – though Knox approved the murder and may have known of the plot. Adam Blackwood and Lord Herries, both contemporaries, wrote later. It was a well-documented atrocity.

On Saturday evening, 9 March, the Queen gave a supper party in a little room some twelve feet square, which opened off her bedchamber in the Palace of Holyrood. The room was almost filled by the dining table, a 'low reposing bed' on which the Queen sat at one end of the table, and the seats for her guests which surrounded it. There was a fireplace on one wall, and the fire both warmed the room and probably overheated those who had their backs to it. There were candles on the table, and though it was Lent there were dishes of meat, because the Queen's pregnancy dispensed her from the obligation of fasting. Her guests were her illegitimate brother and sister, Lord Robert Stewart and Lady Jean Stewart, Countess of Argyll, and two members of her household, the Laird of Creich and Sir Arthur Erskine, her Master of Horse. David Rizzio was seated at the foot of the table, dressed in a 'nightgown', or informal indoor gown, of damask trimmed with fur, a satin doublet and hose of russet velvet. He was wearing his cap, and that he should be permitted to cover his head in the Queen's presence was a privilege that his enemies noted and resented[30].

The Queen's apartments consisted of a Presence Chamber and a bedchamber and the little cabinet. The King had a similar suite of rooms on the floor beneath. The principal staircase connected their Presence Chambers; a private stair led up from the King's bedchamber to the Queen's. While the supper was in progress, Darnley came up the private stair, entered the cabinet, sat down beside the Queen, and put his arm around her. His recent unpleasant behaviour made his arrival surprising, but the Queen received him amicably, and asked him if he had supped. He said he had done so earlier.

Then the heavy tread of steel-clad footsteps was heard, and Lord Ruthven entered the room, a bizarre apparition in full armour with a nightgown over it. His appearance was the more sinister because in recent weeks he had been extremely ill, and was even rumoured to be dying.[31] Pointing dramatically at Rizzio he said, 'Let it please your Majesty that yonder man David come forth of your privy chamber where he has been over long!' Mary demanded, 'What offence hath he done?' Ruthven answered, 'He hath offended your honour, which I dare not be so bold as to speak of. As to your husband's honour, he hath hindered him of the Crown Matrimonial, which your Grace promised him, besides many other things . . .' By his own account, Ruthven launched into a long speech concerning Rizzio's misdeeds, while everyone remained motionless with astonishment.

Then the group suddenly broke into turmoil. Everyone rose simultaneously. Rizzio darted round the table, behind the Queen, and crouched down clutching her skirts for protection. Creich and Erskine drew their daggers to defend her. Ruthven said to Darnley, 'Sir! Take the Queen your wife and sovereign to you!', then drew his own dagger, shouting at Creich and Erskine, 'Lay no hands on me for I will not be handled!' Now the rest of the conspirators surged into the room and rushed at Rizzio, overturning the table, from which the Countess of Argyll, with instinctive fear of fire, quickwittedly snatched one of the candlesticks. Ruthven pushed the Queen into the arms of Darnley, who held her pinioned in a tight embrace, while Rizzio was pulled away from her, his fingers bent back to force him to let go of her skirt, while all the while he shrieked, 'Giustizia! Giustizia, Madame! Save ma vie! Save ma vie!' in polyglot terror. The Queen struggled wildly, and two of the conspirators, Patrick Bellenden and Andrew Ker of Fawdonside, pressed the muzzles of their pistols against her body. Fawdonside, she believed, meant to kill her, but his weapon 'refused to give fire'. George Douglas plucked the King's dagger from its sheath at his side and struck at Rizzio over the Queen's shoulder – later she said she had felt the cold of the steel as the blow passed her neck.

Rizzio was dragged from the room, and in the bloodlust of the mêlée dispatched with many dagger thrusts. His body was later found to have fifty-six wounds, and the King's dagger was left stuck into the corpse, to advertise his responsibility for the murder. It was unlikely that he, controlling the Queen, had had a chance to strike a blow himself, but the murder had been carried out exactly as he intended.

After the turmoil Darnley led the Queen from the wreckage of the supper party into her bedchamber, Lord Ruthven returned, and the

three of them faced one another. A sordid scene of recrimination
ensued. The Queen said to Darnley, 'My Lord, why have you caused
to do this wicked deed to me? Considering that I took you from low
estate and made you my husband? What offence have I given you
that you should do me such shame?' In reply, Darnley poured out
all the pent-up resentments of recent months:

> I have good reason for me, for since yonder fellow David came in
> credit and familiarity with your Majesty, you neither regarded me,
> entertained me or trusted me after your wonted fashion; for every
> day before dinner you were wont to come to my chamber, and
> past the time with me, and this long time you have not done so;
> and when I came to your Majesty's chamber, you bear me little
> company except David had been the third person; and after supper
> your Majesty used to sit up at the cards with the said David till
> one or two after midnight. And this is the entertainment that I
> have had of you this long time.

Mary replied that it was not a gentlewoman's duty to go to her
husband's chamber, but the husband's to visit his wife. This inspired
from Darnley a torrent of sexual jealousy and political resentment,
which, if it was half as eloquent as Lord Ruthven reported, was
almost Shakespearean:

> How came you to my chamber in the beginning, and ever till
> within these six months, that David fell into familiarity with you?
> Or am I failed in any sort in my body? Or what disdain have you
> of me? Or what offences have I done you that you should coy me
> at all times alike, seeing I am willing to do all things that becometh
> a good husband? Suppose I be of mean degree, yet I am your
> husband, and you promised me obedience at the day of your mar-
> riage, and that I should be participant and equal with you in all
> things; but you have used me otherwise, by the persuasion of
> David.[32]

The Queen replied, 'My Lord, all the offence is done [to] me, you
have the wite [knowledge] thereof, for the which I shall be your wife
no longer, nor lie with you any more, and shall never like well till I
cause you have as sorrowful a heart as I have at this present.'
This painful scene ended when Lord Ruthven, 'being sore felled

with his sickness', sat down, or collapsed on a seat, and called for a drink 'for God's sake', and one of the Queen's French servants brought him a cup of wine. The Queen's fury at this insulting behaviour, added to the horrors of the evening, snapped her self-control, and she broke into a hysterical diatribe, threatening the revenge that the King of France, the Cardinal of Lorraine, the Pope and the Princes of Italy would take on her behalf.[33]

She was interrupted by loud banging at the door, and Lord Gray broke in, reporting that Huntly, Bothwell, Atholl, Caithness, Suther-land and others were fighting in the close with Morton and his com-pany 'being on the King's part'. Darnley, no doubt longing to escape from the raw emotions he had unleashed, attempted to go and join the action, but Lord Ruthven told him to stay with the Queen, and staggered off down the stairs 'supported by the arms' – presumably by Lord Gray. Ruthven managed to pacify the combatants, and shook hands with Huntly and Bothwell, who went indoors, and shortly afterwards escaped from the palace by a back window. They rode hard for Bothwell's castle of Dunbar, where they set about planning the Queen's rescue. This was the first indication that the coup might fail.

But the Queen's only chance of rescue that night was quickly foiled by Darnley. The sounds of fighting around the palace had roused the town. 'Then came the Provost of Edinburgh, and a great crowd of townsmen armed, to the outer court of the Palace', and the Prov-ost, Preston of Craigmillar, demanded to see the Queen, to be assured of her safety. Darnley went to the window and called down, 'Provost, know you not that I am King? I command you to pass to your homes.' They obediently dispersed.[34] When the Queen attempted to get to the window to make her own appeal to the Provost, she was, in her own words, 'extremely menaced by the lords, who in our face declared "if we desired to have spoken [to] them, they should cut us in collops and cast us over the walls".'[35]

Gradually an uneasy peace settled on the Palace of Holyrood. The Queen was permitted to go to bed, a prisoner in her own palace, the gates guarded by Morton's men-at-arms, and guards at her chamber door. Despite her bitter words to him earlier, Mary invited Darnley to sleep with her: she had already determined to detach him from his confederates. Darnley's actions were also contrary to his words: having complained vehemently of being deprived of his conjugal rights, he went down to his own bedchamber, lay on the bed, no

doubt intending to take a brief sleep to recover himself, and slept
soundly until the next morning.

Darnley woke early, and endeavoured to repair his lost opportunity;
he put on his nightgown and went up to the Queen's bedchamber,
where he found her still asleep. He sat on the side of the bed and
looked at her – asleep, or pretending to be so.[36] When she opened
her eyes he offered to get into bed with her, but she insisted on
getting up immediately. She faced the day with the remarkable courage which made her so admirable in adversity.

It appeared that the advantage was still with Darnley and the
conspirators. The Queen was kept confined in her chamber while
Darnley joined his confederates and issued a proclamation dismissing
the Parliament on his own royal authority, presumably intending
that it should be reconvened or a new Parliament summoned, to
grant him the Crown Matrimonial.

During the day the Queen's companion was the Dowager Lady
Huntly, widow of the Earl who had died after the Battle of Corrichie,
and mother of the present Earl, for whose restoration to his title and
estates she was grateful to the Queen. She knew of the escape of her
son and son-in-law Bothwell the previous night, and offered to help
Mary escape also. She made the reckless suggestion that a rope ladder
could be brought with the Queen's dinner, under the cover which
kept it warm. Mary declined. She was too heavily pregnant to risk
descending from a window. But she gave Lady Huntly a letter to her
son and son-in-law, informing them of her intended escape and urg-
ing them to be ready to assist her. Conveniently, Lady Huntly was
ordered to leave, lest she and the Queen might be plotting. She was
superficially searched, and sent on her way with the Queen's letter
between her chemise and her skin.

During the afternoon, in order to convince the conspirators that
she had no thoughts of escape, Mary feigned an imminent miscarriage. A midwife was brought, who confirmed the probability, and
the Queen was left in her care to await the outcome, while the
conspirators discussed what should be done with her if she weathered
the immediate danger and kept the child. The consensus was that
she should be confined in Stirling Castle, and 'the King could manage
the affairs of state, along with the nobles'. Someone objected that
an attempt might be made to rescue the Queen by force, to which

Lord Ruthven replied, 'If they cause any uproar by attempting to release her we will throw her to them piecemeal from the top of the terrace.' Darnley, if he had previously dreamed of destroying his wife to serve his own ambition, found such undisguised brutality alarming; he required little imagination to see that he too might become a victim of it.

In the early evening Moray and Lord Rothes, who had moved from Newcastle to Berwick in readiness for the coup, arrived in Edinburgh. The conspirators met again, and this time Darnley brought his father to the meeting, obviously because he felt intimidated, and in need of protection. There was further discussion:

> At last they addressed the King: 'If you wish to obtain what we have promised you, you must needs follow our advice . . . if you do otherwise, we will take care of ourselves, cost what it may.' Hereupon they . . . whispered together, which put the King and his father into great terror, for they did not think their lives were safe . . . as, when they [the lords] were breaking up, they told him that now he must not talk with the Queen save in their presence. They removed his own attendants and left a guard near his chamber.[38]

This was not the treatment Darnley had expected, and he was now frankly terrified. Later that night he crept up the private stair to the Queen's bedchamber and begged for admittance, but she refused to let him in until the morning. He returned at daybreak, and on being admitted, fell on his knees, 'which she was unwilling he should do', and said abjectly, 'Ah, my Mary (for so he was used to call her familiarly) . . . I have failed in my duty towards you . . . The only atonement which I can make . . . is to acknowledge my fault and sue for pardon . . .' and he told her that he had 'consented' to the return of Moray and his confederates, in return for their promise to secure the Crown Matrimonial for him, and showed her the bond they had signed. It will be remembered that this bond made no mention of the murder of Rizzio, which he told her had been no part of his plan. So long as Mary believed this, he was not beyond forgiveness. He told her of the conspirators' plans for her, and concluded, 'Unless you take some means to prevent it, we are all ruined, and that speedily.'[39]

Mary had already determined to make use of him, and had probably expected to need all her arts of persuasion to detach him from his accomplices. But as she found him already desperate to be free of them, she revealed her plan to escape, and told him that he must play his part in this by getting the guards removed. He said that the best thing she could do would be to pardon the conspirators, to which she replied that she could not bring herself to do so – but that he might make any promises on her behalf for the sake of expediency. Darnley then returned to his own bedchamber, without their meeting having been discovered.[40]

Later in the morning the Earl of Moray came to see the Queen, and Mary threw herself into his arms, crying, 'Oh, my brother, if you had been here they had not used me thus!' This was not necessarily play-acting. Mary may have remembered the ascendancy of Moray as a time of law and order, which she now longed to see restored. Moray was so moved by her emotional welcome that 'tears fell from his eyes'.[41]

Mary's next visitors were the midwife and her personal physician, a Frenchman, who was now permitted to visit her for the first time. Both said the Queen ought to be removed 'to some sweeter and pleasanter air'. Darnley relayed this recommendation to the lords, who replied that 'they feared all was but craft and policy'.[42] So the rest of the day was spent in assuring them that Mary had no intention of escape.

In the afternoon Darnley brought Moray, Morton and Ruthven to her Presence Chamber, where they all fell on their knees as she entered. She told them that she would 'remit the whole number that were banished, or were at . . . the death of David, and put all things in oblivion as if they had never been'.[43] She then told them to draw up a deed to this effect, and she would sign it. Morton and Ruthven left, and then Mary took Darnley by one hand and Moray by the other, and walked up and down the room conversing with them, in apparent reconciliation.

The King and Queen had an early supper together, and afterwards Darnley went down to his own Presence Chamber, where the lords gave him 'the articles which were for their security' for the Queen to sign. Darnley took the document, and then asked them to remove their guards, so that the Queen's own guards and servants 'might order all as they pleased'. This led to a revival of suspicion, but Darnley assured them that he would 'warrent for all'. So, after minatory remarks that any 'bloodshed or mischief' would be his fault, they left, to have supper at Morton's house in the town.[44]

When Mary and Darnley were satisfied that only their own people remained in the palace, the Queen sent for the captain of her guard, John Stewart of Traquair, and told him of her plan of escape. Stealth was necessary, for the suspicions of Darnley's erstwhile confederates had been very difficult to quieten. Traquair promised to provide horses at midnight, and Mary chose their small escort: Traquair himself, Sir Arthur Erskine, behind whom she would ride pillion, and Anthony Standen, one of Darnley's Gentlemen of the Chamber,[45] with two or three guards. Darnley wanted to bring his father, but Mary refused to take the extra risk of sending for him. The Queen's plan was to ride to Dunbar, where she hoped that Bothwell and Huntly were already assembling supporters.

At midnight Mary and Darnley stole down the privy stairs and out of the palace by a back door. They crossed the graveyard of the old Abbey of Holyrood, passing close to Rizzio's freshly covered grave.[46] Outside the cemetery their escort was waiting with the horses. Mary was mounted behind Erskine on a pillion saddle, and they galloped off into the night, making first for Seton, where they would change horses. They rode fast, but not fast enough for Darnley, who was full of nervous terrors at the thought of his betrayal of the conspirators. When the pace showed signs of slackening he flogged the hindquarters of Erskine's horse, shouting at the Queen, 'Come on, come on! By God's blood, they will murder both you and me if they can catch us!' Mary begged him to remember her condition, but he answered savagely, 'Come on! In God's name, come on! If this baby dies, we can have more.'[47] Perhaps he was still hoping she might miscarry, and since they were now confederates in escape, might yet grant him the Crown Matrimonial – if so it was a delusion of which he would be soon disabused.

Arrived at Seton, they changed horses, and for the second stage of the journey Mary rode her own horse. The endurance she showed in her advanced pregnancy was astonishing, and suggested that she had never seriously felt the danger of miscarriage. They reached Dunbar at dawn, having ridden thirty miles, safe from immediate danger, and ready to prepare a counter-stroke. Now the escape of Bothwell and Huntly proved to have been decisive, for in response to the Queen's message brought by Lady Huntly, they had begun to summon supporters to the Queen's cause. Bothwell's borderers were swift to respond, and from Dunbar Mary ordered a muster at Haddington on 18 March, to which men were to bring eight days' supply of provisions. This suggests that she anticipated a repetition of the Chaseabout Raid. But after the rendezvous at Haddington she was able to re-enter Edinburgh unopposed, protected by the guns of the castle, riding at the head of an army of eight thousand men, with Darnley at her side. He perhaps, imagined that he had turned the tables on his erstwhile confederates and was sharing Mary's triumph. Shortly after their return he issued a proclamation declaring that he had consented to the return of Moray and the rest of those who had been banished after the Chaseabout Raid, but that he had played no part in the murder of Rizzio. He had, however, left powerful ammunition in the hands of those he had betrayed.

Over the next few weeks a new regime established itself. Loyal lords flocked to join Mary at Dunbar, including Atholl, Fleming, Livingstone and Seton. Of the recent exiles Argyll and Glencairn were swift to make their peace with her. She had no choice but to make her peace with Moray, an imperfect reconciliation, since he had not returned by a royal act of clemency such as she had been urged to make, but at Darnley's invitation and against her will. Furthermore, having welcomed him with emotion and promised him 'remission', she had deceived him and fled. However, at least outward reconciliation had to take place, to ensure the restoration of Mary's authority, or the appearance of it. For, as her most recent biographer has observed, this crisis 'was the effective end of any semblance of policy or government by the Queen'.[48] She returned at the cost of having to restore Moray and his chief confederates Argyll and Glencairn to favour and influence. They in turn were formally reconciled with her chief supporters, Bothwell, Huntly and Atholl. These formed the coalition that governed for the remainder of her reign.

Lennox, who was with justification extremely angry with his son, was banished from court for his ambiguous connection with the recent conspiracy. Lethington, who had had foreknowledge of the murder of Rizzio, though he had played no part in it, went to Dunkeld as the guest of Atholl, whose good offices he hoped would help restore him to favour. He rejoined the government in September 1566. John Knox, who had approved the murder and, according to information supplied by Randolph in late March, also had fore-knowledge of it, fled to Ayrshire.[49]

The Earl of Morton, Lord Ruthven, Lord Lindsay, Ker of Fawdonside, George Douglas, and others involved in the murder itself, found it expedient to flee to England, where Ruthven wrote his vivid account of Rizzio's death and the events that followed it, shortly before he succumbed to his final illness. He died in May, after an impressive deathbed repentance for his evil life. The flight of Morton and his friends was little comfort to either Mary Queen of Scots or Darnley, for in effect Morton and Moray had merely changed places, and since Morton had engineered Moray's return, it could be assumed that Moray would soon endeavour to do the same for him. In the meantime the exiles showed what mercy Darnley could expect from them by sending the Queen the bond of indemnity in which Darnley had taken full responsibility for the murder of Rizzio.[50]

7

'YOUNG FOOL AND PROUD TYRANT'

> Forasmuch as it was thought expedient and most
> profitable for the commonwealth that such a young fool
> and proud tyrant should not reign or bear rule over
> them . . . they all had concluded that he should be put
> off by one way or other.[1]

IN EVERY BREAKDOWN OF MARRIAGE there is a moment of no
return, a point beyond which reconciliation is impossible. In the
marriage of Mary Queen of Scots and Darnley that point was not
the murder of Rizzio, but the moment when Mary read the bond
that proved Darnley's responsibility for it. She might have forgiven
the ambitious folly that he had confessed on his knees, but she could
not forgive the crime of which he had mendaciously sworn he was
innocent. By insisting that the crime be committed in her presence,
he had ensured that she should be exposed to the full shock of it;
the logic of his determination was obvious to her – he had hoped
she would miscarry, he had been ready to risk her death. It was this,
rather than the fate of Rizzio, which rendered him unforgivable.

That Rizzio had not been the Queen's lover is as certain as anything
can be, in the mysterious realm of sexual relations. During his life
the Queen had been blamed for allowing him undue political influence, not for impropriety with him (Darnley's jealousy only distorted
the situation, as jealousy usually does); after his death she did not
behave like a woman who had lost a lover. On the night of the
murder, once she knew exactly what had happened after Rizzio had

been dragged from her presence screaming for mercy, she had sent one of her ladies to his chamber to retrieve a little coffer containing the ciphers used in her French correspondence. After her return to Edinburgh she had had his body exhumed from its hastily dug grave and buried within the Abbey of Holyrood, though not in the royal vault, as a later calumny reported. Mary's immediate reaction to his death showed political prudence; the reburial showed decent respect, not excessive attachment. Less sensible was her appointment of the dead man's younger brother, Joseph Rizzio, as her new French secretary; it was a gesture of defiance to the prevailing disapproval of foreign favourites, when conciliation would have been wiser.[2]

However, Mary was aware that before the birth of her child it was of paramount importance to restore the normal processes of government and the normal life of the court. She appointed Huntly as Lord Chancellor in the place of Morton, and Sir James Balfour as Clerk Register in place of James MacGill, who had been one of the conspirators. The most significant change in the life of the court was that Mary did not return to Holyrood. It was natural that she would not wish to do so after the horror of the events she had witnessed there, but these had also demonstrated that the palace was impossible to defend. After staying a few days in the town house of the Bishop of Dunkeld, the Queen moved to Edinburgh Castle, where the Council resolved that she should stay until her child was born.[3] There was no constraint upon her to stay there, for it was also resolved that if she left the castle in the meantime some of the Lords of Council should accompany her. This was to ensure both her safety and the smooth functioning of government.

It was also important that her relations with the King should appear to be normal, in order to demonstrate that the Rizzio scandal was without substance. In fact, Mary's son, on the evidence of the date of his birth, 19 June 1566, had been conceived in mid-September 1565, before the Rizzio scandal had been imagined, when Mary was still in love with her husband, and the only trouble between them had been the quarrel over whether Lennox or Bothwell should command the royal forces, which would have been forgotten had not other troubles followed. However, after the murder of Rizzio the only way in which the memory of the scandal might be dispelled was by the apparent reconciliation of the King and Queen. Even though Darnley could not be forgiven, Mary had to appear to do so, to ensure that he would acknowledge the paternity of their child.

Accordingly, Mary swallowed her bitterness, concealed her revulsion, and promised him her forgiveness. But it was generally believed that they did not cohabit, for which her advanced pregnancy provided a perfect excuse. Their sleeping apart was indeed sufficiently notorious for an anonymous English balladist to write:

> When this queen see the chamberlain [Rizzio] was slain,
>   For him her cheeks she did weete [wet],
> And made a vow for a twelvemonth and a day
>   The king and she would not come in one sheet.[4]

Darnley had probably been told that his mother had learned of the murder of Rizzio and 'was in great trouble at the news'.[5] Though he could no longer pretend that he had no responsibility for the murder, he tried to ensure that his mother would not suffer in consequence of his actions. He wrote to Queen Elizabeth to assure her that Lady Lennox was not to blame for anything he had done, and knew nothing of his acts. Elizabeth refused to accept the letter from the messenger who brought it, or to write in reply, though she may have permitted it to be read to her. She asked if it were true that Darnley had drawn his dagger in the Queen's presence to stab the secretary, and was assured that he had not. 'She said that she had not believed it, because all the time he was in this country [England] he had never put his hand to a knife.'[6] Not having personally stabbed Rizzio was the only aspect of the crime of which Darnley appeared to be exonerated.

In Scotland it seemed that his kingly authority was unimpaired. The Acts of the Privy Council continued to be promulgated in the names of 'their Majesties', and Darnley continued to sign State papers, or the stamp of his signature was used in his absence.[7] Despite this, there was a rumour that the Queen had sent an envoy named James Thornton to Rome, to enquire into the possibility of a divorce, but nothing came of it.[8]

An annulment probably could have been obtained on the grounds that Mary and Darnley had married before the arrival of the dispensation (if the backdating were ignored); but this would have rendered their child illegitimate, which made annulment unacceptable to Mary, to whom the status of the child was all-important.

Easter approached and was celebrated with full Catholic ritual. On Thursday of Holy Week Mary and Darnley washed the feet of the poor, in imitation of Christ's washing the feet of His disciples. This was part of the traditional Easter duties of royalty, and was called the mandatum, from Christ's words 'Mandatum novum do vobis' – 'I give you a new commandment'. (The French mandé for mandatum is the origin of the name Maundy Thursday.) Darnley, provided with an apron and a towel of cambric, washed the feet of thirteen 'poor virgins', the number symbolizing Christ and the disciples, and after the ceremony gave each of them three-and-a-half yards of fine red cloth.[9] Mary performed the ceremony every year, washing the feet of as many poor girls as the years of her age; but this was the only occasion on which it was done by Darnley, for the previous year he had not been a king, and by the following year he was dead.

The ceremony was witnessed by the French ambassador, Castelnau de Mauvissière, and reported to the Spanish ambassador in London, Guzman de Silva, so that word filtered back to the Catholic powers that whatever his misdeeds, Darnley was a pious Catholic: 'The King continues his devotion to the ancient religion and hears Mass every day'.[10] When Mauvissière left Scotland in early May Darnley took the opportunity of giving him a letter to Charles IX, in reply to one written him by the French King, protesting his innocence of the murder of Rizzio. Presumably he hoped that Charles might accept 'the word of a Prince', or that if he protested his innocence often enough it would eventually come to be accepted. The fact that he had not stabbed Rizzio might have more influence on public opinion than a bond few people had seen.

He wrote to Charles as an equal:

Monsieur mon bon frère,

Jay receu par le Sieur de Mauvissière les lettres que par luy vous a pleu m'escrire; et entendu le credit dicelles qui ne me donne peu de facherie, pour appercevoir par iceluy combien a tort le bruit m'a rendu coulpable dun faict lequel j'aborre tant. Mais dautre part esperant que mon innocence entendue par le susdit Sieur de Mauvissière, auquel jay declairé la verité de tout, ne permettra que imprimer autre que bonne opinion de moy, je suys hors de ceste peyne, me confiant en sa suffisance, pour ne faire tort a laquelle, je finiray la presente. Priant le Créateur vous donner, Monsieur mon bon frère, en bonne santé très heureuse et très longue vie. De Lislebourg ce vj^e jour de May 1566.

Vostre affectioné bon frère Henry[11]

Apart from clearing his reputation for political reasons, Darnley would have wished to avoid being forced by the guilt of murder to return his Order of St Michael to the King of France, which would have been a great public humiliation.

Mauvissière travelled home through England, and in London met the Spanish ambassador who asked him about Darnley, and reported to Philip II, 'The King does not seem bad personally or in his habits, because I asked Mauvissière how he passed his time, and he said mostly in warlike exercises, and he is a good horseman'.[12] Obviously Mauvissière had seen no signs of the drunkenness and debauchery of which Darnley had been guilty the previous winter. The dissolute youth, driven by ambition and jealousy to crime, seemed to bear no resemblance to this pious and athletic young king. It seems that plunging from one extreme to the other, Darnley was now on his best behaviour again, displaying exaggerated piety by his daily attendance at Mass, and working off his energy and aggression in horsemanship and martial sports. But if he believed that good behaviour could restore him to the Queen's good graces he was doomed to disappointment, for the Queen had seen the best and the worst of him, and concluded with reason that the best was a veneer.

As the term of her pregnancy approached Mary prepared for the birth of her child by making her will. If this seems unduly pessimistic, it must be remembered that childbirth was dangerous at the best of times, and many women died in childbed. After the shock of the murder of Rizzio and, as she believed, her own narrow escape from death on that night, Mary may have had premonitions of a fatal labour, or she may have wished merely to make provisions for that eventuality.

The will was drawn up by Mary Livingstone, the Lady of Honour in charge of the Queen's jewels, and Margaret Carwood, the Woman of the Bedchamber in charge of her cabinet.[13] Three copies were made: one for the Queen's executors in Scotland, one for her French kindred who were to be beneficiaries, one for herself.[14] None of these copies is believed to have survived, but some of her intentions are known from a testamentary inventory of her jewels, which she annotated herself.[15] If Mary died and her child survived, the child was to be the sole inheritor; but if, as she seems to have feared, both were to die, the bequests were to take effect. Mary left her grandest jewels to the Crown of Scotland, with the request that an Act be passed annexing them to the Crown in memory of herself, some especially to be worn by future Queens of Scots. A further selection of splendid jewels was bequeathed to the House of Guise and to individual members of the Guise family. But, remarkably, the largest number of bequests to any individual, twenty-six in all, was made to her husband. Among them was the diamond ring in a red enamelled setting, marked in the margin of the inventory with the words '*Cest celui de quoy je fut espousée. Au Roy qui la me donné*'[16] – 'It was with this that I was married. [I leave it] to the King who gave it me', words that sound like an elegy for lost love. Other bequests to him included a watch studded with rubies and diamonds; a 'little dial' (watch) set with diamonds, rubies, pearls and turquoises; a St Michael jewel containing fourteen diamonds, to be worn with the insignia of his French Order; a chain of gold enamelled in white, composed of two hundred links, each set with two diamonds; and several sets of jewelled and enamelled buttons, which could be transferred from one costume to another. A portrait of Darnley painted in 1566 shows him wearing a cream-coloured doublet with pearls for buttons and a magnificent enamelled pendant jewel on a black ribbon, a style of costume which shows that the Queen's bequests (which of course he never received) would have been very much to his taste. The remaining beneficiaries were Mary's illegitimate Stewart kindred, her Lords of Council, and the members of her household, all of whom were to receive bequests appropriate to their status. Apart from the words with which Mary detailed the bequest of her wedding ring, her bequests to Darnley were probably what she considered appropriate to his status as King. There is no reason to suppose that he knew of the provisions of her will.

On 3 June the Queen ceremonially entered her lying-in chamber to await the birth of her child. It was customary to do so some days before the birth was expected, but Mary seems to have anticipated it too soon, for she still had many days to wait. On 19 June, after a long and painful labour, the Queen gave birth to her son 'between nine and ten o'clock in the morning' in the tiny panelled room in Edinburgh Castle, which still contains his portrait, and a painting of the Royal Arms of Scotland, beneath which is a verse in Scots commemorating the event:

Lord Jesu Chryst that Crounit was with Thornse
Preserve the Birth quhais Badgie heir is borne,
And send Hir Sonee Successione to Reigne still
Lang in this Realme, if that it be Thy Will
Als grant O Lord quhat ever of Hir proseed
Be to Thy Glorie Honer and Prais sobied.

[Lord Jesus Christ who wore the Crown of Thorn
Preserve the child whose arms this room adorn.
Send the Queen's son succession, long to reign
Within this realm, if so Thy Will ordain.
Grant also, Lord, that all her deeds till then
Be to Thy glory, honour and praise. Amen.]*

The baby was born in a room full of people, and was strong and healthy. There was no contemporary rumour that he had died at birth and that another baby had been substituted, to prevent Darnley from seizing the crown. At this time Darnley had no supporters who might have helped him to do so had the child died. Nor would Mary have wished a supposititious child to inherit the throne of her ancestors. The so-called 'Coffin in the Wall Mystery', according to which a child's skeleton wrapped in cloth of gold was said to have been found sealed into a wall in Edinburgh Castle and imagined to be Mary's child, was a nineteenth-century invention which attracted connoisseurs of unsolved mysteries. In fact, the falsehood of the story has been demonstrated a number of times, but every few years the 'mystery' is rediscovered and discussed all over again.[17] When the child was born, and throughout his lifetime, no one doubted that he was the son of Mary Queen of Scots; the only contemporary doubt concerning his identity was whether he was the son of Darnley or of Rizzio. Throughout his life the enemies of James VI and I could wound him with jibes about his being 'Davy's son', but the timing of the scandal showed that James had been begotten by Darnley before Darnley began to imagine undue familiarity between Rizzio and the Queen. The scandal could be used to embarrass James, but it is unlikely that anyone seriously believed it.

On the day of her baby's birth Mary was determined that Darnley

---

* English version by CB.

should make a public acknowledgement of his paternity. This extraordinary scene, in which Mary revealed her true opinion of her husband, was reported by Lord Herries:

> About two o'clock in the afternoon, the King came to visit the
> Queen, and was desirous to see the child. 'My Lord (says the
> Queen) God has given you and me a son, begotten by none but
> you!' At which words the King blushed, and kissed the child.
> Then she took the child in her arms, and, discovering his face
> [unwrapping him to show his face], said 'My Lord, here I protest
> to God, and as I shall answer to Him at the great day of judgment,
> this is your son, and no other man's son! And I am desirous that
> all here, both ladies and others bear witness; for he is so much
> your own son, that I fear it shall be the worse for him hereafter!'
> Then she spoke to Sir William Stainley.[18] 'This (says she) is the
> son whom, I hope, shall first unite the two kingdoms of Scotland
> and England!' Sir William answered 'Why, Madam? Shall he suc-
> ceed before your majesty and his father?' 'Because (says she) his
> father has broken to me'. The King was by and heard all. Says he
> 'Sweet Madam, is this your promise that you made to forgive and
> forget all?' The Queen answered, 'I have forgiven all, but will
> never forget! What if Fawdonside's pistol had shot, what would
> have become of him [the child] and me both? Or what estate would
> you have been in? God only knows; but we may suspect!' 'Madam
> (answered the King), these things are all past'. 'Then, says the
> Queen, let them go!'[19]

Darnley's response to the Queen's humiliating words had been
courteous and conciliatory, but he must have been chilled by the
realization that she was not going to forget those terrible events to
which her thoughts had returned in the ordeal of labour, and it did
not sound as though she had truly forgiven them.

Though it was important to Mary that Darnley should make a
public acknowledgement of his paternity before witnesses, it does
not seem to have occurred to him to repudiate it. Apparently there
was no doubt in his mind, for earlier in the day he had written to
the Cardinal of Lorraine, announcing the birth of his son – 'an event
which I am sure will not cause you less joy than ourselves' – and to
the King of France, requesting him to be godfather.[20]

The announcement of the birth to Queen Elizabeth, with the

request to be godmother, was carried by Sir James Melville. He left Edinburgh Castle at noon on 19 June, slept that night at Berwick, and reached London four days later.[21] The same evening Sir William Cecil took the news to Queen Elizabeth at Greenwich, 'where her Majesty was in great merriness and dancing after supper.' Cecil whispered in her ear, and the Queen's mood suddenly changed. She sat down, with her hand on her cheek. The music ceased, and in the ensuing silence her words to her ladies were heard by all, as probably she had not intended – 'The Queen of Scots is lighter of a fair son, while I am but a barren stock'.[22] But the following morning Elizabeth received Melville 'with a merry countenance', thanked him for his diligence in bringing such joyful tidings, and promised to be the Prince's godmother. Melville immediately said, 'Then her Majesty would have a fair occasion to see the Queen, which she had so often desired', but Elizabeth made it clear that she had no intention of coming to Scotland, smilingly wishing that she might, and promising to send 'honourable lords and ladies to supply her room'.[23] Later in the year, as the time of the baptism drew nearer, she wrote to the Countess of Argyll, requesting her to act as her proxy. This was a tactful nomination, for Lady Argyll, though illegitimate, was Elizabeth's cousin and Mary's sister, so their kinship would be stressed by her taking the Queen of England's role.[24]

Darnley was resentful that the Queen of England was to be the godmother of his son, for she had never recognized him as King of Scots, and showed no disposition to do so now. But he took advantage of her generally benevolent mood to write to her again requesting the liberation of his mother, and on this occasion the Queen accepted the letter, which suggests that her attitude to Lady Lennox was softening.[25] Her attitude to Darnley himself might have grown more favourable had he been able to accept his position as the father of the future King of Scots; but his restless ambition to rule, if necessary by using his son as a pawn, soon revived her suspicions of him and ensured that English diplomats would not give him credence when they arrived in Scotland for the baptism.

Though Elizabeth's attitude to Mary was friendly at this time, she showed no more willingness to recognize the son of Mary and Darnley as her heir than she had shown to recognize Mary herself. Indeed, when Patrick Adamson (future Archbishop of St Andrews) wrote a Latin poem hailing the child as Prince of Scotland, England and Ireland, Elizabeth's vehement protest resulted in six months' imprisonment for the poet. After 1568, when Mary had become Elizabeth's prisoner, it was impossible for Elizabeth to acknowledge the rights of Mary's son, for that would have been to acknowledge Mary's own, and thus invite a coup d'état on her behalf. But from the day of his birth Mary's son was always the most convincing candidate as Elizabeth's successor, for he represented the merger of the two strongest claims to the English throne, those of his mother and his father.

After the birth of the Prince, Darnley's position deteriorated. Now that he had fathered an heir to the throne and acknowledged his paternity, he had done all that Mary Queen of Scots required of him. Since she no longer loved him she felt no obligation to maintain the fiction of a reconciliation with him. Thenceforward she did nothing to conceal her contempt for him. She displayed it in small ways, such as pettily upbraiding Sir James Melville for giving Darnley a water spaniel, saying 'she could not trust him who would give any thing to such one as she loved not'. But she also revealed her contempt more forcibly, according to the Earl of Bedford, who reported 'it cannot for modesty nor with the honour of a queen be reported what she said of him'.[26] As once she had used the company of David Rizzio to escape her husband's unwanted attentions, so now she used the unimpeachable excuse of wanting to be with her baby. She watched over James during the day, and had his cradle set beside her own bed at night.

Darnley's response to his continued exclusion from his wife's bed was a renewed plunge into dissipation. Since she would not let him sleep with her, he took to 'vagabondizing' in Edinburgh every night, and returning in the small hours, demanding to have the castle gates opened for him, which the Queen believed put her and her son in danger of a coup, an indication of how insecure she felt.[27] He also showed his chagrin as he had always done by disappearing into the countryside, hunting and hawking. A new cause of anxiety was that he took to swimming alone in the sea, and in lonely lochs and rivers. Swimming was not yet a popular sport, but was considered a dangerous activity to indulge in for any reason except to escape drowning.[28] It was dangerous for other reasons for a man who had many enemies to go away by himself and divest himself of his clothes and weapons;

yet he avoided a fate that might have allowed Mary's story a happier conclusion.

At the end of July Mary decided to take a brief holiday from her anxieties. Without telling anyone but her chosen companions, she went to Newhaven with a few of her ladies, boarded a ship and sailed up the Forth to Alloa, the seat of the Earl and Countess of Mar, to spend a few days with them. When Darnley discovered where she had gone he followed her by land, but received so cold a reception at Alloa that he left again the same day.

Between 13 and 19 August Mary and Darnley were together again, hunting in southern Peeblesshire, close to the Border. While they were staying at Traquair, Darnley's behaviour was said to have been particularly disgraceful:

> While the party was at supper the King . . . asked the Queen to attend a stag hunt. Knowing that if she did so she would be required to gallop her horse at a great pace, she whispered in his ear that she suspected she was *enceinte*. The King answered aloud 'Never mind, if we lose this one, we will make another', whereupon the Laird of Traquair rebuked him sharply, and told him that he did not speak like a Christian. He answered 'What! Ought not we to work a mare well when she is with foal?'[29]

This was distasteful in the extreme, and it was recorded by Claude Nau, Mary's secretary, to whom she gave her reminiscences years later when she was a prisoner. Was it possible that memory had played her false, and the unpleasant episode belonged to a different date? The words attributed to Darnley are similar to his words on the night of their escape after Rizzio's murder. And, if Darnley had persuaded Mary to sleep with him since the birth of their child, it would have been too recently for her to know whether she had become pregnant or not.

On this hunting party the King and Queen were accompanied by Moray, Huntly, Bothwell and Atholl. It was an uneasy group, because Mary's increasingly obvious predilection for Bothwell had by now made him 'the most hated man among the noblemen in Scotland'.[30] Darnley's jealousy, however, at present centred upon Moray, whom he imagined was influencing the Queen against him. Probably in a moment of drunken indiscretion, Darnley told Mary that he was going to kill Moray, 'finding fault that she bears him so much company'.[31] In her open contempt for Darnley, Mary informed Moray of the King's threats, and then forced Darnley to make an embarrassing confession that he had uttered them on misinformation, and repented them. After this humiliation he left the Queen and went to see his father, to whom he poured out his grievances.

Darnley told his father that the Queen did not want to sleep with him, and that a few weeks before their child was born she had recommended him to take a mistress, saying ambiguously, 'I assure you I shall never love you the worse', and had suggested the Countess of Moray. Lennox, a faithful husband, was shocked. He exhorted Darnley never to be unfaithful to his wife, and spoke so earnestly that Darnley was abashed, and replied, 'I never offended the Queen my wife in meddling with any woman, in thought, let be in deed'.[32] He was almost certainly lying, since his 'vagabondizing' was assumed to include visits to Edinburgh prostitutes, and if he was going to be unfaithful Mary would certainly have preferred him to take an aristocratic mistress. Perhaps she hoped that a strong-minded woman might have a civilizing influence on him, and imagined Lady Moray in the role of Diane de Poitiers. Since Darnley got nothing from his father in return for his confidences except a homily, he began to think of abandoning his troubles in Scotland and going abroad.

When the Queen returned from Traquair to Edinburgh she arranged for her child to be removed from Edinburgh to Stirling Castle, where his guardians would be the Earl and Countess of Mar. There was nothing unusual in this arrangement, since the heir to the throne was always placed in fosterage, and the Erskines were hereditary guardians of royalty.[33] What may have been unusual was the haste with which Mary arranged it, possibly reflecting her anxiety that her child might be snatched by his father. Perhaps with this intention already taking shape in his mind, Darnley followed Mary to Stirling, and then refused to accompany her to Edinburgh when she left. But Mary must have decided that her child was sufficiently well guarded to permit her departure, for she went to Edinburgh to attend the audit of the exchequer. Still reluctant to revisit Holyrood, she stayed in the 'Chequer House'. After her downfall it was said that she had begun her adulterous affair with Bothwell there, but there was no contemporary rumour to support this assertion.

While the Queen was in Edinburgh Darnley was visited at Stirling by his father, and probably a scheme to restore his status was devised between them. Lennox wrote to the Queen to tell her that his son was dissatisfied with his status, and that he had resolved to 'retire out of the kingdom beyond sea, and that for this purpose he had just then a ship lying ready'.[34] Lennox was warning Mary, because he had endeavoured to dissuade his son, but found that he was powerless to make him change his mind.[35]

Mary received this letter on 29 September. By now she had returned to Holyrood for the first time since the murder of Rizzio, so it would hardly have added to her peace of mind when Darnley appeared before the gates of the palace the same evening and demanded that 'three or four lords [who] were at that time present with the Queen . . . might be gone before he would condescend to come in'.[36] The implication is that one of them was Moray, whom Darnley would have been particularly anxious to avoid.[37] Mary went out to meet him, and 'conducted him to her own apartment, where he remained all night', and this was the only occasion on which he undoubtedly spent the night with her after the murder of Rizzio. 'When the King and Queen were a-bed together, her Majesty took occasion to talk to him about the contents of his father's letter, and besought him to declare to her the ground of his designed voyage.'[38] But Darnley, having at last got into bed with her, refused to waste time in talk; probably he promised to tell her about it in the morning. Accordingly, next day Mary brought him before the Council and the new French ambassador, Philibert du Croc. The Earl of Lennox's letter was read aloud, and Darnley was asked to explain why he wished to leave the country. The French ambassador added that 'his departure must affect either his own or the Queen's honour'.

Darnley and his father had probably planned this opportunity for Darnley to air his grievances and demand an improvement of his status as a condition of his remaining in the country. But when the opportunity was offered, Darnley did not take it; either his courage failed him, or the bland and insincere faces of his enemies, cynically inviting his complaints, made the whole enterprise seem hopeless. The French ambassador described the unexpected dignity with which he extricated himself from the situation:

The King at last declared that he had no ground at all given him for [his desire to leave the country]; and thereupon he went out of the chamber of presence, saying to the Queen: 'Adieu, Madam, you shall not see my face for a long space'; after which he likewise bade me farewell, and next, turning himself to the Lords in general,

said 'Gentlemen, Adieu'. He is not yet embarked but . . . still holds
to his resolution and keeps a ship in readiness . . .'[39]

Darnley went to Glasgow and, probably at the instigation of his
father, attempted to make good his lost opportunity of airing his
complaints by writing a letter to the Queen, in which he complained
that he was not honoured or trusted with authority, that nobody
attended him, and the nobility avoided his company. Mary took the
trouble to reply, pointing out that the decline in his status was entirely
his own fault, and that 'if the nobility abandon him, his own deport-
ment towards them is the cause thereof: for if he desire to be followed
and attended by them, he must in the first place make them to love
him . . .'[40]

The Lords of Council wrote an account of this extraordinary dispute between the King and Queen to Catherine de' Medici, Queen-
Regent of France, to pre-empt any account Darnley might give, in
case he decided to go to France. Philibert du Croc notified Mary's
ambassador in France, Archbishop Beaton, for the same reason.
However, he had another opportunity to speak to Darnley and his
father, when they asked him to meet them halfway between Glasgow
and Edinburgh, for the purpose of airing Darnley's grievances yet
again, and if possible securing du Croc's assistance in getting them
redressed. This time du Croc 'remonstrated to him every thing that
I could think of' to dissuade him from leaving the kingdom, and
concluded that he had probably succeeded in stopping him. Darnley
and his father returned to Glasgow, still dissatisfied, and du Croc
dispatched his letter to Beaton, before reporting his diplomatic efforts
to the Queen of Scots.

Mary was in Jedburgh, where she had gone to hold a 'Justice Ayre'
or itinerant court of justice. She arrived on 8 October, and was
informed that the previous day Bothwell, who was attempting to
quell an outbreak of disorder in Liddesdale, had been wounded in
a skirmish with a notorious reiver named John Eliot of the Park.
Some days later Mary decided to visit Bothwell, who was recovering
from his wounds in the castle of Hermitage, some twenty-five miles
from Jedburgh. On 15 October, with a strong escort which included
the Earl of Moray, she rode there and back in one day. Mary did
not, as it was later reported, ride madly to Hermitage the moment

she learnt that Bothwell was wounded; but it was remarkable that she made the expedition at all.[41] There was no occasion to do so, other than to reassure herself that Bothwell was recovering. Possibly the visit to his bedside served the same purpose as her vigils at Darnley's bedside the previous year: it demonstrated to her the depth of her own feelings, it marked the progress from cordiality to love.

Two days after her ride to Hermitage Mary suffered the most dramatic and dangerous illness of her life, possibly the result of a haemorrhage from a gastric ulcer, which almost caused her death.[42] The crisis of the illness occurred between 17 and 24 October, and at one time Mary lost consciousness and was thought to have died. Her recovery was credited to the skill of her French physician, who restored her consciousness with vigorous massage, and later administered a 'clyster' (enema). She began to recover after she had vomited a quantity of 'corrupt (old) blood'.[43]

Maitland of Lethington, who had been restored to favour in September, wrote an account of the Queen's illness to Archbishop Beaton:

The occasion of the Queen's sickness, so far as I understand, is . . . displeasure, and . . . the root of it is the King. For she has done him so great honour . . . and he . . . has recompensed her with such ingratitude, and misuses himself so far towards her, that it is heartbreaking for her to think that he should be her husband, and how to be free of him she sees no outgait [way out].[44]

This was the first indication that Mary had expressed a wish to be free of him (apart from the rumour of the messenger who went to Rome shortly after the murder of Rizzio). Lethington's comment was both shrewd and sympathetic, for if Mary's illness was not caused by her unhappiness it was certainly exacerbated by it.

Darnley arrived in Jedburgh on 28 October, when the Queen was already recovering. According to the 'Diurnal of Occurrents' he had been 'halkand and huntand [in] the west pairtis of this realme',[45] where news of her illness had not reached him. When told of it he rode to Edinburgh on the 27th, and came to Jedburgh the next morning. The Queen made no pretence of being pleased to see him, and since he had made the effort to visit her, he took offence. Having stayed one night in Jedburgh, not in the same house as the Queen, he left for Stirling.

Mary stayed in Jedburgh until mid-November, when she had recovered sufficiently to make a tour of the Borders. She was accompanied by Bothwell, who had joined her in Jedburgh as soon as he had been strong enough to leave Hermitage, and by Moray, Huntly, Lethington, Home and an entourage of a thousand horsemen. They reached Craigmillar Castle, three miles from Edinburgh, on 20 November. Mary was still not well, and according to du Croc was 'in the hands of the physicians'. She could scarcely have returned from apparently imminent death to perfect health in less than three weeks, but recovery was not helped by the continuous anxiety caused by Darnley's conduct. Before she left Jedburgh Mary had discovered that he had written to the King of Spain, the Pope, the King of France and the Cardinal of Lorraine, informing them that his wife was 'dubious in the faith'. This was obviously an attempt to undermine her reputation, and it was a plausible accusation since she had done so little for Catholicism in Scotland, but she had to endeavour to undo the harm he had done by sending messages of reassurance to the Catholic powers.[46] It was terrifying to contemplate what he might do next, and Mary was so depressed by her anxiety that she was heard to say 'I could wish to be dead'.[47]

At Craigmillar Mary's Lords of Council gathered round her, and a preliminary discussion was held on a possible solution to the problem of Darnley. The main authority for the 'Craigmillar Conference' is a document known as 'The Protestation of Huntly and Argyll', which was written as pro-Marian propaganda after her downfall, and accordingly needs to be read with caution. It was written at about the end of 1568, two years after the events described, probably by John Leslie, Bishop of Ross, and purported to give Huntly and Argyll's version of what happened at Craigmillar. At the beginning of 1569 it was sent by Mary from her prison at Bolton Castle in Yorkshire for signature by Huntly and Argyll in Scotland, but was captured by Cecil's agents and never reached its intended recipients (and supposed authors). Its intention was to exculpate Mary from any responsibility for the murder of her husband, and to lay as much blame as possible on Moray and Lethington.[48] The 'Protestation' would never have been written but for the enmities that followed Darnley's death; but at the Craigmillar Conference Mary and her councillors were united in their desire to get rid of him.

According to the 'Protestation' the discussion originated in Moray's desire to discharge his obligation to the Earl of Morton, and arrange for him and the other murderers of Rizzio to be pardoned and recalled from exile. Moray and Lethington came to the Earl of Argyll's chamber in Craigmillar in the early morning at the beginning of December to discuss the matter. Argyll agreed that something should be done for Morton and his allies 'provided that the Queen's Majesty should not be offended thereat', to which Lethington replied 'that the nearest and best way to obtain the said Earl of Morton's pardon was to promise to the Queen's Majesty to find any means to make divorcement betwixt her Grace and the King her husband, who had offended her Highness so highly and in many ways'.[49]

The discussion then shifted away from the Rizzio murderers to the question of finding the means 'to make her quit of him' (Darnley). Huntly was brought into the discussion, then 'passed all [everyone went] to the Earl of Bothwell's chamber, to understand his advice on this thing proposed; wherein he gainsaid not more than we'.[50] Lord Herries, echoing the judgement of Sir Nicholas Throckmorton, described Bothwell as 'a man high in his own conceit, proud, vicious and vainglorious above measure; one who would attempt anything out of ambition',[51] and Sir James Melville said that Bothwell 'had a mark of his own that he shot at . . . for apparently he had already in his mind to perform the foul murder of the King, which afterwards he put in execution, that he might marry the Queen'.[52] Both memoirists were wise after the event, and neither could possibly have known at what moment Bothwell's ambition encompassed marriage to the Queen; but the moment when discussion of the means to end the Queen's marriage first took place was as likely as any other.

Mary's councillors now approached her, and Lethington, after reminding her of 'a great number of grievous and intolerable offences' committed by the King, proposed 'that if it pleased her Majesty to pardon the Earl of Morton . . . they should find the means . . . to make divorcement betwixt her Highness and the King her husband, which should not need her Grace to meddle therewith'.[53] Mary's response was cautious. She said that 'under two conditions she might understand the same': the first was that the divorce was lawful, the second that it should not prejudice her son. Bothwell replied that he did not think a divorce would affect the Prince's position, for his own parents had been divorced, yet he had succeeded his father without question. The Queen remained unconvinced; presumably Bothwell did not know of the difficulties posed by the dispensation.

Discussion then moved on to what would happen after the divorce. It was suggested that the King should live alone in one part of the country and the Queen in another; or else that once divorced Darnley should be permitted to live abroad. The Queen said, perhaps yearning for the possibility, that it might be better if she went to live in France. Then Lethington said:

> Madam, soucy you not (do not worry), we are here of the principal of your Grace's nobility and Council, that shall find the means that your Majesty shall be quit of him without prejudice to your son. And albeit that my Lord of Moray here present be little less scrupulous for a Protestant nor (than) your Grace is for a Papist, I am assured he will look through his fingers thereto, and will behold our doings, saying nothing to the same.

To this coded speech Mary replied, 'I will that you do nothing by which any spot may be laid to my honour or conscience, and therefore I pray you rather let the matter be in the estate that it is, abiding till God of his goodness put remedy thereto [than] that you, believing to do me service, may possibly turn to my hurt or displeasure'. This too was a coded utterance, for Mary was warning her councillors not to avoid hurting the King, but to avoid hurting her reputation. No one had uttered the word 'murder', but it must have been in the minds of everyone present. Lethington lightened the mood of the discussion by concluding, 'Madam, let us guide the matter amongst us, and your Grace shall see nothing but good, and approved by Parliament'.[54] Lethington may have meant no more than casual reassurance, but possibly he had in mind that if Darnley were killed Parliament would simply set on record a regretful statement that he had 'happinit to be slane', as had occurred when King James III had been mysteriously murdered after the Battle of Sauchieburn, in 1488. The 'Protestation of Huntly and Argyll' concluded

> so after the premises, the murder of the said Henry Stewart (Darnley) following, we judge in our consciences . . . that the said Earl of Moray and Secretary Lethington were authors, inventors, devisers,

counsellors, and causers of the said murder, in what manner or by whatsoever persons the same was executed.[55]

Though the 'Protestation' was composed to exculpate the Queen from the guilt of murder, it made her unquestionably participant in the discussions of Darnley's fate, and revealed her as concerned only to safeguard her son's status and her own reputation. What would happen to Darnley was left in abeyance.[56] It would have been well for Mary if he had met a mysterious death in the hunting field at the hands of persons unknown, like King William Rufus. But, to take another medieval parallel, Mary had behaved like Henry II, desirous to be rid of a 'turbulent priest', and like Henry she was obliged to abide the consequences.

If Mary was desperate to find a way of escape from an intolerable situation, Darnley was no less so. His life was in ruins, for which he had only himself to blame, a fact which apparently he would not face. He arrived at Craigmillar during the first week in December to see the Queen, then left again, and sent a message to du Croc to come and meet him 'half a league' outside Edinburgh. Du Croc, who was in the city, came out and had another long talk with him, and concluded that 'things go still worse and worse'. Darnley said that he was going to 'go away', he did not say where, and that he was not going to attend the Prince's baptism. He seemed to be in a state of mental confusion, but still hoping that du Croc would solve his problems for him. The ambassador told Archbishop Beaton that he doubted if the King and Queen could be reconciled: 'I shall name only two reasons against it: the first is, the King will never humble himself as he ought; the other that the Queen cannot perceive him speaking with any noblemen but presently she suspects some plot among them'.[57]

Since she had discovered Darnley's attempts to discredit her with the Catholic powers, she had good reason to suspect him of plotting. Darnley's head was full of fanciful schemes for self-aggrandizement, which had replaced his ambition to acquire the Crown Matrimonial of Scotland. Disappointed of an honour to which he had a reasonable claim, he imagined himself elevated to the throne of England, or even of all Britain, by a rebellion of the English Catholics, possibly with the support of Spain. In the summer of 1566 a spy named

William Rogers who had infiltrated Darnley's household reported the wild talk within it: Darnley would seize Scarborough Castle as a base for his supporters, or he would occupy the Scilly Isles. As the heir of Britain he had a claim to the ordnance that protected the Scillies ... All this nonsense was reported to Sir William Cecil.[58] Mary Queen of Scots may not have heard of it, but she was informed of a more frightening because more realistic rumour, that 'the King, by the assistance of some of our nobility, should take the Prince our son and crown him; and being crowned, as his father should take upon him the government'.[59] This was a plausible plot; it was no wonder that Mary feared and resented the sight of Darnley talking with any noblemen.

Mary went up to Stirling for the baptism of the Prince on 12 December. It was probably sometime in the preceding week that some of her councillors who had been present at the 'Craigmillar Conference' signed a bond committing themselves to the murder of Darnley. This bond subsequently disappeared, but it was seen by one of Bothwell's henchmen, the Laird of Ormiston, who was executed for participation in the murder. Before his execution in 1573 Ormiston said that the substance of the bond was 'forasmuch as it was thought expedient and most profitable for the commonwealth that such a young fool and proud tyrant should not reign or bear rule over them ... they all had concluded that he should be put off by one way or other'.[60] He said that it was signed by Huntly, Argyll, Bothwell, Lethington and Sir James Balfour.

While Darnley's fate was in preparation behind the scenes, the last festivity of Mary's reign was celebrated with great magnificence. The baptism took place on Tuesday, 17 December, having been delayed for almost a week to await the arrival of the ambassador of the third godparent, the Duke of Savoy; but since he still failed to appear, it was celebrated without him. The Earl of Bedford headed the English embassy, and brought Queen Elizabeth's present of a splendid gold font weighing 333 ounces and decorated with jewels and enamel 'designed so that the whole effect combined elegance with value'.[61] The French embassy, led by the Comte de Brienne, brought Mary a necklace and earrings of pearls and rubies. The ambassador of Savoy, Count Moretta, when he eventually arrived, brought her 'a fan of large size with jewelled feathers, of the value of four thousand crowns'.[62] At the ceremony Moretta was represented by Monsieur du Croc.

The christening was celebrated with full Catholic ceremonial, which enabled Mary to counteract Darnley's propaganda by stressing her orthodoxy. The Prince was carried from his chamber to the Chapel Royal of Stirling Castle by the Comte de Brienne 'betwixt two rows of barons and gentlemen, each holding a pricket of wax in his hand'.[63] Then followed a procession consisting of the Earl of Atholl bearing the 'great serge' [grand cierge – a large wax candle], the Earl of Eglinton bearing the salt, Lord Sempill the 'rood' (the cross), and Lord Ross the ewer and basin. At the entrance of the chapel the Prince was received by Archbishop Hamilton, who was to baptize him, attended by the Bishops of Dunkeld, Dunblane and Ross, the Prior of Whithorn, and other Catholic clergy, in their vestments.[64] The Countess of Argyll, as Queen Elizabeth's proxy, held the baby at the font, and the Archbishop baptized him with the names Charles James, after his godfather the King of France and his ancestors the Kings of Scots, though he was always known by the Scottish royal name. One detail of the ceremony was omitted: James said many years later that his mother had declared that she would not have 'a pocky priest' spitting in her child's mouth, which was then part of the ritual. She had reason to say so, for Archbishop Hamilton had recently received treatment for venereal disease.[65] After the baptism there was a fanfare of trumpets, and the Prince's names and titles were proclaimed three times by heralds: 'Charles James, James Charles, Prince and Steward of Scotland, Duke of Rothesay, Earl of Carrick, Lord of the Isles and Baron of Renfrew. Then did the musick begin, and after it had continued a good space the Prince was again conveyed to his apartment'.[66]

The Countess of Argyll was presented with a ruby valued at five hundred crowns for acting as the Queen of England's proxy; but as she was a Protestant the Kirk required her to do penance for participating in a Popish ceremony. The Earl of Bedford, who was a Puritan or evangelical Protestant, stood outside the Chapel Royal with Moray and other Scottish Protestant lords, whose example Queen Elizabeth had advised him to follow 'for which they have the permission of that Queen'.[67] Mary had shown her favour to these lords by providing magnificent clothes for them at her own expense: Moray was dressed in green, Argyll in red, Bothwell in blue.[68]

Darnley was to have outshone everyone in clothes of cloth of gold, but he perpetrated his ultimate offence to the Queen by refusing to attend the baptism. It was an insult that could be interpreted as casting doubt on the Prince's legitimacy, by suggesting that the baptism was that of the Queen's son, not his.[69] However, as he had already acknowledged his paternity, this obviously was not his motive. He knew that as Queen Elizabeth had not recognized him as King of Scots the Earl of Bedford could not do so. He knew also that Mary would not defend his status as she had done in the early days of their marriage. Knowing that the English ambassador would greet him only as 'the Lord Darnley', he determined to avoid the slur on his status and the insult to his pride by remaining in his chamber. But the fact that he had come to Stirling at all, which he had probably done at the persuasion of du Croc, made his unseen presence more offensive to the Queen than his complete absence would have been. If there are gradations in being unforgivable, Darnley had rendered himself even more so.

In the course of the baptismal day Darnley made three unsuccessful attempts to see du Croc, though it is difficult to imagine for what purpose. Hitherto the French ambassador had been very patient with him, meeting him in inconvenient places when requested, listening to his complaints and attempting to give him good advice. Now du Croc's patience snapped, and he sent Darnley a message saying that his chamber had two doors 'and if he should enter by the one, I should feel myself compelled to go out at the other'.[70] Du Croc can hardly be blamed, but his message must have added to Darnley's misery and sense of isolation.

A pleasanter episode followed. Darnley went out of the castle by a back door 'to take the air', and met a member of Bedford's suite, one of Queen Elizabeth's Gentlemen Pensioners named Mr Wiseman, who 'did the King reverence, and having been very familiar with him in the court of England, used some speeches with him by way of compliment'. The encounter was witnessed and reported to Bedford, who gave Wiseman a severe reprimand for disobeying Queen Elizabeth's command not to acknowledge Darnley as King. Wiseman was unrepentant, and 'stoutly replied that it was pity that such was her commandment'.[71] It is to be hoped that Darnley, who performed few graceful acts in his life, appreciated Wiseman's courtesy, and did not merely accept it as his due. Though it was a small gesture it required great courage, and would have done Wiseman's career no good at all.

The festivities continued with a banquet and a Latin masque by George Buchanan. This was the last masque in which Buchanan honoured Mary Queen of Scots. After the death of Darnley he became her most vitriolic calumniator. For this he has been castigated as 'the basest hireling scholar of all the ages'[72]; but Buchanan was a Lennoxman, born on the Lennox estates and owing loyalty to Darnley's father. After Darnley's death, convinced that Mary shared the guilt of it, his hatred of her was the more virulent because of his previous admiration of her, which might make him appear to have been a hypocrite and a sycophant. Desiring to protect his reputation from those accusations, he destroyed it entirely.

The master of revels at the festivities was a Frenchman, Bastien Pagès, a member of the Queen's household, who devised a dance of nymphs and satyrs. This led to an unfortunate incident when the satyrs, by wagging their tails, caused two members of Bedford's suite to imagine that an insult was intended, by a reference to an old racist joke that all Englishmen were born with tails. In the resulting uproar, according to Sir James Melville, 'the noise was so great behind the Queen's back, where her Majesty and my Lord of Bedford did sit, that they heard and turned about their faces to learn what the matter meant. I informed them that it was occasioned by the satyrs, so that the Queen and my Lord of Bedford had both enough to do to get them appeased . . . my Lord of Bedford was discreet and interpreted all things to the best'.[73] Further festivities followed, and when the English embassy headed for home, Bedford declared that 'the service was great, and great welcome'.[74]

When it was over there was also great reckoning. Taxation of £12,000 had been raised to pay for the Prince's christening, and the Queen had spent additional money of her own on clothes for her nobles and presents for the ambassadors, amongst which had been a chain of diamonds for Lord Bedford worth two thousand crowns, and appropriate presents for the members of his suite.[75]

The Queen's great display of Catholic orthodoxy was followed by what appeared to be another gesture to fortify the power of the Roman Catholic Church in Scotland: on 23 December she restored Archbishop Hamilton to his consistorial jurisdiction, which enabled him to pronounce judgement in matrimonial causes. He used it just once, to pronounce a decree of nullity between the Earl of Bothwell and his wife Lady Jean Gordon, after which it was again revoked.[76] But the Queen also appeared to be desirous to win the support of the Kirk: on 3 October she had conceded that all benefices with less than three hundred merks (approximately £200) should go to

Protestant ministers, and on 20 December she made a gift to the Kirk of £10,000, and of an equal value of foodstuffs, presumably to help in providing for underpaid clergymen. A modern historian has commented, 'this looks like an attempt to buy support in a crisis which the Queen could forsee'.[77]

Mary's next move looked like a gesture intended to precipitate the crisis. On 24 December, in response to the bargain outlined at the 'Craigmillar Conference', Mary pardoned the murderers of Rizzio. She excepted Andrew Ker of Fawdonside and George Douglas, the Postulate of Arbroath, both of whom she considered had endangered her own life; but the pardon of a group of men who had been betrayed by Darnley, and who by currently accepted mores could be expected to seek revenge on him, was a gesture that could be regarded as tantamount to his death sentence.

Darnley regarded it as such. As soon as he heard of it he left Stirling and went 'without goodnight, toward Glasgow to his father'. On his journey Darnley fell ill, which inevitably led to the accusation that he had been poisoned:

he was hardly a mile out of Stirling when the poison – which had been given him – wrought so upon him that he had very great pain and dolour in every part of his body. At length, being arrived at Glasgow, the blisters broke out, of a bluish colour; so the physicians presently knew the disease to be by poison. He was brought so low that nothing but death was expected; yet the strength of his youth did at last surmount the poison.[78]

Poison was the first hypothesis of the cause of his illness, smallpox the next and more convincing diagnosis; but the distressing probability, of which the apparent attack of measles the previous year had been a premonitory sign, was that he was suffering from syphilis.[79]

8
THE MURDER OF THE KING
AND ITS AFTERMATH

MARY: .... Well I know him
It is the bleeding Darnley's royal shade
Rising in anger from his darksome grave,
And never will he make his peace with me
Until the measure of my woes be full ...
KENNEDY: You did not murder him – 'twas done by
others.
MARY: But it was known to me; I suffer'd it
And lured him with my smiles to death's embrace.[1]

DARNLEY'S INSTINCT, in unhappiness, danger or sickness, was to
flee to his father, on whom he could rely for protection, and for a
sympathetic and uncritical reception. Lennox had been briefly angry
with his son when Mary and Darnley escaped together after the
murder of Rizzio, leaving Lennox to the dubious mercy of the
betrayed conspirators. But this had not been Darnley's own desire,
as doubtless he was able to convince his father when they met again.
Later, by his own account, Lennox had been shocked when his son
confided to him the Queen's suggestion that Darnley should take a
mistress, and had given him a lecture on marital fidelity. This was a
typical example of a moral hiatus between generations, causing
a father and son to be unable to have a straightforward discussion
on sexual matters. But, despite these misunderstandings, the relationship of Lennox and Darnley was remarkably close.

As the elder of two sons who were the only survivors of a family of eight, and as 'a youth of most worthy carriage . . . and of a most sweet behaviour'[2], it was no wonder that his father doted on him, nor that when he grew to be 'remarkably handsome . . . and almost the tallest man in the isle of Britain'[3], a demi-god in appearance and appropriately accomplished, he became the object of his father's uncritical adoration. Lennox not only adored his son for his looks and his qualities, he was also incapable of seeing his very obvious faults, because he shared them: if his beloved 'Harry' was proud, so was he; and if Harry had a violent temper, that too seemed natural, for so had he. If his son did or said anything to disturb his golden opinion (as in the two instances mentioned) he was immediately ready to be reassured. If he heard any rumours of Darnley's evil conduct he did not believe them: to him his son was always an 'innocent lamb'.

Margaret Lennox may have been as doting as her husband, but she was a woman of forceful character, and may have been the sort of mother a son would hesitate to offend. Perhaps it is significant that until Darnley left the English court he was always regarded as promising and praiseworthy; it was only after the removal of his mother's influence that he began to display his excessive arrogance, his violent passions, and his taste for bad company. His devotion to his mother was shown by his continued and commendable efforts to obtain her liberation, and had he obtained it, and had she been able to join him in Scotland, possibly her influence might have prevented his worst excesses. However, though his mother might have had a better influence on his moral conduct than his father, both parents were culpable of making him obsessively ambitious. The impending tragedy, which was to cause them overwhelming grief, had its origin at the beginning of Darnley's conscious life, when they began to indoctrinate him with the belief that he was destined for kingship. Mary Queen of Scots' refusal to grant him the Crown Matrimonial may have impelled him towards the crime that led directly to his downfall, but the first impulse in that fatal direction derived from the ambition of his parents.

According to Lennox, Darnley had left Stirling after the baptism of the Prince in response to a warning sent by Lennox himself. The Earl had heard a rumour of the 'Craigmillar Conference', at which he believed the Queen and her councillors had concluded that Darnley should be 'apprehended and put in ward [prison]'.[4] But Darnley had an equally cogent reason for flight in the pardon of the murderers of Rizzio. He fled to his father 'being fully resolved to have taken ship shortly after and to have passed beyond the sea',[5] and it would have been well for him if had kept to that resolution as soon as his recovery permitted it.

Over the Christmas season Darnley lay between life and death, and in the course of January slowly began to recover. The suddenness with which he had been taken ill between Stirling and Glasgow gave rise to the rumour that he had been poisoned, which according to Lord Herries seemed to be confirmed by the fact that 'his hair fell off, and [by] some other symptoms that were observed'.[6] Dr Karl Pearson, in his curious work *The Skull and Portraits of Henry Stewart, Lord Darnley*, suggests that the loss of his hair 'may well have been *alopecia syphillitica*, following on an inflammatory condition of the cranial bones'.[7] The skull purporting to be Darnley's, which Pearson examined and illustrated in his book, is pitted with small hollows identifiable as the 'cranial caries of syphilis'. Since this condition is usually associated with the tertiary stage of the disease it seemed to Pearson surprising that the skull had reached this condition if Darnley had contracted syphilis after his marriage, during his first reported plunge into debauchery in the autumn of 1565. But if his attack of measles had indeed been an early manifestation of syphilis, indicating that he had most likely contracted it when he was a fugitive in France, then by the end of 1566 the disease could have progressed sufficiently to produce its 'characteristic erosion of the cranial bones' visible on the skull.[8] A distinguished venereologist consulted more recently by Dr M. H. Armstrong Davison, confirmed these conclusions, but added that 'destructive bone changes' could occur 'earlier in the process of the disease' and produce an appearance of 'precocious tertiarism'.[9] Darnley's misery was increased by the disfigurement of his face, which he concealed behind a taffeta mask.[10]

If Lennox accepted that his son had not been poisoned, no doubt he clung resolutely to the belief that his sickness was smallpox, for it was unthinkable that the 'innocent lamb' who had assured him that he had never been unfaithful to the Queen could have indulged in casual sexual adventures which had infected him with 'the pox'.

While Darnley lay ill in Glasgow the Queen spent Christmas and the ensuing days at Stirling. On the last day of December she rode to Tullibardine in Perthshire and spent two nights as the guest of her Comptroller, Sir William Murray of Tullibardine, and then returned to Stirling.[11] Throughout this period Bothwell was with her, but no scandal-mongering comments were made about their companionship until later. Since it had been resolved, when the Queen returned to Edinburgh in March 1566 having recouped her position after the murder of Rizzio, that she should always be accompanied by a group of her Lords of Council, whoever else attended her, the resolution explained Bothwell's presence.

From Stirling, on 9 January 1567, the Queen sent her own physician to Glasgow to see Darnley. This was reported by the Earl of Bedford, who had heard that the King was 'full of the smallpox'.[12] The pretext was no doubt to offer Darnley expert care; the purpose would have been to secure an accurate report on his illness. Years later, when Bothwell wrote a brief vindication of his own actions in French, entitled *Les Affaires du Conte de Boduel*, he stated that Darnley had suffered from '*petite vérole*' [smallpox]. He had probably dictated this, and reading it over to correct it, crossed out the words and inserted '*roniole*' [syphilis].[13] Bothwell did not see Darnley at the height of his illness, and even had he done so, there is no reason to think that he could have made an instant diagnosis. His comment must mirror the view of Mary's physician, possibly relayed to him by the Queen herself. The doctor's mission to Glasgow did not imply a mellowing of Mary's attitude towards Darnley, for Bedford reported 'the agreement between the Queen and her husband is nothing amended'.[14]

However, Mary sent a message offering to visit Darnley. His initial response was courteous, but non-committal: 'If she come it shall be to my comfort and she shall be welcome. If she tarry even as it pleaseth her, so be it'. Then he suddenly burst out to the messenger: 'But this much you shall declare unto her, that I wish Stirling to be Jedburgh, Glasgow to be the Hermitage, and I the Earl of Bothwell as I lie here, and then I doubt not that she would be quickly with me, undesired'.[15] If this were true, and it has the sound of reality, it shows that Darnley was already aware of the attachment between the Queen and Bothwell, and was festering with jealousy. He had been jealous of Rizzio, almost certainly without cause, but because he had a jealous nature. And for that very reason he had instinctively grasped the significance of Mary's ride to Hermitage. He had not intended to speak of it, but he had betrayed his thoughts, as the violence of his emotions so frequently led him to do. There is no indication as to whether this message was relayed to the Queen, or tactfully suppressed.

On 13–14 January Mary removed her son from Stirling and brought him to Holyroodhouse. This demonstrated her anxiety concerning plots to seize him on Darnley's behalf (as obviously Darnley could do nothing for himself at present), but it was a curious decision, since Holyrood was notoriously vulnerable, as Mary had good cause to remember. It has often been said that she wanted her baby under her own protection, yet she left him again the following week when she went to Glasgow to visit Darnley.

On 20 January Mary wrote to Archbishop Beaton reporting her efforts to uncover the plot that was troubling her:

> Lately a servant of yours, named William Walker, came to our presence . . . at Stirling, and . . . declared to us . . . he had heard by report of persons who he esteemed lovers of us, that the King, by the assistance of some of our nobility, should take the Prince our son and crown him; and being crowned, as his father should take upon him the government.[16]

'Lately' was evidently some time ago, as many fruitless enquiries had followed. Walker, 'being pressed, named William Hiegait, also your servant' as his chief informant, and also reported that Hiegait had said 'the King could not [be] content and bear with some of the noblemen that were attending in our court but either he or they behoved to leave the same'. This would have reminded the Queen of Darnley's earlier threat to kill Moray which she had forced him to retract, and it would have sounded to her like a rumour to be taken seriously. Hiegait, besides being the Archbishop's servant, was the town clerk of Glasgow, well placed at the very centre of Lennox influence to hear every rumour. He was sent for and questioned but denied that he had said anything that Walker reported, though he confessed he had 'heard a bruit [rumour] that the King should be put in ward'. Further questioning only produced more men – including the Lord Provost of Glasgow – who agreed that they had heard rumours, but denied knowledge of any plot. The Queen concluded her letter with bitter comments on her husband and his father:

And for the King our husband, God knows always our part towards him; and his behaviour and thankfulness to us is semblably well known to God and the world; specially our own indifferent [impartial] subjects see it, and in their hearts, we doubt not, condemn the same. Always we perceive him [Darnley] occupied and busy enough to have inquisition of our doings, which, God willing, shall always be such as none shall have occasion to be offended with them, or to report of us any ways but honourably, howsoever he and his father and their folk speak, which we know want no good will to make us have ado [make trouble], if their power were equivalent to their minds.[17]

Having dispatched her letter the Queen set off for Glasgow, to visit Darnley, evidently with no friendly feelings towards him. She was escorted by a guard of mounted arquebusiers, and took with her an empty horselitter, in which to bring Darnley back to Edinburgh. She was accompanied by Bothwell and Huntly as far as Callendar, the house of Lord Livingstone, where they spent the night. The next day the two earls returned to Edinburgh and Mary continued her journey to Glasgow with her escort.

A short distance from Glasgow she was met by Thomas Crawford of Jordanhill, one of Darnley's gentlemen-in-waiting, and a faithful adherent of the House of Lennox.[18] He presented Lennox's commendations to the Queen, and his apologies for not coming to meet her, since he himself was ill. Also 'he presumed not to come in her presence till he knew her mind', since she had spoken sharp words about him to one of his servants at Stirling. Mary replied that there was no recipe against fear, and that Lennox would not fear to face her if he were not culpable. Crawford answered, 'His Lordship would the secrets of every creature were written on their face', to which Mary's response was an angry enquiry as to whether Crawford had any further commission. 'I said "No" and she commanded me to hold my peace'.

Indignant at this encounter, which seemed redolent of the Lennoxes' pride and duplicity, Mary approached the town. Glasgow in the sixteenth century was very small, a cluster of houses, gardens and orchards, dominated by its cathedral and its castle. The Clyde, which would provide its future prosperity, was dominated not by the town but by the strategically placed fortress of Dumbarton on its great rock. Lennox and Darnley were both lying ill in the castle of Glasgow when Mary arrived; she took up residence in the palace of the absentee Archbishop. Then she went to visit Darnley, still out of temper, but determined to discover the truth about the rumoured plot from him, and persuade him to return with her to Edinburgh.

Darnley had had plenty of time to think since he had received Mary's offer to visit him. Despite his outburst to her messenger, he had hoped she would come. He wanted, as he had wanted since the murder of Rizzio, to be reconciled with her. At Easter 1566 he had believed, or at least hoped, that they were reconciled. The Queen's humiliation of him after the birth of their child had disabused him, and his situation during the celebrations of the baptism had brought him close to despair. At the lowest point of his illness he had thought of appealing once more to the Queen's former love, and entreating her forgiveness with unprecedented humility. His verbal appeal to her makes it plain that he had already written to her, seeking reconciliation, and reproaching her for cruelty to him. Thomas Crawford reported that after the Queen's first visit to him Darnley recounted what he had said to her, to be repeated to the Earl of Lennox. Evidently it was an elaborately prepared speech:

You asked me what I meant by the cruelty specified in my letter. It proceedeth of you only, that will not accept my offers and repentance. I confess that I have failed in some things, and yet great faults have been made to you sundry times, which you have forgiven. I am but young, and you will say you have forgiven me diverse times. May not a man of my age, for lack of counsel, of which I am very destitute, fall twice or thrice, and yet repent, and be chastized by experience? If I have made any fail [committed any fault], howsoever it be, I crave your pardon, and protest that I shall never fail again. I desire no other thing but that we may be together as husband and wife. And if you will not consent thereto I desire never to rise forth of this bed. Therefore I pray you, give me an answer hereunto. God knoweth how I am punished for making my god of you and for having no other thought but of you. And if at any time I offend you, you are the cause, for that [because] when any offendeth me, if for my refuge I might open my mind to you I would speak to no other, but when anything is spoken to me and you and I not being as husband and wife ought to be, necessity compelleth me to keep it in my breast and bringeth me to such melancholy as you see me in.[19]

This extraordinary outpouring represented what Darnley intended to say to the Queen, even if he expressed it less coherently. However, as he was by all accounts an eloquent speaker, he probably said something like it. His most striking utterance was 'I am punished for making my god of you', for he had behaved so badly to the Queen that no one could have imagined his feeling such emotions. Even as a suitor he had not been an adoring lover, and not until he was banished from Mary's bed had he been obsessed by desire for her. Only in the sense of becoming an obsession had she become a deity to him, like the mistress of a poet whose amorous thraldom inspires him to address her as a goddess.

Mary was not moved by Darnley's ardour, and with the feeling she had so recently expressed in her letter to Archbishop Beaton, she probably found it repellent. She said somewhat perfunctorily that 'she was sorry for his sickness', and then began questioning him about his intended departure by ship and his rumoured plots. If these had ever been more than wild talk, he now wished to forget them. He gave her evasive answers, but hinted at knowledge of her plots, saying the Laird of Minto (the Lord Provost of Glasgow) had told him 'a letter was presented to her in Craigmillar made to her own devise and subscribed by certain others, who desired her to subscribe the same which she refused to do', but 'he would never think that she who was his own proper flesh would do him hurt, and if any other would, they should buy it dear unless they took him sleeping'.[20]

In response to this Mary became 'very pensive'. No doubt she was taken aback to discover that any information had leaked out concerning the 'Craigmillar Conference', whether accurate or not. Darnley next said he had heard that she had brought a litter with her (which Crawford would have told him before her arrival). She answered smoothly that she had brought it to carry him more softly than on horseback; she was going to take him to Craigmillar 'to be with him and not far from her son'. She might have expected him to baulk at the mention of Craigmillar, but he seized the opportunity to drive the bargain that was uppermost in his mind:

He said he would go, if they might be at bed and board as husband and wife, and she to leave him no more . . . She said if she had not been so minded, she would not have come so far, and gave him her hand and faith of her body, that she would love him and use him as her husband.[21]

It must have been difficult to make this promise convincingly to a man so repulsively disfigured by his illness, and there is something pathetic in Darnley's eagerness to believe her. But she told him that 'before they could come together he must be purged and cleansed of his sickness', and for this purpose 'she minded [intended] to give him the bath at Craigmillar'.

When the Queen had left him, Darnley relayed the interview to Crawford, and asked what he thought of Darnley's agreement to go with the Queen. Crawford replied forthrightly. 'I said I liked it not, for if she had desired his company, instead of to Craigmillar she would have taken him to his own house in Edinburgh . . . therefore my opinion was that she took him more like a prisoner than her husband'. Darnley agreed that he would think much the same, except for his confidence in Mary's promise: 'yet he would put himself in her hands, though she should cut his throat . . .'[22]

When Darnley was ready to travel, influenced by Crawford and his father, and by his own lurking misgivings, he refused to go to Craigmillar.[23] Mary did not want to bring him to Holyrood, and Darnley, still disfigured, did not wish to be seen there.[24] The lesions on his face were healing, but he was still wearing his taffeta mask. If he would not go where Mary had planned, another lodging would have to be found for him. It has been said that Darnley himself chose to go to Kirk o' Field,[25] but he could only have made his choice in response to the suggestion that it might be suitable. The location was on the southern edge of Edinburgh, on high ground, an area considered healthier than the low-lying environs of Holyrood.[26] South of the Cowgate, and just within the town wall, lay the old collegiate church of St Mary-in-the-Field, commonly known as the Kirk o' Field, and a quadrangle of houses, the erstwhile lodgings of the residentiary canons. Adjacent to the quadrangle was the Duke's Lodging, the town house of the Duke of Châtelhérault, who was in France, exiled since the Chaseabout Raid. By two accounts, Darnley thought the suggestion that he should stay at Kirk o' Field implied at the Duke's Lodging,[27] and it might have given him satisfaction to take temporary possession of the house of his absent enemy. It was, however, presently occupied by Châtelhérault's brother, the Archbishop. For Darnley, Mary Queen of Scots intended another house in the quadrangle, known as the Old Provost's Lodging, which she had recently gifted to Robert Balfour, brother of her councillor Sir James Balfour, and which was currently empty.[28] Once Darnley had decided on Kirk o' Field, it was easy to arrange for him to stay in this house and to send a messenger to Edinburgh with orders to move some furniture from Holyrood to the Old Provost's Lodging.

Darnley and Mary with their escort left Glasgow on 27 January, and travelled slowly, transporting Darnley as gently as possible in the horse-litter. They moved only a few miles each day, probably staying at Kilsyth, Callendar, and Linlithgow Palace, where they may have spent two nights, depending on whether they reached Edinburgh on 30 or 31 January.[29] When they arrived at Kirk o' Field, and Darnley saw that the intended destination was the Old Provost's Lodging, 'which was so little in his sight as he in no wise liked of', he indicated the Duke's Lodging and said 'he would lodge in that house, for he misliked the other she [had] prepared for him'. The Queen took him by the hand, assuring him that it had been handsomely furnished for him, and he 'being bent [inclined] to follow her will in all things . . . entered the house where he continued unto the time of his death'.[30]

The Old Provost's Lodging, though smaller than the Duke's Lodging, was a substantial house. It lay on the south side of the quadrangle, so close to the town wall that a gallery extending from the main bedchamber projected over it. A garden within the town wall and an orchard outside it belonged to the house. The principal room, described as the *salle*, became the Presence Chamber during Darnley's occupation. There were two bedchambers, one above the other; the upper one, with the projecting gallery, was Darnley's. Two other small rooms were designated *garderobes*. On the ground floor, beyond the *salle*, lay the kitchens. Cellars ran beneath the whole house.[31]

Darnley's bedchamber contained a bed with black velvet hangings, which may have belonged to the previous occupant of the house. He evidently objected to it, and it was removed and replaced with a magnificent bed from Holyroodhouse, with curtains of violet velvet trimmed with gold and silver *passementerie* [braid], and with a coverlet, pillow and pillowcase of blue taffeta.[32] The rest of the furniture was equally rich and bright: sixteen pieces of tapestry covered the

PLATE XVII: HENRY, KING OF SCOTS

Henry Stuart, Lord Darnley, King of Scots, c.1566.

PLATES XVIII AND XIX: THE MURDER OF DARNLEY AND ITS CONSEQUENCES

A contemporary drawing of the events at Kirk o'Field: centre: the Old Provost's Lodging reduced to rubble by the explosion; top left: Prince James praying for vengeance on his father's murderers; top right: the bodies of Darnley and William Taylor in the garden; lower left: a crowd watches the removal of the bodies; lower right: Taylor is buried in the precincts of Kirk o'Field [Darnley's body was taken to lie briefly in state, and embalmed].

Above right The design of the banner carried by the Confederate Lords at Carberry Hill, 1567. The banner shows the body of Darnley as it lay under the tree in the garden at Kirk o'Field, and Darnley's son Prince James praying with the words "Judge and avenge my cause, O Lord"; the monogram of the Holy Name of Jesus above signifies that his prayer is heard.

Below right The confrontation of the Confederate Lords and the Queen's army at Carberry Hill. The Confederate Lords' army is on the left in the picture; they carry two versions of the banner, one showing the version illustrated above, the other with only the body of Darnley on it. In the ranks of the Queen's army her position is shown by the royal banner of the lion rampant. In the centre of the picture a later incident is shown; the Queen, having surrendered is led towards the rebels by Kirkaldy of Grange.

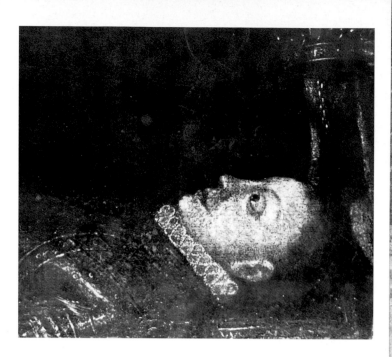

MAGNATES ET HEROES SANGVINE REGALI SCOTIAE ET ANGLIAE PROGNATI.
HENRICI DARNLEY SCOTORVM Regis effinguntur Parentes ejus MATTHAEVS Comes LENOXIAE cum filio MARGARETA Pietor, CAROLVS
...ine SCOTIAE postea vero BRITANNIAE Rex ejus nominis primus: Omnes flexis genibus DEVM orantes nefariae caedis vindices
MATTHAEI STVART Comitis Lenoxiae anno MDLXXI defunctum, Serenissima Regina CAROLINA anno MDCCXXXI in Palatio Kensingtoniense postera sacrum
...volo RICHMONDIAE LENOXIAE et ALBINIACI Duci, Stabuli Regalis Comiti, nobilissimique Ordinis Periscelidis Equiti.
                                                        omni cultu et obsequio devotissimus D. D. D. Georgius Vertue.

PLATES XX AND XXI: THE DARNLEY MEMORIAL – A VENDETTA PICTURE

Above The Darnley Memorial Picture, engraved by George Vertue, in which the details are clearer than in photographs of the original painting. An effigy of Darnley lies on the catafalque, while his parents, brother and son pray for divine punishment on his murderers. The intention of the picture is that the onlooker will 'read' its message, and agree that Darnley ought to be avenged.

Above left Close-up of the head of Darnley's effigy, from the picture illustrated below; it was probably of carved and painted wood.

Below left The Darnley Memorial Picture by Lieven de Vogelaar; there are two versions of the picture, one in the Goodwood Collection, and the other in the Royal Collection; this is the Goodwood version, from which Vertue made his engraving.

The most illustrious Prince Henry, Lord Darnly, King of Scotland, father to our Soueraigne lord King James. He died at the age of 21. 1567. · The most excellent Princesse Marie, Queene of Scotland, mother to our Soueraigne lord King James. She died. 1586. and intombed at Westminster

Are to be soulde in Popes head Alley at the white horse by John Sudburye and George Humble.

R. Elstrack sculp.

PLATE XXII: JAMES VI AND I REHABILITATES THE MEMORY OF HIS PARENTS

The Elstracke engraving of Darnley and Mary as King and Queen of Scots, which was on sale in Jacobean London. The biographical notes beneath the figures give their ages at death, but do not mention how either of them died. The likeness of Darnley is based on the earlier engravings of him in the robes and insignia of the Order of St Michael; that of Mary Queen of Scots is based on portraits of her in later life, and she is wearing clothes of a fashion at least a decade later than his.

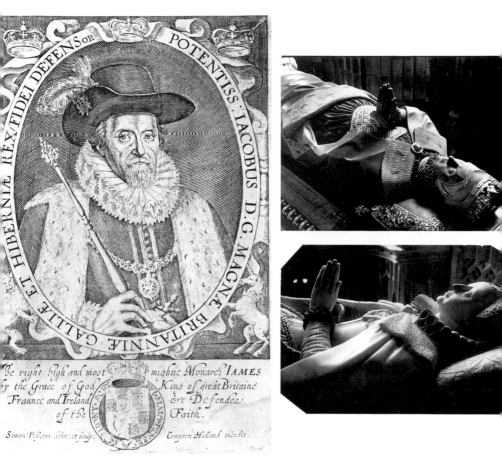

PLATE XXIII: THE TRIUMPH OF AMBITION

Above left Engraving of James VI and I as 'The Right High and Most Mightie Monarch James by the Grace of God King of Great Britaine . . .'

Above right Alabaster and polychrome effigy of Margaret, Countess of Lennox, James's grandmother; inscriptions on her tomb list all the Kings and Queens to whom she was related.

Below right White marble effigy of Mary Queen of Scots by William and Cornelius Cure. James had his mother's body exhumed from her original grave in Peterborough Cathedral and reburied in Westminster Abbey, in a tomb equal in splendour to that of Queen Elizabeth I.

The inscription reads:

HENRY SECOND SONNE TO THIS LADY WAS K OF SCOTTS.
AND FATHER TO IAMES THE 6 NOW KING THIS HENRY
WAS MVRTHERED AT THE AGE OF 21 YEARES. CHARLES
HER YOVNGEST SONNE WAS EARLE OF LEVENOX
FATHER TO THE LADIE ARBELL. HE DYED AT THE
AGE OF 21 YEARES AND IS HERE INTOMBED.

PLATE XXIV: A ROYAL MONUMENT

Statues of Darnley and his younger brother, Lord Charles Stuart, as 'weepers' on
the plinth of the tomb of their mother, Margaret, Countess of Lennox, in Westminster Abbey. Darnley's royal status is shown by the crown above his head, and
by his ermine-lined royal mantle. The inscription beneath reports the events of his
brief life.

walls of the Presence Chamber, the King's bedchamber, and the adjacent *garderobe*. There were two high-backed chairs, one covered in violet velvet, the other in leather; and there was a *chaise percée garnye de deux bassin* (a commode furnished with two – interchangeable – containers). In the Queen's bedchamber was a small bed with hangings of green and yellow damask, and a coverlet of green taffeta.[33] A bath was placed in the King's bedchamber, to facilitate the frequent bathing that was part of his treatment, and one of the doors of the house was removed from its hinges to provide a cover for the bath, which would then do double duty as a seat. There was a small table with a green velvet cloth – a gaming table – which presumably was in the King's bedchamber; there was also a small Turkish carpet, and a chamber pot. While the King's chamber was colourful and crowded with furniture, the Presence Chamber was apparently empty, except for its tapestries – unless it contained some furnishings belonging to the house, for nothing else was brought from Holyrood.[34]

In these surroundings, comfortable by the standards of the time, and probably typical of the town houses of the Scottish aristocracy, Darnley spent his last days. Though George Buchanan later described the Old Provost's Lodging as semi-ruinous, and unsuitable quarters for a king, the inventory of its furnishings proves the contrary, and the Queen herself found it adequately comfortable to stay in for two nights in early February, sleeping in the green and yellow bed.

On 7 February Darnley wrote to his father, reassuring him that he had not been unwise to leave Glasgow with the Queen, and expressing the hope that their reconciliation would endure:

My Lord,
  I have thought good to write unto you by this bearer of my good health, I thank God. Which is the sooner come to, through the good treatment of such as hath this good while concealed their good will, I mean my love the Queen. Which I assure you hath all this while and yet doth use herself like a natural and loving wife. I hope yet that God will lighten our hearts with joy that have so long been afflicted with trouble. As I in this letter do write unto your Lordship so I trust this bearer can certify you the like. Thus thanking Almighty God of our good hap, I commit your Lordship into his protection.

From Edinburgh the vii of February, your loving and obedient son

Henry, Rex[35]

Lennox was told that the Queen read the letter over Darnley's shoulder, put her arm round his neck and kissed him, before he handed it to the messenger.[36] The anxious father would have been cheered to read Darnley's assurances of returning health and happiness, and his hopes that past afflictions might be forgotten. Darnley himself was encouraged by the attentions he received at Kirk o' Field, for according to Crawford he had complained to the Queen in Glasgow that she 'would never abide with him past two hours at once',[37] but now she seemed content to sit at his bedside and talk to him, as she had done when he fell ill before, and she fell in love with him. And he was visited by many of the lords who had shunned him at Stirling and avoided him during most of the past year. It seemed as though the court had transferred itself to Kirk o' Field, and the recently despised King was at the centre of it.

Sir James Melville, writing his memoirs long afterwards, said that 'many suspected that the Earl of Bothwell had some enterprise against him',[38] but were reluctant to warn him because of his notorious indiscretion. However, Lord Robert Stewart, contemptuous of Bothwell and at least fleetingly pitying Darnley, 'told him that if he retired not hastily out of that place, it would cost him his life'. Unfortunately Darnley, now trusting the Queen completely, reported the warning to her, and 'my Lord Robert denied that he ever spoke it.'[39] Thus passed Darnley's last chance of escape.

Presumably it was a medical decision when Darnley's convalescence was pronounced complete: on 10 February he could leave Kirk o' Field and return to public life. His last day at the Old Provost's Lodging was the Sunday before Lent, and as such a day of festivity. He began the day by hearing Mass. Evidently he was in one of his religious phases, for recently 'he had promised to set up the Mass again, and caused say Mass in Glasgow'.[40] During the morning the Earl of Moray left Edinburgh, telling the Queen that he must go to his wife, who had had a miscarriage. Having visited her he did not return to court, but soon left Scotland and stayed away until after the Queen's downfall; thus did he fulfil Lethington's prophecy that he would 'look through his fingers' at the King's fate.

After the departure of Moray the Queen attended the marriage feast of Bastien Pagès and his bride Christian Hogg, and promised to attend the masque Bastien had devised for the occasion, which would be performed at night. In the afternoon Mary went to another formal dinner, given in honour of Count Moretta, the ambassador of Savoy, who was about to leave Scotland. From the dinner Mary and her entourage rode to Kirk o' Field to spend the evening with Darnley. The Queen's companions were Argyll, Cassillis, Huntly and Bothwell. It was probably a relief to Darnley that Moray was not with them, for his contempt and Darnley's hatred were at best lightly veiled. Now there were no enemies near him that he was aware of: his uncle the Postulate of Arbroath remained unpardoned, and his cousin Morton was still forbidden to approach the court. With the Queen's recent show of love his jealousy of Bothwell had faded. The evening passed pleasantly and Darnley expected the lords to take their leave and Mary to remain and sleep in the room beneath. He was disappointed and probably angry when she told him that she had promised to attend Bastien's masque, and prepared to leave him. Then Bothwell, glitteringly clad in black and silver, a swarthy man with dark, suspicious eyes, now 'with a good countenance', reminded the Queen that she had arranged to ride to Seton early in the morning, evidently stressing that it would not be worth her while to return to Kirk o' Field that night.[41] Mary sought to restore Darnley's good humour with 'very loving words' and gave him a ring in pledge of her promise that the following night she would sleep with him.[42]

Mary went into the quadrangle, followed by the lords, and there as she was about to mount her horse she saw a man named Nicholas Hubert, known as 'French Paris', formerly Bothwell's servant and now a member of her household. Mary noticed his blackened face and hands and exclaimed, 'Jesu, Paris, how begrimed you are!', at which he blushed vividly.[43] This tiny incident, turning on details surprisingly visible in the dark, was told by Mary to Nau for inclusion in his narrative. Its purpose was to stress her ignorance of what had 'begrimed' Paris, and consequently of what was to happen later: Paris had been blackened by the gunpowder he had been helping to stow in the cellars of the Old Provost's Lodging.

When the Queen had left him Darnley 'commanded that his great horses should be in readiness by five of the clock in the morning'. Early morning activity was customary, but five o'clock seems unusually early for a dark winter morning. But Darnley was determined to be ready to

ride with the Queen to Seton. To banish his low spirits he called for
wine and said to his servant William Taylor, 'Let us go merrily to bed in
singing a song before'. Taylor asked him to play the lute to accompany
them, but Darnley said his hand was not inclined to the lute that night.
As Taylor had a book of psalms, he selected the fifth psalm and they
sang unaccompanied. It contains the lines:

> Ponder my words O Lord . . . For thou art the God that hast no
> pleasure in wickedness . . . Lead me O Lord in thy righteousness,
> because of mine enemies . . . Their throat is an open sepulchre;
> they flatter with their tongue. Destroy them O God; let them perish
> through their own imaginations . . . For thou Lord wilt give thy
> blessing unto the righteous; and with thy favourable kindness thou
> wilt defend him as with a shield . . .

It was not a likely choice for a man who wanted to 'go merrily to
bed', and perhaps was included in the story of Darnley's last night
for dramatic effect. Whatever they sang, Darnley then 'drank to his
servant bidding him farewell for that night and so went to bed'.[44]
Darnley slept in his great bed behind the violet velvet curtains; Taylor
slept on a little 'pallet' bed beside it. Another servant, Thomas Nelson, slept in the gallery. What happened next can be reconstructed
from what Count Moretta heard before he left Scotland, and afterwards recounted to his contacts in France, the Bishop of Mondovi,
Papal Nuncio-Designate to Scotland, and the Venetian ambassador
in France, Giovanni Correr. In the depth of the night Darnley awoke,
disturbed by noises outside the window; he got up to look out, and
saw men milling about below. Instantly he would have remembered
Lord Robert Stewart's warning, and understood that these men
intended his death. He may have feared that they meant to burn the
house over his head, a common form of murder, but the presence of
gunpowder he would not have guessed. He had looked out of the gallery window, over the town wall. Without hesitating, without even
waiting to dress, he and Taylor got out of the other window, into the
garden within the town wall. How they descended is uncertain, possibly with an improvised rope of sheets, though Taylor may have low-
ered Darnley first on a chair which was found outside with them. He
also paused to gather up the King's purple velvet nightgown furred
with sables.[45] But Darnley did not have time to put it on. Out in the
garden, still in their nightshirts, the King and his servant found that

the house was surrounded. More men appeared out of the darkness, flung themselves on Darnley and overpowered him. As he struggled with them 'certain women who lodged near the garden affirm that they heard the King cry "O my brothers [kinsmen], have pity on me for the love of Him who had mercy on all the world"',[46] last words which imply that he recognized his murderers as members of his Douglas kindred. According to Moretta, 'they strangled him with the sleeves of his own shirt under the very window from which he had descended',[47] but it is more likely that they smothered him with someone's cloak, or even with his magnificent nightgown, for there was no mark of strangulation on his throat. Taylor, the witness who could not be permitted to survive and tell the tale, suffered the same fate.

The murderers knew, as Darnley had not, that the cellars of the house were piled with gunpowder, towards which a slow fuse was probably already burning. It would have been folly to remain in the garden under the walls of the house. They gathered up the two bodies, and fled through a door in the town wall into the orchard beyond. They laid the body of Darnley beneath a tree, and unceremoniously dropped that of Taylor nearby, before disappearing into the night.[48] One of them left a velvet 'mule' (backless shoe) at the scene of the crime, which was afterwards said to have belonged to Darnley's kinsman Archibald Douglas, one of the pardoned murderers of Rizzio.

Scarcely had they fled when the house exploded, with 'a tremendous noise . . . as of a volly of twenty-five or thirty cannon, arousing the whole town.'[49] Lord Herries reported, 'The blast was fearful all about. Many rose from their beds at the noise, and came in multitudes to look upon the dead corpse, without knowing the cause'.[50] But one thing was obvious, that while the solid stone house was reduced to a heap of rubble, with the mutilated remains of three or four of Darnley's household servants buried in it, the explosion had not killed the King or William Taylor, who lay on the grass, their semi-nakedness revealing them uninjured by the blast, 'neither were their shirts singed . . . nor their skins anything touched with fire.'[51] The murder had been intended by one means, and committed by another. Thomas Nelson, the servant who had slept in the bedchamber gallery, had not followed Darnley and Taylor out of the house. Miraculously he survived its destruction, saved by the overhang of the gallery, and was found later standing dazed on the town wall, the only witness to Darnley's last hours.[52]

The murder of the King had the unexpected result that, by the savagery and pathos of his end, Darnley was transformed from a widely detested young man into a sacrificial victim, as widely pitied.

The Earl of Lennox received the news of his son's death so soon after the arrival of his optimistic letter that the shock was the more devastating. Immediately he thought of the Queen's kiss as she leant over Darnley's shoulder to read that letter, and it seemed to him that she had 'kissed him as Judas did the Lord his Master'. He had no doubt that the Queen had taken Darnley away from the safety of Glasgow to meet his death: 'This tyrant having brought her faithful and most loving husband, that innocent lamb, from his careful and most loving father to the place of execution, where he was a sure sacrifice unto Almighty God'.[53] The news was brought to Margaret Lennox in the Tower of London, and she was equally certain of the guilt of Mary, for the logic of her actions seemed inexorable. Margaret was in such an agony of grief that Queen Elizabeth sent a doctor to attend her, and within a few days released her from the Tower and sent her to stay with her former gaolers, the Sackvilles, where her surviving son Lord Charles Stuart was allowed to join her.[54] The Spanish ambassador, de Silva, commented to Philip II that Margaret was not the only person who suspected Mary's guilt: 'Every day it becomes clearer that the Queen of Scotland must take steps to prove that she had no hand in the death of her husband . . .'[55] She failed to do so. Her explanation of the murder for the consumption of foreign courts was that the explosion at Kirk o' Field had been intended to kill both her and her husband, but her life had been miraculously saved by her departure to attend the masque. However, this tale was received with scepticism, since the fact that Mary had brought Darnley to Kirk o' Field and departed so opportunely looked more like good management than good fortune or, as she claimed, divine intervention.

Mary began by obeying the conventions. She ordered the court into mourning, and retired to the black-draped mourning chamber where etiquette demanded she should remain for forty days. On 12 February spices to the value of £40 were ordered for the 'oppyning and perfuming of the Kingis grace majesteis umquhile [late] bodie',[56] and when embalmed the body was buried in the Abbey of Holyrood, in the royal vault of James V. These provisions were seemly, if shorn of ceremony. The following month, somewhat tardily, a Mass was offered for the repose of Darnley's soul, and a dirge was sung. But, after only five days, Mary emerged from her mourning chamber and rode to Seton. It was given out that her departure was for reasons of health, but it created a bad impression. Scant ceremonies and skimped mourning were not appropriate responses to the murder of a king: it demanded vengeance. Queen Elizabeth wrote Mary an urgent letter, exhorting her to do the duty which was essential to preserve her reputation:

> Madam,*
> My ears have been so astounded and my heart so frightened to hear of the horrible and abominable murder of your late husband and my slaughtered cousin, that I have scarcely spirit to write . . . I should not do the office of a faithful cousin and friend, if I did not urge you to preserve your honour, rather than look through your fingers at revenge on those who have done you such pleasure, as most people say . . .[57]

This was a far more forthright letter than any diplomat would have dared to write, and Mary would have done well to heed Elizabeth's advice and act upon it. But she could not bring herself to do so, for the chief suspect as murderer of the King was the Earl of Bothwell, and Mary's actions proved that she was utterly subservient to his ambition, even without the evidence of the controversial 'Casket Letters' and the sonnet sequence attributed to her, which will be mentioned in the context of their discovery.

In the later part of February cartels began to appear accusing Bothwell of the King's murder. Anonymous and damaging, they were fixed at night to the doors of churches and the Tolbooth, and to the gates of Holyroodhouse. Bothwell 'declared that if he knew who were the setters up of the bills he would wash his hands in their blood',[58] a characteristic response which merely confirmed that Bothwell was not a man to shrink from murder. Of course, if Moretta's account of the murder were substantially correct, the explosion of the Old Provost's Lodging had not killed Darnley; but Bothwell's generally credited murderous intent and organization of the

---

* The original letter was in French, and the beginning 'Madame' instead of the more intimate 'Ma Chère Soeur' may suggest that Elizabeth shared the suspicions that she reported.

explosion made him the murderer in the public mind. Many people may have supposed that it was he who had killed the King in the garden. The contemporary ballad 'Earl Bothwell' is probably an accurate mirror of public opinion, if not of the events:

> To bed the worthy King made him bowne [laid him down]
>   To take his rest, that was his desire;
> He was no sooner cast on sleep,
>   But his chamber was on a blazing fire.

> Up he lope, and a glass window broke,
>   He had thirty feet for to fall . . .
> 'Who have we here?' said Lord Bothwell,
>   'Answer me now I do call'.

> 'King Henry the eighth my uncle was;
>   Some pity show for his sweet sake!
> Ah, Lord Bothwell, I know thee well,
>   Some pity on me I pray thee take!'

> 'I'll pity thee as much' he said
>   'And as much favour I'll show to thee
> As thou had on the Queen's chamberlain
>   That day thou deemest him to die . . .'[59]

It was significant of the change in attitude to Darnley that though the balladist held him responsible for the death of Rizzio ('the Queen's chamberlain'), nonetheless he had become 'the worthy King'. This tilt of opinion in Darnley's favour was extremely dangerous to Mary Queen of Scots, but far more dangerous was her continuing inaction in the face of it. Modern historians are agreed that the Queen could have survived the scandal caused by the murder of Darnley, and even the imputation of culpability, if she had played the part of a sorrowing widow and outraged sovereign, and brought the culprit, or any plausible culprit, to justice.[60] But Mary now possessed no vestige of control over affairs. She was wholly reliant on Bothwell, and certainly she lacked the power to single out anyone of status to sacrifice on the altar of her reputation. The participants in the 'Craigmillar Conference' and others who were rumoured either to have joined the plot against Darnley or to have had foreknowledge of it – these included Archbishop Hamilton and the Earl of Morton – had nothing to fear from the Queen.

The anonymous accusations directed at Bothwell grew more strident, and at last in response to the appeals of Lennox for justice and to the pressure of public opinion, the Queen was forced to permit the trial of Bothwell for the murder. The prosecution, which should have been initiated by the Crown, was left to the Earl of Lennox. The result was a travesty of justice. The trial was set for 12 April, and Lennox, who had left Glasgow with three thousand followers, had reached Linlithgow when he received 'commandment that he should not come to Edinburgh (with) above six in his company',[61] and since Edinburgh was thronged with Bothwell's armed followers, Lennox sent a protest that he dared not enter the city for fear of his life, and this was courageously presented to the court by his servant Robert Cunningham. As a result, Bothwell was acquitted since 'no evidence . . . had been brought by the pursuer [plaintiff]'.[62] This verdict did nothing to clear Bothwell's reputation, while the Queen's was further tarnished by her failure to administer justice.

Henceforward increasingly lewd pasquils began to appear in Edinburgh, linking the Queen's name with Bothwell's in accusations of adultery and murder. A famous example was a drawing of a mermaid poised above a hare which crouched in a circle of daggers. The design derived from *Symbola Heroica* by Claude Paradin (the emblem book which may have been presented to Darnley), in which it is accompanied by the motto *Mala Undique Clades* ['Destruction awaits the wicked on every side'].[63] The mermaid represents the siren or symbolic temptress; the hare conveniently happened to be a heraldic animal of the Hepburns. So that the message should not be missed, the pasquil stressed it by initials to label each figure: the mermaid was marked MR (Maria Regina), and the hare IH (James Hepburn). A more outspoken pasquil simply demanded:

Is it not aneuch the pure king is deid
Bot the mischand murthararis occupand his steid
And doubell addultrie hes all this land schamit . . .[64]

[Is it not enough that the poor king is dead
But the wicked murderers are occupying his place
And double adultery has all this land shamed.]

For Mary Queen of Scots the débâcle was now rapidly approaching. On 19 April Bothwell gave a supper at Ainslie's Tavern to a large gathering of the nobility, and induced them to sign a bond to persuade the Queen, now 'destitute of a husband', to marry him. In later life Mary thought that her enemies had signed the bond and encouraged her to marry Bothwell 'so that they might charge her with being in the plot against her late husband . . . this they did shortly after, appealing to the fact that she had married the murderer'.[65] The signatories were the Earls of Argyll, Huntly, Cassillis, Morton, Sutherland, Rothes, Glencairn and Caithness, 'Eglinton subscribed not but slipped away'. Among the lords were Boyd, Seton, Sempill, Herries, Gray and Hume.[66] The motives of the signatories must have varied. Some may have schemed as Mary imagined; some may have been influenced by Bothwell's men-at-arms outside the tavern; some may have drunk too well to think much about it.

On 21 April Mary rode to Stirling, where her son was once more in the care of his guardians, and this visit was the last time she saw him. On her way back to Edinburgh she was intercepted by Bothwell, with a much larger armed escort than her own, and carried off to Dunbar. While she was held captive at Dunbar Bothwell supposedly raped her, thus according to contemporary thinking obliging her to recover her honour by marrying him. Sir James Melville, who was in attendance on the Queen, heard Bothwell boast that 'he would marry the Queen, who would or would not; yea, whether she would herself or not';[67] but Melville's own captor told him that it was done with the Queen's consent, and the rumour of collusion clung to the episode. Certainly collusive was Bothwell's divorce from Lady Jean Gordon, for which she petitioned on the grounds of his adultery with her maid Bessie Crawford, a liaison she would have been expected to ignore under other circumstances. For the Queen's satisfaction a decree of nullity was pronounced by Archbishop Hamilton, on the grounds that Bothwell and Lady Jean, who were related, had married without a dispensation; but as Hamilton had provided a dispensation himself the whole transaction was both fraudulent and absurd.

If the nobility had fleetingly countenanced the marriage of Bothwell and the Queen on a drunken evening, the ensuing tales of ravishment and collusive divorce caused a revulsion of feeling. On 1 May a new bond was signed at Stirling by Argyll, Morton, Atholl and Mar, proclaiming their resolution to rescue the Queen 'ravished and detained' by Bothwell, to preserve the Prince and to pursue the King's murderers.[68] The four earls were supported by most of the signatories of the 'Ainslie's Tavern Bond'. They were joined at Stirling by M. du Croc, recently returned to Scotland, who told them that he had attempted to dissuade the Queen from marrying Bothwell, but 'she will give no ear'.[69]

On 15 May Mary Queen of Scots and Bothwell were married at Holyrood by Protestant rites. It was the nadir of Mary's reign at which she was not even able to demand the exercise of her own religion, though previously she had always insisted on her right to practise it, even if she disregarded the rights of her Catholic subjects. After the marriage she wept copiously and talked wildly of suicide. If she loved Bothwell obsessively she also recognized that in marrying him she faced political ruin. She may also have felt that in consenting to the Protestant ceremony she imperilled her immortal soul.

The Queen was well aware that she could not create her unacceptable husband King; it was sufficiently intolerable that she created him Duke of Orkney. Their married life lasted exactly a month, before they were forced to face their adversaries arrayed for battle on the field of Carberry Hill, near Musselburgh. The signatories of the bond signed at Stirling had occupied Edinburgh and issued a proclamation summoning the townsmen to assist them in delivering the Queen, preserving the Prince and avenging the murder of the late King, all of which required the overthrow of Bothwell. Avenging Darnley's murder provided the rallying cry of the party now called the 'Confederate Lords'. Their forces marched to Carberry Hill with a large painted banner depicting the dead body of Darnley as it had been found, lying half naked beneath a tree, and beside it a small child representing Prince James, praying for divine vengeance, a scroll issuing from his lips inscribed 'Judge and avenge my cause, O Lord'. It was a powerfully emotive image, and a brilliant example of propagandist art and political adroitness. For among the Confederate Lords were men involved in Darnley's death or suspected of foreknowledge of it, and they were casting the opprobrium on Bothwell, with whose guilt the Queen was now inextricably linked by marriage.

There was no battle at Carberry Hill. There was a day-long confrontation, in which Bothwell and the Queen were defeated by the power of propaganda. At the end of the day the Queen surrendered to the Confederate Lords on condition that Bothwell was permitted to depart unharmed. To his credit, he would have preferred to decide the issue by single combat, but agreed to leave the field in the hope of fighting on more advantageous terms another day. He and Mary parted with a public embrace, little imagining that it was their final separation. Before riding away, Bothwell gave the Queen the Craigmillar Bond against Darnley; this was a great mistake, for inevitably it was taken from her and destroyed.[70] Kirkaldy of Grange took the Queen's surrender, and assured her of honourable treatment. But if the Confederate Lords had intended it they could not control the taunts of their own soldiery, nor, when they escorted the Queen into Edinburgh, the passions of the mob which screamed, 'Burn the whore! Burn the murderess of her husband!' If Mary had imagined that she could ignore accusations of complicity in Darnley's death, she was terrifyingly disabused. It had been a rapid descent to disaster from the oblique discussions at Craigmillar, where Mary had stressed the importance of protecting her honour, to this dishonoured return to her capital threatened with death for the murder, at which she had at best 'looked through her fingers', at worst had deliberately facilitated.

Mary was removed from Edinburgh and imprisoned in the island castle of Lochleven, Kinross-shire, in the care of Sir William Douglas of Lochleven, half-brother of the Earl of Moray, and their mother the Lady of Lochleven, the erstwhile mistress of James V. Her disappointed hope that the King would marry her and that her son would succeed made her a willing gaoler of James V's daughter.

In late July Mary Queen of Scots miscarried of twins. She was said to have been five months pregnant, and the foetuses were sufficiently developed to be described as 'deux enfants', which implies that their conception must have antedated Bothwell's abduction of the Queen, thus further suggesting that it was collusive.[71] While the Queen was still weak from the after-effects of her miscarriage she was forced, with some brutality, to sign her abdication, which was euphemistically described as her 'voluntary demission'. She did so on 24 July, comforting herself with the belief that a document extorted under duress could not be legally binding. On 29 July the thirteen-month-old Prince James was crowned as King James VI, in the parish church of Stirling. It was a Protestant coronation, expunging the effects of his Catholic baptism. The Earl of Morton took the oath on his behalf to 'reule in ye faith, fear, and love of God, and maintain ye religion then professed in Scotland',[72] thus emphasizing that James was to be a Protestant king. John Knox, who had recently returned after a long absence in England, preached a sermon on a suitable text from the Old Testament, in which Joash was crowned King of Judah as a young child, and his mother Athaliah was slain with the sword.[73] The message was obvious to his congregation. On 11 August the Earl of Moray returned to Scotland and visited his captive sister at Lochleven. It was no longer necessary for him to treat her with conventional reverence, and what he said to her over the course of the next two days reduced her to tearful pleas that he would accept the regency. He was proclaimed Regent of Scotland on 22 August.

The following spring, on 2 May 1568, Mary escaped with the connivance of Moray's younger half-brother, George Douglas, who had fallen in love with her, and of a young orphaned kinsman, Willie Douglas, who, more humbly captivated, remained in her service to the end of her life. Immediately a remarkably strong party rallied to Mary's cause, a reaction in her favour which mirrored disapproval of her enforced abdication and imprisonment, once Bothwell was out of the way. Nine earls, nine bishops, twelve commendators and eighteen lords formed the nucleus of her party, bringing her a force of some five thousand men.[74] Mary's recovery of liberty was brief but magnificent. 'All historians', commented Professor Gordon Donaldson, 'are familiar with the Hundred Days of Napoleon ... perhaps equally memorable should be the Eleven Days of Mary Stewart ... between her escape from Lochleven on 2 May 1568 and the battle of Langside on the 13th'.[75]

On 13 May Mary's forces, marching to take possession of Dumbarton, were intercepted by the forces of the Regent Moray, and decisively defeated. In temporary despair, and in deadly fear of recapture, Mary rode some ninety miles from the battlefield to the Abbey of Dundrennan, near the shores of the Solway Firth. On 16 May, from nearby Abbeyburnfoot, she crossed the Solway in a fishing boat, to seek refuge in England, a flight which took her to the long incarceration which ended only with her life.

*   *   *

The government of the Regent Moray asserted its credentials as a virtuous regime by chasing Bothwell from the kingdom, establishing a Protestant monarchy, and pursuing and executing the murderers of the King. Those who suffered were, of course, associates of Bothwell, whose confessions, extracted under torture or the threat of torture, all incriminated Bothwell and avoided blaming anyone now associated with the government.

What had happened at Kirk o' Field had always been mysterious, and it was not clarified by these exemplary trials and executions, which were intended to serve the purposes of policy, not of justice. Ingratiating and contradictory tales of the purchase and transportation of gunpowder, its unloading at the Old Provost's Lodging, the incompetent laying and firing of the slow fuse, and Bothwell's investigating its progress immediately before the explosion, created an impression of bungling improvisation which would have been laughable had it not been deadly. It resembled a modern terrorist crime in being an extravagant and haphazard attempt on the life of the intended victim and a reckless destruction of other innocent lives.[76]

When Mary fled to England her intention was to appeal for Elizabeth's aid to secure her restoration. She had some justification for her hopes, since during her imprisonment at Lochleven Elizabeth had displayed sympathy with her cause, and had sent Sir Nicholas Throckmorton to Scotland, to ensure that her life was not in danger. But Elizabeth did not receive her in England as a defeated monarch but as a fugitive from justice, and accordingly refused to receive her personally, or decide whether or not to aid her until she had been cleared of the accusation of complicity in the murder of her husband. Immediately it became Moray's chief concern to justify the continued existence of his government and the reign of James VI by proving Mary's guilt. Queen Elizabeth appointed an enquiry, which though it had no judicial status became a trial of Mary Queen of Scots for the murder of Darnley. The enquiry opened at York in October 1568, transferred to Westminster, and concluded at Hampton Court in January 1569.

Mary was not permitted to appear before the enquiry, but was represented by John Leslie, Bishop of Ross, and by Lord Herries, both of whom were loyal defenders, but by no means as subtle as Mary's enemies, who presented the case against her in the devastating 'Book of Articles', an inextricable blend of lies and half-truths based in part on the first draft of Buchanan's *Detectio Mariae Reginae Scotorum*.[77] But the Regent Moray's prize exhibit was undoubtedly the 'Casket Letters', a collection of eight letters together with two contracts of marriage between Mary and Bothwell, and a sonnet sequence addressed to him, all of which were claimed to have been taken from George Dalgleish, Bothwell's servant, in a silver casket belonging to Bothwell, which he had sent Dalgleish to retrieve from his apartment in Edinburgh Castle in June 1567.

The letters are controversial chiefly because of the length of time which elapsed between their discovery and their revelation, and because the originals disappeared in 1584, when they passed into the possession of James VI, who presumably destroyed them.[78] They exist now only in copies and translations, which make it impossible to tell whether there have been interpolations. They have served the purposes of controversy for so long that all the arguments for and against their genuineness are outworn with repetition. It is only certain that if Mary wrote the Casket Letters – in particular Letter Two, the 'Long Glasgow Letter' – there is ineluctable proof that she plotted Darnley's death and brought him to Edinburgh to be murdered. The letter bears a close, some would say an unnaturally close, resemblance to the 'Declaration of Thomas Crawford': possibly one text was adjusted with reference to the other, but which was the earlier narrative is open to theory. Crawford's narrative was previously quoted as giving Darnley's perspective on the Queen's visit to Glasgow, which could not penetrate the workings of her mind. The 'Long Glasgow Letter' gives the Queen's perspective, and reveals her as guilty of planning Darnley's death, as the helpless pawn of Bothwell's ambition, and tormented in her conscience.[79] No one who wishes to believe her entirely innocent will accept the genuineness of the Casket Letter; the Crawford narrative leaves her role more ambiguous.

Equally ambiguous was Queen Elizabeth's verdict at the conclusion of the court of enquiry. In January Moray returned to Scotland to continue his regency as Elizabeth's ally; Mary remained in England, though Elizabeth declared that nothing had been proved against her honour. Without pronouncing it, or having the right to do so, Elizabeth imposed on her a sentence of life imprisonment.

The Earl of Lennox, craving vengeance for the murder of his son, was bitterly resentful that he was not permitted to appear at the court of enquiry. The longing for vengeance that united the Earl and Countess of Lennox as much as their ambition and their devotion to their son had done was enshrined in a remarkable painting which they commissioned from the Dutch painter Lieven de Voglaar. It shows the interior of a chapel, hung with heraldic banners. On a painted catafalque lies an effigy of Darnley encased in ornate armour, the face and hands probably of carved wood painted in polychrome. In front of the catafalque James VI, a crowned infant, kneels at a *prie dieu*, uttering a prayer for divine vengeance inscribed on a scroll: *Exurge Domine et vindica sanguinem innocentem Regis patris mei meq[ue] tua dextra defendas rogo* ['Arise Lord and avenge the innocent blood of the King my father, and me, I entreat thee, defend with thy right hand']. Behind him on the inlaid marble floor kneel his grandparents the Earl and Countess, and behind them kneels Lord Charles Stuart, praying that he may become the instrument of divine vengeance.[80]

Beyond the confines of the picture he never aspired to avenge his brother. Since he died at the age of twenty-one in 1577 his life was as short as Darnley's, though perhaps pleasanter. After the death of his father in 1571, he inherited the Lennox title, and in 1574, with the connivance of his mother, he married Elizabeth Cavendish, daughter of Elizabeth Countess of Shrewsbury, the renowned 'Bess of Hardwick'. They were the parents of Lady Arabella Stuart, whose existence would trouble James VI, as a possible rival claimant to the English throne. Queen Elizabeth imprisoned Margaret Lennox yet again in the Tower of London for arranging the marriage of her younger son without royal permission. The ageing countess commented with world-weary resignation, 'Thrice have I been cast into prison, not for matters of treason, but for love matters. First, when Thomas Howard . . . was in love with myself; then for the love of Henry Darnley, my son, to Queen Mary of Scotland; and lastly, for the love of Charles, my younger son, to Elizabeth Cavendish'.[81] During her imprisonment, lonely and bereaved, Margaret allowed herself to be persuaded that the Queen of Scots had played no part in Darnley's death, and conducted an epistolary reconciliation with her.

Besides the 'Memorial Picture' Darnley may be commemorated in his mother's famous jewel, known as the 'Lennox or Darnley Jewel'. It used to be believed that Margaret Lennox had commissioned this exquisite enamelled pendant as a memorial to her husband after his death in 1571. But Hugh Tait in a learned article, 'Historiated Tudor

Jewellery',[82] stated that the style belonged to the previous decade, therefore possibly it had been commissioned in 1564 while Margaret was at the English court and Lennox in Scotland, to be sent to him conveying messages regarding their dynastic policy. However, since their ambition was so perfectly understood between them as to require no such complex communication, it appears more likely that the jewel was commissioned in 1567 or 1568 to commemorate the death of Darnley and express the hope of his son's accession to the English throne. Such messages might be deduced from its complex tissue of symbolism.[83]

The Lennox family's prayer for vengeance did not go unanswered. Darnley continued to haunt Scotland like the ghost of Hamlet's father, demanding to be avenged, and providing a pretext for eliminating people, in a comprehensive if somewhat random manner.

The earliest to go were those lesser associates of Bothwell who were the exemplary victims executed by the regency to prove its zeal to punish Darnley's murderers. The first to die were Bothwell's servants: William Powrie, who confessed to having delivered gunpowder to the Old Provost's Lodging, and George Dalgleish, who had attended Bothwell at Kirk o' Field and had been arrested with the silver casket. 'French Paris' was caught and executed a little later. John Hay of Tala and John Hepburn of Bolton, kinsmen of Bothwell, paid the price of being close to him and associated with the events at Kirk o' Field. The Laird of Ormiston and his nephew survived longer, and were tried and executed in 1573. Bothwell himself, after his flight from Carberry Hill, made his way first to Orkney and thence to Scandinavia, where he had the misfortune to encounter the powerful kinsmen of an abandoned mistress. He was imprisoned in Denmark, and King Frederick II held a consultation on what was to be done with him. Moray's request for his extradition was refused, and Frederick's treatment of him was similar to Elizabeth's treatment of Mary: Frederick made no formal decision on Bothwell's fate, but transferred him from prison to prison, gradually increasing the rigour of his incarceration. Incapable of enduring isolation and inactivity, Bothwell sank into insanity and died in 1578.[84]

The Earl of Moray, acknowledged as 'The Good Regent', was assassinated with the connivance of Archbishop Hamilton in 1570, and was succeeded by the Earl of Lennox, who thus attained his old ambition, though perhaps following upon too many sorrows to afford him much pleasure. He was assassinated in turn in 1571, but his short regency was marked by the capture of Dumbarton Castle from the Queen's partisans, a brilliant feat of arms achieved by Thomas Crawford of Jordanhill, who led a small force up the precipitous rock and broke in on the astonished garrison with cries of 'A Darnley! A Darnley!' Archbishop Hamilton was captured in the castle and hanged, having been linked with the murders of both Darnley and Moray. Edinburgh Castle, the last fortress held by partisans of Mary Queen of Scots, was captured by Morton, now Regent in his turn, in 1573. Its defenders were Kirkaldy of Grange, who had transferred his allegiance to the Queen's party, who was hanged, and Lethington, who was believed to have committed suicide. The general slaughter omitted two deserving candidates in Archibald Douglas and Sir James Balfour, whose nefarious lives were ended by natural causes.

The last and most spectacular trial for Darnley's murder was that of the Regent Morton in 1581. Accused of being 'art and part' in the murder of Darnley, he denied the charge, but admitted foreknowledge and concealment. He confessed that on his return to Scotland early in January 1567 he had been met by Bothwell and Lethington at Whittinghame Castle, the home of a kinsman, and invited to participate in the plot against the life of Darnley. He had declined on the ground that having been pardoned for his part in one murder (that of Rizzio) he did not want to be involved in another, unless he were shown the Queen's written approval of it. His cousin Archibald Douglas approached Mary to request her handwrit, which she naturally refused. Though Morton declined to take further action, Archibald Douglas probably represented him and the rest of the aggrieved Rizzio murderers at the Kirk o' Field enterprise, and may have been Darnley's actual murderer. In a sense, Morton and the Queen were in the same position, for as a result of Archibald Douglas's mediation, both were aware that the plot against Darnley was being formulated, and both were silent. Morton was tried at the instigation of Darnley's cousin Esmé Stuart d'Aubigny, who arrived from France in 1579, to become the favourite of the young James VI, who created him Duke of Lennox.[85] It was so many years since he had met his young cousin Henry Darnley in France and taken him hunting in the forests around La Verrerie that it is unlikely that a personal feeling for vengeance was uppermost in his mind; he was an ambitious man, whose own rise to power was blocked by Morton, but vengeance provided the pretext to destroy the Regent. The total of victims was now almost complete.

When Mary Queen of Scots went to the block in England on 8 February 1587, the accusation of complicity in Darnley's murder had not been revived. She was condemned to death for complicity in plots against the life and throne of Elizabeth. She protested her innocence and claimed that she died a martyr for the Catholic faith. However, when her body was buried in Peterborough Cathedral, the Dean of Peterborough, who preached the funeral oration, touched upon the old accusation in terms that expressed no doubts concerning it:

> The day [of her execution] being very fair did, as it were, show favour from Heaven, and commended the justice. The eighth day of February that judgment was repaid home to her, which the tenth day of the same month, twenty years past, she measured to her husband.[86]

After James VI had succeeded to the throne of England he achieved the remarkable feat of rehabilitating both his parents. An engraving of them by Elstracke, on sale in Jacobean London, shows them standing side by side, as they might have appeared at the court of Scotland; the caption beneath the figures gives the dates of their deaths, without mentioning how either of them died. Darnley was left in peace in his grave in the Abbey of Holyrood;[87] but Mary Queen of Scots was exhumed from hers in Peterborough Cathedral, and reburied in Westminster Abbey, beneath a beautiful effigy in white marble. Nearby, Margaret Lennox was given a tomb only a little less splendid, with an alabaster effigy painted in polychrome and adorned with a gilded coronet. Elaborate inscriptions enumerate her royal relations. A statue of Darnley, in armour and an ermine-lined mantle, kneels as a 'weeper' on the plinth of his mother's tomb, with a statue of his brother behind him. Above his head is suspended a crown, symbolic of his royal status; below him an inscription recounts his brief kingship and his tragic fate. He has his place among the monuments that commemorate the triumph of his family's ambition, attained at the cost of so much individual suffering.

EPILOGUE

The life of Darnley was brief and tempestuous, and he died unloved and unlamented by anyone except his parents. His existence, in the words of one of his son's biographers, was 'eminently miserable'.[1] This was certainly true of his last year, and in particular of his last months, during which his misery must have been extreme. But it is a judgement which takes no account of Darnley's childhood, spent in the tranquil splendours of Temple Newsam, which was probably unusually happy and untroubled for one so near the succession; nor of his adolescence which, with his secret journeys to France, was a time of excitement and hope. Ambition is admittedly a painful emotion if unfulfilled; but Darnley experienced the pleasure and the triumph of fulfilment, before it was soured by disappointment when the Crown Matrimonial was denied him. The resentment, caused by denial of what he conceived as his right, and his continuing obsession with it, wrought immeasurable damage to his marriage and to his character, and led him to actions that were ultimately as self-destructive as they were criminal. He passed so rapidly from promising boyhood to dissolute youth and thence to criminal manhood that it was easy to forget the attractive and accomplished impression he had fleetingly given. His actions were so deplorable that he seemed to deserve the condemnation most historians accorded him.

But one contemporary, writing shortly after his death, delivered a balanced judgement, which recorded his good qualities as well as his vices. The continuator of John Knox's History wrote:

[He was] a Prince of great lineage, both by mother and father. He was of a comely stature, and none was like unto him within this island. He died under the age of one and twenty years; prompt and ready for all games and sports, much given to hawking and hunting, and running of horses, and likewise playing on the lute, and also to Venus' chamber. He was liberal enough; he could write and dictate well; but he was somewhat given to wine, and much feeding, and likewise to inconstancy; and proud beyond measure, and therefore contemned all others. He had learned to dissemble well enough, being from his youth misled up in popery . . .[2]

Most of this, from evidence previously adduced, seems to have been true, except that Darnley was singularly incapable of dissembling; but dissembling belonged so much to the traditional character of a 'papist' that the Protestant chronicler felt compelled to include it as an aspect of his portrayal. Besides giving him credit for the agreeable characteristics of being sporting, musical and generous, it is noteworthy that the author remembered that 'he could write and dictate well', to which his letters bear witness. Despite his degenerate behaviour, the good effects of his education had not disappeared. Whenever his spoken words are quoted by diplomat or memoirist, or reported in correspondence, it is obvious that he spoke lucidly and eloquently, which can never be the characteristics of a complete fool.

He was described by the men who plotted his death as 'a young fool and proud tyrant', which is reminiscent of the description of his maternal grandfather, Archibald, Earl of Angus as 'a young witless fool'; yet Angus matured sufficiently to become capable of governing Scotland – tyrannically, in the opinion of his stepson James V. A similar development of Darnley's character may be imagined, if ever he had governed Scotland for his son.

In the last weeks of his life, however egotistical and obsessed with his ambitions he had been, Darnley apparently began to have some awareness of his faults, if his appeal to Mary Queen of Scots was truthfully reported by Thomas Crawford: 'May not a man of my age, for lack of counsel, of which I am very destitute, fall twice or thrice, and yet repent and be chastized by experience?'[3] These words suggest that he acknowledged his need for amendment, even if the Queen had been too much wounded by his conduct to credit the possibility of a change of heart. Perhaps it is not necessary to see him as beyond redemption, but rather as a prodigal who might have redeemed himself, given time. Unfortunately, through the ill will of his enemies, which he had done much to deserve, he was not given time; nor, if the diagnoses of medical experts were correct, might he have been given time by his disease.

Darnley is a tragic figure as the victim of a brutal and ruthless crime; but he is even more tragic as a figure of unfulfilled promise.

APPENDIX

Note on Unpublished Verses
Concerning the Murder of Darnley

The Calendar of State Papers (Scottish) Volume 2 No. 507 details a ballad on the death of Darnley, published in May 1567 by Robert Lekprevik of Edinburg, under the heading 'Heir followis ane ballat declaring the nobill and gude inclinatioun of our king'.[1] It is described in the Calendar as 'Three columns of doggerel'. No doubt it has remained unpublished because it is indeed of little literary merit; but it is of great interest as an example of propaganda verse. Written after the death of Darnley and before the fall of Mary Queen of Scots, it represents the tilt of public opinion which played so influential a part in her downfall, and demonstrates the skill with which propaganda was deployed by her enemies. In this verse Darnley is shown as an entirely praiseworthy young man, the victim of her treachery, malice and wickedness.

The anonymous author of the poem opens with a well-worn literary device whereby the poet has a chance encounter with the person who tells the story embodied in the poetic narrative:

To Edinburgh about vi houris at morne
As I was passand pansand out the way,
Ane bony boy was soir makand his mone
His sory sang was oche and wallaway
That ever I sould byde to se that day –
Ane King at evin with sceptur, sword and crown,
At morne bot ane deformit lump of clay.

[To Edinburgh, near six o'clock in the morn
As I was going, thinking on the way,

A bonny boy was sadly making his moan,
His sorry song was 'Ochone and wellaway
That ever I should live to see that day –
At eve a King, with sceptre, sword and crown,
At morning but a deformed lump of clay!']

The 'bonny boy' went on to lament the King's murder, and to praise his character and his prowess in feats of arms:

His cruell murther ye will call monsterous
For in meiknes he did all men excell,
And unto no man was he odious.
To meet his marrow he was audatious
On sturdie steid with craftie feat of weir.
Mars favourit him as fair Ascanius,
Aeneas' sone that weill a steid could steir.
In deidis he soulde have bene lyke Deiphobus
Had feinzeit Fourtoun favourit him to King;
Or Theseus or gentill Julius,
In gentill featis servand for ane King.
Dartis about him swiftlie could he fling,
And rin ane rais and shortlie turne ane steid;
Cunning of crossbow [?cutthrot] and culvering
And flaine let flie with bow in tyme of neid . . .

[His cruel murder you will call monstrous,
For in meekness he did all men excel,
And unto no man was he odious.
To meet his match he was audacious
On sturdy steed with crafty feats of war;
Mars favoured him as fair Ascanius,
Aeneas' son, that well a steed could steer.
In deeds he should have been like Deiphobus
Had fickle Fortune favoured him as King –
Or [like] Theseus or gentle Julius [Caesar]
In gentlemanlike feats, fit for a King.
Darts about him swiftly he could fling,
And run a race, or neatly turn a steed.

Cunning with crossbow he was . . . and with culverin
And arrow could speed from bow in time of need.]

But, the narrator went on, the Queen's unkindness to him caused
him to 'be sad and pance' – to be unhappy and to think sombre
thoughts:

Yet nevir did scho se his maik in France . . .
Not her first spous for all his greit puissance
In portratour and game might be his peir.

[Yet never did she see his like in France . . .
Not her first spouse, for all his mighty power
In appearance or at sport might equal him.]

Darnley is then praised in somewhat confused language for his
prowess as a musician and singer, a Latin scholar, a hunter and a
falconer. The narrator then returns to his intellectual attainments:

With Romaine hand* he could well leid ane pen
And storyis wryte of auld antiquitie;
Nobill himself and nobill of ingyne,
And lovit weill concord and unitie.
He swoumit in the fluidis of poetrie
And did exerce the science liberall,
The facund phrase did use of oratrie.
His gude ingyne was rycht celestiall.
In pulchritude to Paris perigall
With browis brent and twinkland cristell eine
Off face formois and vult heroicall,
He mycht have been ane marrow to ane Quene.

[With the Roman hand he well could use a pen
And stories write of old antiquity.
Noble himself and of noble intellect,
Well-loved by him were concord and unity.

* Italic handwriting.

He plunged into the flood of poetry,
Had expertise in science liberal,
And used the fertile phrases of oratory;
His intellect was indeed celestial.
In handsomeness he was Paris's equal,
With his straight brows and eyes like bright crystal,
With facial beauty and heroic height,
To be counted a Queen's equal, well he might!]

Having described Darnley as such a paragon of charm and ability, the narrator suddenly turns to the moment of the Queen's departure from Kirk o' Field on the night preceding Darnley's death, and her gift of a ring as her pledge of her promise to sleep with him the next night. It was a gesture which, if fictitious, entered popular mythology, and, if true, was a gift to anti-Marian propaganda:

At ten o'clock on Sunday at even
Quhen Dalila and Bothwell bad gudnycht
Off hir finger fals she threw ane ring
And said my Lord ane taikin I you plycht . . .

[At ten o'clock at night on Sunday evening
When Delilah and Bothwell bade goodnight,
Off her unfaithful finger she drew a ring
And said, 'My Lord, a token I you plight . . .']

As a betrayer, a murderer's paramour, and an accomplice in murder, the Queen was characterized as Delilah, the betrayer of Samson, Jezebel, the Queen and accomplice of Ahab, and Clytemnestra, the murderer of her husband Agamemnon. Vengeance upon her is demanded from every partisan of the houses of Douglas and Lennox:

Now every Dowglas of ane hartsum mynde
Think on Dame Margaret sum tyme in the Tower,
And of young Charles, prudent of ingyne,
I pray God lat them se a joyfull houre.

[Now every Douglas of courageous mind
Think of Dame Margaret, once prisoner in the Tower,
And of young Charles, so prudently inclined,
I pray God let them see a joyful hour.[2]]

That hour would be when Darnley was finally avenged.

The second unpublished poem is a lament for his death, in twenty-four
stanzas of five lines each, entitled 'the Complaint of Scotland'. It is in
the form of a woman's lament for her dead love: Scotland (or her tutel-
ary deity, Scotia) laments Darnley, and exhorts the lords of Scotland
to avenge him. It is very repetitive, but four of the twenty-four stanzas
will convey the flavour of it:

Adew all glaidnes, sport and play
Adew fair well baith nycht and day
All thing that may make mirrie cheir
Bot sich rycht sair in hart and say
    Allace to graif is gone my deir . . .

Bot lang allace I may complaine
Befoir I find my deir againe
To me was faithfull and inteir
As turtill on me tuke paine
    Allace to graif is gone my deir . . .

Revenge his deith with ane assent
With ane hart, will, mynde and intent,
In faithfull freindship perseveir
God will you favour and thame shent
    Be work or word that slew my deir . . .

With sobbing sych I to you send
This my complaint with dew commend,
Desyring you all without feir
Me pure Scotland to defend,
    Since now to graif is gone my deir.

[Adieu all gladness, sport and play,
Adieu, farewell both night and day
All things that may make merry cheer,
But sorely sigh in heart and say
   Alas, to the grave is gone my dear.

But long alas may I complain
Before I find my dear again,
Who faithful was beyond compare
As turtle-dove who bore my pain;
   Alas to the grave is gone my dear . . .

Revenge his death with one assent,
With one heart, mind, will, and intent,
In faithful friendship persevere,
God will you favour, shame them send
   By work or word that slew my dear . . .

With sobbing sighs I to you send
This my complaint, with due commend [commendation]
Desiring you, without all fear,
Me, poor Scotland, to defend,
   Since now to the grave is gone my dear.[3]]

The most fulsome and laudatory of all the poems of lament composed for Darnley is inscribed on the Darnley Memorial picture. Among the many inscriptions on the picture the only ones readily legible are the prayers of the infant James VI, The Earl and Countess of Lennox and Lord Charles Stuart, which are inscribed on the scrolls issuing from their mouths and billowing around their heads. But within the imaginary chapel represented in the picture, on the wall directly above and behind the effigy of Darnley, and below the saltire banner, is a *trompe l'oeil* representation of a mural tablet with a Latin verse inscribed on it:

In interitum excellentissimi Henrici Scotorum Regis
carmen heroicum.

Quem iam depictum videas hac mole iacentem
Grande Britanorum quondam resplenduit astrum
En heros Darnleius erat flos Deorum
Qui modo Regina rutilans uxore Maria
Scotorum celebrum Rex est memorabilis ortus
Sacrato Britonum de stemmate Regum
Indole magnifica venerandi cultor honesti
Ingenio praestans linguarum numine fusus
Flosculus eloquii literis insigniter altus
Musicus armipotens animosus mitis in omnes
Innumero celsae florebat munere mentis
Corporis en compes quantus quamque beatus
Vultus membrorum vario superante decore
Emicuit certe coelestis imaginis instar
Extitit heu vitae brevis heu finisque dolendi
Quem sors annis uno tulit esse viginti
Et pater infantis fuerat cum principis almi
Spe Rex eximia mira pietate maritus
Occidit o tristis sors conspirante Maria
Coniuge Regina truculento volnere caesus
Occidit hoc rutilum lumen sed corpore tantum
Mente Deo vivit longe quoque vivit honore.

HEROIC POEM UPON THE DEATH OF THE MOST
EXCELLENT HENRY KING OF SCOTS

He whom you may see depicted lying upon this bier
Once shone in splendour, the bright star of the Britons.
Behold, he was great Darnley, darling of the Gods,
Who but lately, resplendent with Queen Mary his wife,
Arose as illustrious King of the famous Scots.
A luminary of the sacred line of British Kings,
Magnificent in nature, a worshipper of honour,
Pre-eminent in mind, filled with the power of language,
A very flower of eloquence, and remarkably learned,
Musical, skilled in arms, courageous, gentle to all,

He blossomed with uncounted mental gifts.
Behold how superbly formed was his body,
How fair his face, how graceful all his limbs!
He shone with the radiance of a celestial being.
But alas, he had a short life and a sorrowful end.
He whom Fate had brought to twenty-one years of age,
When he had fathered a child, a noble Prince,
As a King of great promise and a husband of rare devotion
He was slain, O unhappy fate! (Mary the Queen
His wife conspiring against him), slain with a savage wound!
Slain was this shining light – but only his body –
His soul dwells with God, and long lives his honour.*

On the version of the Darnley Memorial picture in the Royal Collection the references to Mary's participation in Darnley's death were
obliterated, presumably at the desire of James VI and I, in his attempt
to rehabilitate his mother's reputation. On the Goodwood version of
the picture the inscriptions remained undamaged, but they were non-
theless extremely difficult to decipher, not least because of the
inclusion of many sixteenth century manuscript contractions, and
because of later clumsy restoration of the lettering. However, the
inscriptions were faithfully transcribed by Vertue in his engraving of
the picture.

The verse was transcribed by D. Hay Fleming and W. A. Craigie,
with the assistance of Vertue's engraving; the original translation was
by W. A. Cragie.⁴ Who was the author of the Latin verse? Given his
close connection with the Earl of Lennox, and his animus against
Mary Queen of Scots, surely the most likely candidate for authorship
was George Buchanan.

* English version by CB.

NOTES AND REFERENCES

Abbreviations:

BL – British Library
CSP – Calendar of State Papers
DNB – Dictionary of National Biography
PRO – Public Record Office
SP – State Papers

References to printed books will cite the full name of the author and title of the book in the first reference, e.g. Gordon Donaldson, *Mary Queen of Scots*; in subsequent references this will appear as Donaldson, op. cit. In the case of books with long titles, a short title will be given in the Notes and References, and the full title will appear in the Bibliography.

PROLOGUE

1. There is a biographical essay on Darnley in George Chalmers, *Life of Mary Queen of Scots* (1818), and another in William Fraser, *The Lennox* (1874). The former is very inaccurate; the latter is well documented.
2. Antonia Fraser, *Mary Queen of Scots and the Historians*, Royal Stuart Papers VII (Royal Stuart Society, 1974), p. 1.
3. Jenny Wormald, *Mary Queen of Scots: a Study in Failure*, (1988), pp. 12–13. In the 1962 printed catalogue Dr Wormald counted a mere 455 entries.
4. For an account of the opposed delineations of Mary's character see J. E. Phillips, *Images of a Queen: Mary Stuart in Sixteenth Century Literature* (1964); Ian B. Cowan, *The Enigma of Mary Stuart* (1971); Antonia Fraser, *Mary Queen of Scots and the Historians* (1974).
5. The most striking contemporary example of the portrayal of Mary as saint and martyr is in a verse by the Jesuit poet Saint Robert Southwell:

Alive a Queene, now dead I am a Sainte;
  Once Mary calld, my name nowe Martyr is;
From earthly raigne debarred by restraint,
  In liew thereof I raigne in heavenly blisse . . .

See Cowan, op. cit., p. 212.

6. The progress of Marian studies during the seventeenth, eighteenth and nineteenth centuries can be followed in the works previously listed, by Cowan and Fraser, and also in Gordon Donaldson, *Mary Queen of Scots*, Chapter Eight, 'The Continuing Debate'
7. P. Hume Brown, *George Buchanan, Humanist and Reformer*, p. 194.
8. *The Lennox Narratives*, Mahon, *Mary Queen of Scots, a Study of the Lennox Narratives*, p. 127
9. Agnes Strickland, *Lives of the Queens of Scotland*, Vol. V, pp. 198–9.
10. T. F. Henderson, *Mary Queen of Scots*, Vol. I, pp. 306–7. The ellipsis represents the omission of a digression on the opinion that Darnley, Moray and Mary were all fair in colouring; but this is incorrect, as Moray was dark, Mary was auburn, and Darnley was blond or reddish-blond. The reference to a 'heart of wax' is to the controversial Casket Letter II, here assumed to be a genuine letter from Mary Queen of Scots to Bothwell: '. . . if I had not proofe of his hart [heart] to be as waxe and that myne weare not as a dyamant, no stroke but comming from your hand, could make me but to have pitie of him'. See CSP (Scottish), Vol. II, Appendix II, p. 724.
11. Stefan Zweig, *The Queen of Scots*, pp. 92–4.
12. Karl Pearson, *The Skull and Portraits of Henry Stewart, Lord Darnley, Biometrika*, Vol. XX pt I (July 1928), p. 52 (offprint, bound as volume).
13. Antonia Fraser, *Mary Queen of Scots*, pp. 220–3.
14. Ibid, pp. 222–3.
15. Edith Sitwell, *The Queens and the Hive*, p. 206.
16. Donaldson, op. cit., p. 80.

CHAPTER ONE: DANGEROUS INHERITANCE

1. Captain Borthwick to the Comte de Noailles, French Ambassador in England, 1559. See Strickland, op. cit., Vol. II, pp. 362–3.
2. Ralph A. Griffiths and Roger S. Thomas, *The Making of the Tudor Dynasty*, p. 164.
3. J. P. Hodges, *The Nature of the Lion*, p. 41.

4. Strickland, op. cit., Vol. I, p. 80; Henry Ellis, *Original Letters*, Vol. I, Series I.

5. This was Gavin Douglas, Bishop of Dunkeld, translator of the Aeneid into Scots, and one of the leading poets of his time.

6. This marriage had lasted eighty-six days when Louis died on 1 January 1515.

7. Herbert Maxwell, *History of the House of Douglas*, Vol. 2, p. 72.

8. Strickland, op. cit., Vol. 2, p. 275.

9. Maxwell, op. cit., p. 76.

10. Albany's sister-in-law, Madeleine de la Tour, married Lorenzo de Medici, Duke of Urbino. Their daughter Catherine de' Medici was the ward of Pope Clement VII. Albany later suggested her as a bride for James V – an interesting historical 'might have been'. The link with the papacy enabled Albany to help Margaret gain her divorce.

11. The murderer was said to have been Sir James Hamilton of Finnart, known as the 'Bastard of Arran', an illegitimate son of the first Earl of Arran, and therefore a half-brother of the Governor Arran. Despite his notoriously violent character he was a man of culture and ability who later became a favourite of James V.

12. Captain Strangeways to Cardinal Wolsey, 26/1/29, cit. Strickland, op. cit., Vol. 2, p. 279. Wolsey was godfather to Lady Margaret Douglas.

13. Thomas Howard, second Duke of Norfolk, was born in 1444 and died in 1524, an unusually long life for this period. His first wife was Elizabeth Tilney of Ashford Thorpe, Norfolk; his second was her cousin, Agnes Tilney. Lord Thomas Howard was his eighth child and second son by his second wife. See *Dictionary of National Biography; Who's Who in History*, Vol. 2, which contains a simplified genealogical table of the Howards; Strickland., op. cit., Vol. 2, p. 284.

14. Antonia Fraser, *The Six Wives of Henry VIII*, p. 235.

15. Strickland, op. cit., Vol. 2, pp. 288–9.

16. Ibid.

17. BL Add. MS 17492 (The Devonshire Manuscript), fol. 26.

18. Ibid, fol. 28.

19. Ibid, fol. 29.

20. Cit. Strickland, op. cit., Vol. 2, pp. 292–3.

21. BL Add. MS 17492, fol. 88. In this poem Margaret imagines herself addressing the friends and relations gathered around her deathbed, and saying to her father Angus:

Therffor swet father, I you pray
  Ber thys my deth with pacyence,
And tourment nat your herys gray

But frely pardoun myn offence . . .

22. BL Cott. Vespasian F xiii; Strickland, op. cit., Vol. 2, pp. 296–7.
23. The poem is quoted by Strickland, op. cit., Vol. 2, p. 300, who also states that Lord Thomas Howard's mother, Agnes, dowager Duchess of Norfolk, requested leave to have her son's body for burial. This was granted, but she 'buried her son so privately that no notation exists of the place of his interment'. Ibid, p. 301.
24. BL Cott. Vespasian F xiii: 'And my Lord, as for resort [visitors at Syon] I promise you I have none, except it be gentlewomen that cometh to see me . . . if any resort of men had come, it would neither have become me to have seen them nor have kept them company, being a maid as I am'. But it was apparently perfectly becoming that she should have brought several men servants.
25. Fraser, *Six Wives of Henry VIII*, p. 334.
26. Mary Howard was the widow of Henry VIII's illegitimate son Henry Fitzroy, Duke of Richmond, who had died on 22 July 1536.
27. *Letters and Papers of Henry VIII*, Vol. 16, pt 2, p. 613. Privy Council to Cranmer and others; also Sir Ralph Sadler to Cranmer and others, 12/11/41. Ibid, p. 615.
28. Katharine Parr was the widow of Lord Latimer, who had died on 2 March 1543. The King began to pay court to her only two weeks after Latimer's death. Fraser, op. cit., pp. 366–7.
29. Berault Stuart was a soldier and diplomat of high reputation. He had contributed a body of soldiers to the force that Henry of Richmond led to victory at Bosworth in 1485. In 1508 he visited England in person, and was received by Henry VII with great honour, as one who had helped to ensure his victory. Griffiths and Thomas, op. cit., pp. 130–1, 174. He then went on to the court of James IV, and died in Scotland.
30. More detailed histories of this family may be found in Lady Elizabeth Cust, *Some Account of the Stuarts of Aubigny in France* (1891); and Eileen Cassavetti, *The Lion and the Lilies: the Stuarts and France* (1977).
31. Lindsay of Pitscottie, *History of Scotland*, edition of 1778, cit. Fraser, *The Lennox*, Vol. 1, p. 369.
32. According to England's ambassador in Scotland, Sir Ralph Sadler, Angus's brother Sir George Douglas called Arran 'the most wavering person in the world'. Sadler to English Council, 31/3/43, *L and P Henry VIII*, Vol. 18, pt 1, p. 189. But the editor of this volume, James Gairdner, comments, 'There was a curious agreement everywhere to disparage Arran's mental endowments . . . [but] . . . It was not that the Governor was weak, though perhaps he did not mind being so

considered. The state of Scotland was weak and he could but temporise . . .' Ibid, Introduction, pp. xxxii–xxxiii.

33. Fraser, *The Lennox*, Vol. 1, p. 370. Angus had no option but to 'remit' the matter to Henry VIII, since Margaret was in his hands.

34. Ibid, p. 371. At this period 'Majesty' and 'Highness' were forms of address used interchangeably.

35. Ibid, Vol. 1, p. 347. Much of this letter is about a dispute between Lennox and the Bishop of Caithness, which he reported with great fury, though the quarrel was apparently short-lived.

36. Cust, op. cit., pp. 72–3; Maitland Club Miscellany, Vol. 1, pp. 214–6.

37. Fraser, op. cit., Vol. 1, pp. 377–8.

38. Ibid, p. 378.

39. Strickland, op. cit., p. 317; Frederick Madden, *Privy Purse Expenses of the Princess Mary*, pp. 175, 177, 193.

40. Strickland, op. cit., Vol. 2, p. 320.

41. Madden, op. cit., p. 198.

42. This brass does not appear in Mill Stephenson's *List of Monumental Brasses in the British Isles* (1964); possibly it no longer exists.

CHAPTER TWO: DESTINED FOR KINGSHIP

1. John Jewel, Bishop of Salisbury to Peter Martyr Vermigli, 7/2/62, Zurich Letters, Vol. 1, p. 125.

2. F. W. Crossley, 'A Temple Newsam Inventory, 1565', *Yorkshire Archaeological Journal* XXV (1918–19), pp. 91–2. Crossley calls the original grantee Mary de Santo Paulo, and her husband Aymer de Valencia, and does not mention the Countess's lasting claim to fame as the foundress of Pembroke College, Cambridge.

3. *L and P Henry VIII*, Vol. 19, pt 1, pp. 627–8. Many other properties were also granted to the Lennoxes, including the manor of Settrington, previously the property of Sir Francis Bigod, executed for his part in the Pilgrimage of Grace. Settrington became the Lennoxes' favourite home after Temple Newsam, but their whole estate comprised some thirty-five properties, manors and farms, and 'appurtenances of the premises'.

4. *Guide to Temple Newsam* (1989), p. 3.

5. Edmund Spenser, *The Faerie Queene*, Book 1, Canto IV. A description of the House of Pride, a faerie palace or allegorical construct, in turn deriving from the 'prodigy house' of the period.

6. The present park is by Capability Brown, and it now prevents the house from being engulfed by the encroaching suburbs of Leeds.

7. Richard Fawcett, 'The Early Tudor House [Temple Newsam] in the light of Recent Excavations', *Leeds Arts Calendar*, No. 70 (1972), pp. 5–11.

8. Crossley, op. cit. The Inventory is, of course, open to various readings, and others may disagree with my interpretation of it.

9. BL Harleian 6815, 'Orders of service belonging to the degrees of a duke, a marquess, and an erle used in there owne howses', an unpublished manuscript of household ordinances; Mark Girouard, *Life in the English Country House* (1978), pp. 46–50. Girouard's account of aristocratic life at this period also draws on other books of household ordinances, but the Harleian manuscript is the one most relevant to the life lived at Temple Newsam.

10. No attempt was made to restore them to legitimacy; it was too complex an issue. Mary had been bastardized by the annulment of her parents' marriage (an annulment that she had refused to acknowledge); Elizabeth had been conceived before that annulment, and was supposed to be legitimized by Henry's subsequent marriage to Anne Boleyn. She was bastardized once again when that marriage was annulled before Anne's execution. Most people, whatever their religious persuasion, saw that whatever legal contortions Henry had gone through, Mary was legitimate and Elizabeth illegitimate. Henry married Jane Seymour as a widower, so Edward VI was indisputably legitimate. Elizabeth succeeded as the strongest claimant, not as the legitimist one.

11. Strickland, op. cit., Vol. 2, p. 320. The author's dry comment was 'Such profession was sufficient to make those predict who knew Henry VIII best, that he would, by every means in his power, prevent his niece, Lady Margaret, from taking her natural place in the regal succession'.

12. Thomas Bishop to Sir William Cecil, 9/2/62, *Selections of Unpublished Manuscripts*, ed. Joseph Stevenson, Maitland Club (1837), p. 98.

13. Strickland, op. cit., Vol. 2, pp. 326–7.

14. William Fraser, *The Douglas Book*, Vol. 4, p. 171.

15. Lennox to Somerset, 27/6/48. He wrote, 'If it shall please your Grace that I may have the keeping of the Master of Morton and the Laird of Glenbervie with the others, I shall answer [be responsible] for the sure keeping of them'. Cit. Strickland, op. cit., Vol. 2, p. 331.

16. The total number of Glenbervie's children was ten, of whom, unusually, nine survived. He had two wives, Agnes Keith, daughter of the second Earl Marishal, and Elizabeth Irvine of Drum. Despite his poor health he survived until 1570. Fraser, op. cit. Vol. 2 pp. 117–18.

17. Morton and his wife had ten children, seven of whom died young. The Countess survived her husband, and at his death in 1581 she was declared by a jury to have been insane for the past twenty-two years. This suggests an unendurably horrible married life for them both. Poss-

ibly she suffered from post-natal dementia, and with endless childbearing, never had a chance to recover. Ibid, Vol. 2, p. 321.

18. He was promoted to the benefice by Governor Arran and the Privy Council on 13/12/46. Ibid, Vol. 2, p. 253.
19. 'He was . . . prompt and ready for all games and sports; much given to hawking and hunting, and running of horses . . .' John Knox (continuator). *Works of Knox*, ed. David Laing (Bannatyne Club, reprint, 1966), Vol. 2, p. 551.
20. BL Royal MS 18a xxxviii; also *Bannatyne Miscellany* (1827) pp. 7–18. This has often been quoted in works on Highland dress, because Elder called the Highlanders 'Redshanks', and explained that this nickname had arisen as a result of their making themselves buskins of red deerskin.
21. BL Cott. Vespasian F III fol. 378: also Ellis, *Original Letters* (1827), Vol. 2, pp. 249–50.
22. Sidney Lee, 'Sir Thomas Wyatt', DNB, Vol. XXI, p. 1103.
23. Tissue was woven of gold and silk threads, and is sometimes called 'cloth of gold of tissue'. The silk might be of different colours, so the tissue might be purple/gold, green/gold, white/gold, or any colour combination. Cloth of gold was woven of gold thread and of gold thread and gold-coloured silk, or occasionally of fine gold wire only. Both these fabrics were worn principally by royalty. C. Willet Cunnington and Phyllis Cunnington, *Handbook of English Costume in the Sixteenth Century*, pp. 192, 204.
24. One of them was a valuable Venetian instrument of 'emery' – presumably ebony, used as a veneer or inlay. Strickland, op. cit., Vol. 2, p. 344.
25. John Elder, *The Copie of a Letter sent in to Scotlande*, (London, 1555), no pagination.
26. Ibid.
27. *The Apophthegmata Regis* were recorded by Peter Young on the flyleaves of the book in which he listed the books collected for the young James VI. BL Add. MSS 34275; published in George F. Warner, 'The Library of James VI', *Miscellany of the Scottish History Society*, Vol. 1, pp. lxxii–lxxv.
28. George Clement Whittick, 'Valerius Maximus', *Oxford Classical Dictionary* (1949), p. 935.
29. BL Egerton 2805 fol. 7. To Charles IX of France, *vide infra* Chapter Seven.
30. Lady Margaret Beaufort, after the accession of Henry VII, adopted the signature 'Margaret R', to define her role as Queen Mother, though she was in fact only the King's mother, and had never been a Queen. Perhaps Margaret Lennox would have felt justified in doing the same.

31. Fraser, *The Douglas Book*, Vol. 4, pp. 173–4; Strickland, op. cit., Vol. 2, p. 336.
32. At a pageant held at the Palace of Les Tournelles, Paris, a Latin verse was displayed together with the arms, and was translated as follows:

> The Armes of Marie Queen Dolphines of France
> The nobillest lady in earth for till [to] advance
> Of Scotland Quene, of Ingland also,
> Of Ireland also God hath providit so.

It was not a message that Queen Elizabeth could either forget or forgive. BL Cott. Caligula BX 16 fol. 18 – a beautiful coloured illumination.

CHAPTER THREE: 'YONDER LONG LAD'

1. Sir James Melville, *Memoirs*, ed. Gordon Donaldson (1969), pp. 3–6.
2. James Laver, *Nostradamus* (1942), p. 51 (his translation of verse, p. 58), this trans. CB; Theophilus de Garancières (trans.), *The True Prophecies of Michael Nostradamus* (London, 1672), p. 25.
3. Strickland, op. cit., Vol. 2, p. 363; Fraser, *The Lennox*, Vol. 1, p. 469.
4. Cassavetti, op. cit., p. 51. The author had access to the archives of La Verrerie and has provided fresh information on the Stuarts of Aubigny.
5. Fraser, op. cit., Vol. 1, pp. 388–90.
6. PRO SP/12/23 No. 14; Deposition of William Forbes; also cit. Strickland, op. cit., Vol. 2, p. 367.
7. This was Garancières, op. cit.
8. *Les Propheties de M. Michel Nostredame* (Lyons, Macé Bonhomme MDLV), containing three 'centuries' and fifty-three quatrains of the fourth, and an introductory epistle to Nostradamus's son, Cesar.
9. PRO SP/12/23 No. 14.
10. What Nostradamus had written was as follows:

> Le sang du juste a Londre fera faute
> Brulez par foudres de vingt trois les six
> La dame antique cherra de place haute
> De mesme secte plusieurs seront occis
>
> [The blood of the just shall be required of London
> Burnt by fire in three times twenty and six
> The aged lady shall fall from her high place
> And many of the same sect shall be destroyed]

After 1666 commentators on Nostradamus decided that the verse referred to the Great Fire of London, the blood of the just being that of Charles I and 'la dame antique' being St Paul's Cathedral (because Nostradamus referred to the Church, or a church, as 'the lady' – the female figure of Ecclesia being the allegorical personification of the Church – a typical Nostradamian obfuscation). Lallart would have regarded one of the Henrician Catholic martyrs as the 'just' whose blood demanded vengeance, and assumed that the heretic Elizabeth would fall from her high place when she was a 'dame antique'. He could not have seen any significance in 'vingt trois les six', unless he had imagined it to refer to the age of 'la dame antique' and not to the date of the event. (Nostradamus made things very difficult by referring to '66 and omitting to say to which century it belonged!) The 'plusieurs' Lallart might have supposed to have been some of Elizabeth's fellow heretics, whereas later commentators identified them as several of the city churches destroyed in the Great Fire, which belonged to the same 'sect' as St Paul's. Forbes's contempt for Lallart's ingenious interpretation sprung from his own belief that the prophecy referred to the destruction of the steeple of St Paul's early in Elizabeth's reign (1561), and that the 'plusieurs' were 'IX of my Lord Robert's men with divers of the Queen's guards ... suddenly struck dead in St James's Park'.

11. Laver, op. cit., p. 66; Garancières, op. cit., p. 419; this trans. CB.
12. Louis A. Barbe, 'The Song of Mary Stuart', in *Byways of Scottish History* (1912), pp. 79–90; Caroline Bingham, 'The Poems of Mary Queen of Scots', Royal Stuart Papers X (1976), pp. 2–4.
13. Wormald, op. cit., pp. 102–4.
14. Strickland, op. cit., Vol. 2, p. 369.
15. Knox, *History of the Reformation*, Vol. 1, pp. 354–6; Gordon Donaldson, *Scotland: James V–James VII*, pp. 107–8.
16. Fraser, *Mary Queen of Scots*, p. 131.
17. Claude Paradin, *The Heroical Devices of M. Claudius Paradin*, trans. PS (London, 1591); information on this book in Rosemary Freeman, *English Emblem Books* (1948), p. 62, and Duncan Thomson, *Painting in Scotland 1570–1650*, p. 44.
18. 14/9/61, *vide* D. Hay Fleming, *Mary Queen of Scots* (1897), Itinerary, p. 515.
19. PRO SP/12/23 No. 33, Confession of Arthur Lallart.
20. Thomas Randolph to Sir William Cecil, 7/4/62, 'It is bruited [rumoured] that Lord Darlie [sic] is conveyed to France'. CSP (Scottish), Vol. 1, p. 616.
21. Jasper Ridley, *The Tudor Age* (1988), p. 30.
22. Sir Richard Sackville was first cousin to Anne Boleyn. Though Queen Elizabeth seldom or never spoke of her mother, she maintained close

relations with her maternal kindred, and seems to have trusted them especially in guarding state prisoners.

23. Strickland, op. cit., Vol. 2, p. 384.

24. Ibid, p. 386.

25. The Lieutenant of the Tower to Cecil, 20/9/62, PRO SP/12/24 No. 49

26. The dangerous task of nursing the Queen was undertaken by Lord Robert Dudley's sister, Lady Mary Sidney, who caught the Queen's smallpox and recovered so disfigured that thenceforward she 'chose rather to hide herself . . . than come upon the stage of the world with any manner of disparagement'. Contemporary comment, quoted by Robert Dunlop, 'Sir Henry Sidney', DNB, Vol. XVIII, p. 216.

27. Report on the State of Scotland, trans. of early Latin copy of Barberini MS XXXII 210 (1197), Appendix 1 in Claude Nau, *History of Mary Stuart*, ed. Revd Joseph Stevenson, p. 126.

28. Fraser, *Mary Queen of Scots*, p. 218 fn and ref. note to Roy Strong, *Hans Eworth: A Tudor Artist and His Circle* (exhibition catalogue, 1966), p. 22. Fraser attributes to Strong the statement that the picture is painted in tempera on linen; Strong in the catalogue says that it is in watercolour on fabric. At any rate, it was intended for easy transportation.

29. Knox, op. cit., Bk IV, p. 228.

30. Lord John Stewart was born *c.* 1532, illegitimate son of James V by Catherine Carmichael. On 4 January 1562 he married Lady Jean Hepburn, sister of James Hepburn, fourth Earl of Bothwell, who would become the third husband of Mary Queen of Scots. Shortly after his marriage, Mary granted to Lord John some of the lands of the still-exiled Earl of Lennox, and the title of Lord Darnley. This seems very odd, considering that Lennox was even now petitioning for the restoration of his lands, and that she had already shown some favourable inclination towards his request, in addition to having shown some favour to his son Lord Darnley. Perhaps the explanation is that Henry Darnley's title was a courtesy title, and if his father were restored his official style in Scotland would be 'Master of Lennox' (though, in fact, he was never known by it). Lord John Stewart died in October or November 1563, and his son Francis was briefly known as Lord Darnley; but after the restoration of Lennox he was granted the lordship of Badenoch, and was thereafter called Lord Badenoch. He was named after Mary's first husband, and was her godson. In 1581 James VI created him Earl of Bothwell. He was a turbulent subject, who caused the King a great deal of trouble. He died in exile in 1612, having supported himself during his last years in Naples by 'feats of arms, fortune-telling and necromancy'. *The Scots Peerage*, ed. Sir James Balfour Paul, Vol. II, pp. 168–71.

31. *Register of the Privy Council of Scotland*, Vol. 1, pp. 226–7.
32. Sir James Melville, *Memoirs*, p. 12.
33. Philip II wrote to the Pope: '. . . Since, for my sins, it has been God's will that the Prince should have such great and numerous defects, partly mental, partly due to his physical condition, utterly lacking as he is in the qualifications necessary for ruling, I saw the grave risks that would arise were he to be given the succession . . . in short, my decision was necessary'. Geoffrey Parker, *Philip II* (1979), p. 91.
34. Contemporary words quoted by J. E. Neale, *Queen Elizabeth and Her Parliaments*, Vol. 1, p. 106.
35. Simon Adams, 'The Release of Lord Darnley and the Failure of the Amity', in *Mary Queen of Scots, Queen in Three Kingdoms*, ed. Michael Lynch (1988), p. 133.
36. Quadra to Philip II, 16/6/63, CSP (Spanish) Vol. 1, p. 339.
37. Elizabeth to Mary, 16/6/63, CSP (Scottish) Vol. 2, p. 14.
38. Silva to Philip II, 27/6/64, CSP (Spanish) Vol. 1, p. 364.
39. Silva to Philip II, 12/8/64. Ibid, p. 374.
40. *Diurnal of Occurrents*, Anon. (Bannatyne Club, 1833), pp. 77–8 (spelling anglicized).
41. Melville, op. cit., p. 35.
42. Ibid, pp. 35–6.
43. Cecil to Moray and Lethington, 16/12/64, CSP (Scottish) Vol. 2, pp. 104–5.
44. Adams, op. cit., p. 132.
45. Melville, op. cit., p. 40.

CHAPTER FOUR: 'HENRICUS ET MARIA'

1. BL Add. MSS 17492 fol. 57.
2. Inscription on obverse of silver ryal of 1565 current for thirty shillings, issued on the marriage of Mary Queen of Scots and Lord Darnley. R. W. Cochrane-Patrick, *Records of the Coinage of Scotland* (1877), Introduction, pp. cxli–cxlii; also *Dolphin Coins Fixed Price List No. 1* (1991), cover illustration and p. 37, coin no. 652, illustration and description.
3. John Stow, *The Chronicles of England* (1580), p. 1126. It will be noticed that Stow refers to 1 January as the beginning of the New Year, although the dating of 1565 would not begin until 25 March. Stow is using the Latin Calendar, in which the year begins on the Kalends of January (1 January in the Gregorian Calendar adopted in England in 1752). How the Latin Calendar was dated is explained very clearly

in Archibald H. Dunbar, *Scottish Kings* (1899), pp. 316–23 with a conversion table of dates.

4. Stow, op. cit., p. 1126.
5. Ridley, op. cit., p. 80.
6. Randolph to Cecil, 12/2/65, CSP (Scottish) Vol. 2, pp. 124–5; Randolph to Leicester. Ibid, p. 125.
7. Ibid.
8. Melville, op. cit., p. 45.
9. BL Add. MSS 19401 fol. 101.
10. Randolph to Cecil, 27/2/65, CSP (Scottish) Vol. 2, p. 128.
11. Ibid.
12. Ibid, p. 126.
13. Sir Richard Maitland wrote:

> And gif they Heines plesis for to marie,
>   That thow haive help I pray the Trinitie
> To cheis and tak ane husband without tarie,
> To thy honour, and our utilitie;
>   Quha will, and may, mantein our libertie;
> Repleit of wisdome and of godlienes;
>   Nobill, and full of constance and lawtie;
> With guid successioune, to our quyetnes.

> [And if thy Highness pleases for to marry
>   That thou have help I pray the Trinity
> To choose and take a husband without tarry
> To thy honour and our utility;
>   Who will, and may, maintain our liberty;
> Replete of wisdom and of godliness;
>   Noble, and full of constancy and loyalty;
> With good succession, to our quietness.]

Cit. Cowan, *Enigma of Mary Stuart*, pp. 47–8.

14. *Lennox Narrative*, para. 2, cit. R. H. Mahon, *Mary Queen of Scots: a Study of the Lennox Narrative*, p. 120.
15. BL Add. MSS 17942 fol. 57.
16. Helena Mennie Shire, *Song, Dance and Poetry of the Court of Scotland* (1969), pp. 71–2.
17. Bannatyne MS cccv fol. 244a, cit. John McQueen, *Ballattis of Luve: the Scottish Courtly Love Lyric 1400–1570* (1970), pp. 132–3.
18. The origins and development of the Bannatyne Manuscript are discussed in Alasdair A. MacDonald, 'The Bannatyne Manuscript – A

Marian Anthology', *Innes Review*, Vol. XXXVII, No. 1, (Spring 1986), pp. 36–47.

19. Melville, op. cit., p. 45.
20. Fraser, *The Lennox*, Vol. 1, p. 442.
21. Randolph to Sir Henry Sidney, 31/3/65, cit. F. A. Mumby, *Elizabeth and Mary Stuart* (1914), p. 356.
22. Randolph to Bedford, 7/4/65, CSP (Scottish) Vol. 2, p. 141.
23. Throckmorton to Leicester and Cecil, 11/5/65. Ibid, pp. 158–9.
24. BL Cott. Caligula BX (16) fol. 295, 'The Oath of an Earl that the said Henry made'; also Robert Keith, *History of the Affairs of Church and State in Scotland* (1845), Vol. 2, p. 289.
25. BL Cott. Caligula BX (16) fol. 295; also CSP (Scottish) Vol. 2, p. 161.
26. Throckmorton to Queen Elizabeth, 21/5/65, CSP (Scottish) Vol. 2, p. 163.
27. 8 September 1565, PRO Special Commissions and Returns of the Exchequer, cit. F. W. Crossley, op. cit.
28. Randolph to Leicester, 3/6/65, CSP (Scottish) Vol. 2, p. 171.
29. Randolph to Cecil, 23/5/65. Ibid, p. 154.
30. Ibid, p. 171.
31. Randolph to Cecil, 21/5/65. Ibid, p. 168.
32. Ibid, p. 166.
33. Randolph to Cecil, 3/6/65. Ibid, p. 172.
34. M. H. Armstrong Davison, *The Casket Letters*, Appendix A, 'The Maladies of Mary Queen of Scots and her Husbands', p. 314.
35. 'Hutaudeau' was an Old French word for a young chicken or pullet; it entered the Scots language as 'howtowdie'. *Vide* F. Marion McNeill, *The Scots Kitchen* (2nd ed., 1963), p. 133.
36. J. H. Pollen, 'The Dispensation for the Marriage of Mary Stuart with Darnley, and its Date', *Scottish Historical Review*, Vol. IV, No. 15 (April 1907), pp. 241–8.
37. Randolph to Cecil, 8/5/65, CSP (Scottish) Vol. 2, p. 156.
38. Randolph to Cecil, 3/6/65. Ibid, pp. 172–3.
39. Randolph to Leicester, 21/5/65. Ibid, p. 166; also Mumby, op. cit., p. 378.
40. Randolph to Queen Elizabeth, 16/7/65, CSP (Scottish) Vol. 2, p. 181.
41. Randolph to Cecil, 16/7/65, cit. Hay Fleming, op. cit., pp. 346–7.
42. The title of Duke of Albany had been held previously by Robert, Duke of Albany (d. 1420), brother of King Robert III and Governor of Scotland during the minority and English imprisonment of King James I; then by his son Murdac (executed 1425). The next creation was of Alexander, Duke of Albany (d. 1485), brother of King James III. The title passed to his son John, Duke of Albany, Governor of Scotland in

the minority of King James V, and he died childless in 1536. The next creation was of Henry Stuart, Lord Darnley.

43. Accounts of the Parish of the Canongate, cit. Fraser, *The Lennox*, Vol. 1, p. 483.

44. Keith, op. cit., Vol. 2, pp. 342–3.

45. Zwetkovitch to Emperor Maximilian II, 6/8/65, cit. Victor von Klarwill, *Queen Elizabeth and some Foreigners* (1928), p. 251.

46. Pollen, op. cit. The papal letter, whatever it was, would have revealed the fact that the Pope had not as yet received the application from the Cardinal of Lorraine; so Mary would have realized that she might have to wait a long time for the dispensation. If she felt that the best way to deal with the opposition was to marry quickly, she had no choice but to do so without the dispensation. The back-dating of it must have been a great relief to her when the document finally arrived – though it was to pose a different set of problems later on. *Vide infra* Chapter Seven.

47. Rosalind K. Marshall, *Virgins and Viragos: a History of Women in Scotland*, p. 32: 'It is important to notice that the plighting of the troth was what actually constituted the marriage ceremony. It might be done in public or in private, with or without mass, and the presence of the priest was not strictly necessary. Obviously the Church was anxious that weddings should be held in the priest's presence . . . and marriage was certainly a sacrament, but strictly speaking the husband and wife were themselves ministers of that sacrament.' This makes Darnley's non-attendance of the nuptial mass of less significance than is sometimes supposed.

48. Randolph to Leicester, 29/7/65, cit. Mumby, op. cit., p. 388.

49. Ibid, pp. 388–9.

50. Ibid.

51. Ibid.

52. This possibility is discussed in detail by Fraser, *Mary Queen of Scots*, pp. 126–8.

CHAPTER FIVE: THE QUEST FOR THE CROWN MATRIMONIAL

1. Randolph to Leicester, 3/7/65, cit. Fraser, *The Lennox*, Vol. 1, pp. 480–1.

2. Keith, op. cit., Vol. 2, p. 347.

3. Knox, *History of the Reformation* (ed. McGavin, 1831), Bk. V, p. 332.

4. Joseph Robertson, *Inventaires de La Royne Descosse*, Preface, pp. lxxxiv–lxxxv.

5. Sir Thomas Craig, 'An Epithalamium on the Marriage of Henry Duke

of Albany . . . and Mary, Most Serene Queen of Scots', in *Epithalamia Tria Mariana*, trans. Revd Francis Wrangham (1837), no pagination.

6. Randolph to Leicester, 31/7/65, cit. Mumby, op. cit., p. 387.
7. Melville, op. cit. So far as the picture itself is concerned, its date is controversial. Sir Roy Strong has described it as 'the only contemporary painting depicting them as husband and wife', Roy Strong and Julia Trevelyan Oman, *Mary Queen of Scots* (1972), p. 75; but Mark Girouard describes it as a 'composite image', in *Hardwick Hall* (National Trust, 1989), p. 75. The picture is No. 126 in the Hardwick Hall collection and presently it is deplorably badly hung for such an important picture; it is in the lobby between the Blue Room and the North Staircase, badly lit and difficult to study.
8. Randolph to Cecil, 27/8/65, CSP (Scottish) Vol. 2, p. 197.
9. Martin Hume, *The Love Affairs of Mary Queen of Scots* (1903), p. 276 fn.
10. Professor Gordon Donaldson's view was that 'Possibly, if English help had been forthcoming and if Moray had received wider Scottish support, some kind of council might have been imposed upon Mary, but that would have been all'. Donaldson, *Mary Queen of Scots*, p. 88. If this was the case, Moray was taking a great risk for a plan that still would not provide for the elimination of Darnley, the pivot of his resentment.
11. Fraser, *Mary Queen of Scots*, p. 282.
12. Knox, 'A Sermon on Isaiah xxvi, 13–21, preached in St Giles Kirk 19th August 1565', in *Works of John Knox*, ed. David Laing, Vol. VI, pp. 234–73 – this passage p. 256.
13. Ibid, p. 272.
14. Knox, *History of the Reformation*, Bk V, p. 332.
15. Ibid.
16. Ibid, p. 333.
17. Ibid.
18. Ibid, p. 334.
19. Ibid.
20. Hay Fleming, *Mary Queen of Scots*, Itinerary, pp. 515–43. This detailed itinerary of the Queen's movements throughout her reign shows that this is the only occasion on which she and Darnley could have been at Crookston together.
21. John Wilson, 'Clyde', cit. David Semple, *The Tree of Crocston*, p. 25.
22. Walter Scott, *The Abbot* (Nelson annotated edition, no date), pp. 517–18. The author's note on this passage is: 'The real place from which Mary saw the rout of her last army was Cathcart Castle . . . [but] a tradition[al] report of Mary having seen the battle from the Castle of Crookstone . . . seemed so much to increase the interest of the scene

that I have been unwilling to make . . . the fiction give way to the fact'. Ibid, pp. 552–3.

23. *Register of the Privy Council of Scotland*, Vol. 1, p. 413.

24. Margaret Swain, *The Needlework of Mary Queen of Scots*, p. 39. This emblem does not appear in either of the editions of Paradin's *Symbola Heroica* which I have consulted, but it belongs to the same emblematic tradition and style as those illustrated in that work, which date from the late fifteenth to mid-sixteenth century, and certainly antedate the coin.

25. Randolph to Cecil, 25/12/65. C.S.P (Scottish) Vol. 2 p. 248

26. This is the superior example, which was sold by Dolphin Coins, England's Lane, London NW3, in 1991. *Vide supra*, Chapter Four, ref. note 2.

27. T. F. Henderson, 'James Hepburn, fourth Earl of Bothwell', DNB, Vol. IX, p. 599.

28. *Register of the Privy Council of Scotland*, Vol. 1, p. 379.

29. Mauvissière to Charles IX, cit. Strickland, op. cit., Vol. 4, p. 207.

30. *The Bannatyne Manuscript*, ed. W. Tod Ritchie (1928), Vol. 4, pp. 227–8. The poem that precedes 'Be Governor Both Good and Gracious' in the Bannatyne Manuscript, ibid, Vol. 4, pp. 224–6, is 'Contra Septem Peccata Mortalia [Against the Seven Deadly Sins]'. Could this also be by Darnley? It contains several of the same phrases as the poem that is certainly his, e.g. 'be blyith in hart' and 'be just to pure'; and it has the same stanza form – eight lines each being a short admonition to virtue beginning with the word 'Be', and the final line repeated at the end of each stanza. It seems probable that either Darnley wrote both poems, or knew 'Contra Septem Peccata Mortalia', and based 'Be Governor Both Good and Gracious' upon it. In my own view, the poems sound like the work of the same author. Here, for comparison, follow two stanzas, 'Aganis Ire', p. 225, and 'Aganis Licherye', p. 226:

Be pacient quhen thow art movit to Ire
Be reasoun wirk that wit oursett thy will
Be nocht malicious nor crewell of desyre
Be no occasioun of mannis blude to spill
Be sufferance thy purpois thow fulfill
Be wyiss counsall tak ay thy gouernall
Be red for blame with schame to hald thee still
Be reddye ay quhenevir the judge will call

[Be patient when thou art provoked to ire
By reason work that wit controls thy will

Be not malicious nor cruel of desire
Be no occasion of man's blood to spill
By forbearance thy purpose thou fulfill
By wise counsel take always thy governall [governance]
Be counselled, for blame, with shame to hold thee still
[Be cautioned to restrain yourself or you will be blamed]
Be ready always whenever the Judge will call
[i.e. God, the Judge on the Last Day]

Be nocht inclynd to fleschlie foull delyte
Be sensuall lust thy silly saule to sla
Be temperans refrane thy appetyte
Be chaste of lyfe, or sett thy mortall fa
Bethink the als of dreidfull domisda
Befoir the world quhen suffer schame thay sall
Be moment syn to win eternal wa
Be reddye ay quhen evir the judge will call.

[Be not inclined to fleshly foul delight
By sensual lust thy simple soul to slay
By temperance, restrain thy appetite
Be chaste of life, overcome thy mortal fae [foe – i.e. the Devil]
Bethink thee also of the dread judgment day
Before the world when suffer shame they [the damned] shall
Be moment then to win eternal way
[Be ready at that moment to win eternal salvation]
Be ready always whenever the Judge will call.]

If Darnley wrote 'Contra Septem Peccata Mortalia', it is an unhappy irony that he was guilty of all the Deadly Sins, with the exception of avarice.

31. Lord Herries, *Historical Memoirs*, pp. 74–5; also Knox, *History of the Reformation*, Bk V, p. 342.
32. Ibid, p. 440.
33. Randolph to Cecil, 25/12/65, CSP (Scottish) Vol. 2, p. 248.
34. A. F. Pollen, 'Francis Yaxley', DNB, Vol. XXI, pp. 1220–1; Hume, op. cit., p. 294.
35. Donaldson, op. cit., p. 84.
36. The Queen's apologist Adam Blackwood described Rizzio as very ugly, though intellectually gifted. His motive was to make it clear that Mary could not possibly have loved Rizzio, but had good reason to value him: 'He was a man of no beauty or outward shape, for he was mis-shapen, evil favoured, and in visage very black; but for his fidelity,

wisdom, prudence, virtue and his other good parts and qualities of mind he was richly adorned' (spelling anglicized). Adam Blackwood, *History of Mary Queen of Scots, A Fragment* (Maitland Club, 1834), pp. 9–10.

37. Ida Macalpine and Richard Hunter, 'Porphyria in the Royal Houses of Stuart, Hanover and Prussia', in *Porphyria, A Royal Malady* (1968), pp. 35–8; Armstrong Davison, op. cit., Appendix A, 'The Maladies of Mary Queen of Scots and Her Husbands', passim.

CHAPTER SIX: THE KING AS MURDERER

1. Vincenzo Laureo, Bishop of Mondovi, Papal Nuncio-Designate to Scotland, to the Cardinal of Alessandria, 21/8/66, cit. A. F. Mumby, *The Fall of Mary Stuart*, p. 61.
2. Randolph to Cecil, 25/12/65, CSP (Scottish) Vol. 2, p. 247.
3. Keith, op. cit., Vol. 1, Introduction, p. xcix; Strickland, op. cit., Vol. 4, p. 238. Keith dates the letter to 1566, but then Darnley was in Glasgow with his father, and too ill to go anywhere; *vide infra* Chapter Eight. Strickland is obviously right in dating it to 1565, when Darnley certainly did go to Peebles just before the New Year (Roman style).
4. Blackwood, op. cit., pp. 10–11.
5. Ibid, p. 11.
6. Randolph to Cecil, 7/2/66, CSP (Scottish), Vol. 2, p. 254.
7. Strickland, op. cit., Vol. 4, p. 247. She says that the robe was afterwards given to the herald for his fee.
8. BL Harleian 6815 fol. 8. This document gives the oath as it was administered to Norfolk and Leicester; but it would have been substantially the same as administered to Darnley.
9. Knox, op. cit., Bk V, p. 342.
10. *Diurnal of Occurrents*, p. 87.
11. Drury to Cecil, 16/2/66, Keith, op. cit., Vol. 2, p. 404.
12. Ibid. Keith thought the mention of the coin was 'an evident mistake', for he had not seen an example of it, and did not believe it had ever been minted, even if commissioned. We now know that he was wrong, from the survival of the two examples.
13. It was actually signed by Moray, Rothes, Ochiltree, Kirkaldy of Grange, Wishart of Pitarrow and Haliburton of Pitcur. Mumby, op. cit., p. 39.
14. Details of both bonds, CSP (Scottish) Vol. 2, pp. 260–1; also Mumby, op. cit., pp. 39–40.
15. Mary Queen of Scots to Queen Elizabeth, 12/2/66, CSP (Scottish) Vol. 2, p. 256.
16. Mary Queen of Scots to Queen Elizabeth, 20/2/66. Ibid, p. 257.

17. Robertson, *Inventaires de La Royne Descosse*, p. 162.
18. Randolph to Leicester, 13/2/66, Keith, op. cit., p. 402 fn.
19. Knox, op. cit., Bk V, p. 342.
20. Ibid.
21. Blackwood, op. cit., p. 12.
22. Melville, *Memoirs*, p. 51.
23. A sidelight to the idea that the murder was a Douglas plot was added by Pietro Bizari, an Italian man of letters, who was for a time in the service of the Earl of Bedford, at Berwick, when he visited the court of Scotland. Bizari wrote an account of the murders of Rizzio and Darnley, which contains some details unsubstantiated by other sources. According to Bizari, Rizzio seduced a lady of the Douglas family, thus drawing the enmity of that powerful kindred upon himself; and Darnley fathered a child on one of the ladies of the court, and likewise made for himself powerful, unnamed enemies. There were enough political reasons for enmity to both Rizzio and Darnley, without reducing their deaths to the level of sexual vendettas. However, Bizari was a contemporary, and his account is therefore at least worth mentioning; *vide* G. F. Barwick, *A Sidelight on the Mystery of Mary Stuart: Pietro Bizari's Contemporary Account of the Murders of Riccio [sic] and Darnley* (SHR XXXI, 1924), passim.
24. Lord Ruthven, 'A relation of the Death of David Rizzio', in *Miscellanea Antiqua Anglicana* (1816), pp. 16–18.
25. Ibid, pp. 17–18.
26. Knox, *History of the Reformation*, Bk V, pp. 342–3; also Keith, op. cit., Vol. 2, p. 409.
27. Melville, op. cit., p. 49.
28. BL Cott. Caligula BX (16) fol. 392.
29. Mary Queen of Scots to the Archbishop of Glasgow, Strickland, *Letters of Mary Queen of Scots*, cit. Mumby, *The Fall of Mary Stuart*, pp. 42–4; Lord Ruthven, 'A Discourse of the late troubles that happened in Scotland ... written at Berwick, the last of April 1566', cit. Keith, op. cit., Vol. 3, pp. 260–78; also in *Miscellanea Antiqua Anglicana*, pp. 12–35; Randolph and Bedford to Cecil, 27/3/66, BL Cott. Caligula BX (16) fols 387–93; also transcribed Mumby, op. cit., pp. 48–56.
30. Ruthven, 'A Discourse', cit. Keith, Vol. 3, p. 266.
31. By his own account he had been suffering from 'inflammation of the liver and consumption of the kidneys'; Ruthven, 'A Discourse', op. cit., p. 260.
32. Ibid, pp. 267–8.
33. Ibid, p. 269.
34. Knox, op. cit., Bk V, p. 343.

35. Mary Queen of Scots to the Archbishop of Glasgow, cit. Mumby, op. cit., p. 43.
36. Ruthven, 'A Discourse', Keith, op. cit., Vol. 3, p. 275.
37. Claude Nau, *History of Mary Stuart*, ed. Stevenson (1863), p. 4. Nau was Mary's secretary during her imprisonment in England. She gave him an account of the dramatic events of her life in Scotland. He wrote it down with plenty of reported speech and tendentious arguments. But his style probably mirrors the Queen's vivid account, and if it acquired some highlights here and there, it is still the closest version of her own recollections.
38. Ibid, loc. cit.
39. Ibid, p. 7.
40. Ibid, p. 9.
41. Melville, *Memoirs*, p. 52.
42. Lord Ruthven, 'A Discourse', Keith, op. cit., Vol. 3, p. 276.
43. Ibid.
44. Ibid, p. 277.
45. Darnley was served by two brothers both called Anthony Standen. When families wished to ensure the perpetuation of a Christian name, parents frequently gave it to two of their children, so that if one died the name would continue in that generation; this is in itself an indication of the expectation of infant mortality. However, the elder Anthony Standen survived to be associated with the Gunpowder Plot. G. M. Thomson, *The Crime of Mary Stuart* (1967), pp. 50–1.
46. Darnley may have said 'In him I have lost a good and faithful servant . . . I have been miserably cheated', as reported in Nau's narrative. But, as Lady Antonia Fraser rightly observes, 'It seems inconceivable that Mary should have told Darnley bluntly that he himself would go the same way before a year was out – as Lennox announced in his own narrative written after Darnley's death'. Fraser, *Mary Queen of Scots*, p. 256 fn.
47. Nau, op. cit., p. 16.
48. Wormald, op. cit., p. 159.
49. Randolph to Cecil, 21/3/66, CSP (Scottish) Vol. 2, pp. 269–70. The postscript to this letter is a list of 'persons implicated' in the murder of Rizzio. It concludes with the names 'John Knox, John Crag [Craig], preachers'. The question of Knox's foreknowledge or implication is discussed by Sir Edward Parry in his chivalrous if tendentious defence of Mary, *The Persecution of Mary Stewart* (1931), pp. 68–173. Parry makes a strong case that Knox not only had foreknowledge of the murder, but prepared public opinion to rejoice at it, with some suitable propaganda from the Old Testament.

50. Morton and Ruthven to Cecil, 2/4/66, CSP (Scottish) Vol. 2, p. 273; Randolph to Cecil, 4/4/66. Ibid, p. 275.

CHAPTER SEVEN: 'YOUNG FOOL AND PROUD TYRANT'

1. The Confession of the Laird of Ormiston, 13/12/73, cit. Robert Pitcairn, *Criminal Trials in Scotland* (1833), Vol. 1, pp. 511–12. Ormiston claimed to recollect that the 'Craigmillar Bond' shown him by Bothwell, signed by Huntly, Argyll, Maitland and Sir James Balfour, contained the words quoted in the epigraph (spelling anglicized).
2. Joseph Rizzio arrived in Scotland at Easter 1566 in the entourage of the French Ambassador, Castelnau de Mauvissière.
3. *Register of the Privy Council of Scotland*, Vol. 1, p. 443.
4. *English and Scottish Popular Ballads from the Collection of James Francis Child*, ed. Sayer and Kitteredge (1905), No. 174, 'Lord Bothwell', pp. 423–4.
5. De Silva to Philip II, 23/3/66, CSP (Spanish) Vol. 1, p. 534.
6. De Silva to Philip II. Ibid, p. 541.
7. As late as 21/7/66 the King and Queen of Scots wrote jointly to Pope Pius V, to recommend Alexander Campbell for appointment as Bishop of Brechin. BL Royal MSS 18 BVI fol. 240; CSP (Scottish) Vol. 2, p. 296.
8. Randolph to Cecil, 4/4/66, CSP (Scottish) Vol. 2, p. 274; and mentioned again, Randolph to Cecil, 25/4/66. Ibid, p. 276.
9. *Inventaires de La Royne Descosse*, Introduction, p. lxiv; *Accounts of the Lord High Treasurer of Scotland*, Vol. 2, p. 491.
10. De Silva to Philip II, 29/4/66, CSP (Spanish) Vol. 1, p. 546.
11. Henry King of Scots [Darnley] to Charles IX, King of France, 6/5/66, BL Egerton 2805 fol. 7; CSP (Scottish) Vol. 2, p. 277.

> Monsieur my Good Brother,
> I have received from the Sieur de Mauvissiere the letter which you were good enough to write me, which has caused me great distress, since I learn from it that I am greatly wronged by a rumour which makes me guilty of a deed which I truly detest.
> But on the other hand, I hope that my innocence, fully accepted by the Sieur de Mauvissiere, to whom I have told the whole truth, will reaffirm your good opinion of me, and then I shall be free from anxiety.
> Entrusting myself to his capacity to right this wrong, I conclude this letter, praying the Creator to give you, Monsieur my Good Brother, in good health a very long and happy life.
> From Edinburgh this 6th day of May 1566,
> Your affectionate Good Brother,
> Henry.

The contemporary convention was that kings addressed each other as 'Brother' and Queens as 'Sister'.

12. De Silva to Philip II, 18/5/66, CSP (Spanish) Vol. 1, p. 549.
13. *Inventaires de La Royne Descosse*, Introduction, pp. xxxi–xxxii.
14. Ibid, p. xxxi.
15. Ibid, pp. 93–115; also a facsimile of two folios, between Introduction pp. xxxii and xxxiii.
16. Ibid, p. 112.
17. The definitive demolishment of the story is 'The Coffin in the Wall: An Edinburgh Castle "Mystery"' by Frank Gent, *Chambers Journal*, September/October 1944, and pamphlet reprint. See also, Grant R. Francis, *Scotland's Royal Line* (1929), pp. 53–61; Antonia Fraser, *Mary Queen of Scots* (1969), p. 267 fn; Gordon Donaldson, *Mary Queen of Scots* (1974), p. 89; Caroline Bingham, *James VI of Scotland* (1979), pp. 19–21.
18. This name may be an error by Lord Herries for Sir Anthony Standen, who had helped Darnley and Mary to escape after the murder of Rizzio. Mary had later commanded Darnley to knight him, as his reward for the part he played in saving their child's life. Causing Darnley to give the accolade also could be regarded as causing him to acknowledge paternity of the child.
19. Lord Herries, *Memoirs*, p. 79.
20. Strickland, op. cit., Vol. 4, p. 344. Strickland quotes the letter in English, without giving the source reference; presumably the original was in French. The text as given by Strickland is as follows:

To Monsieur the Cardinal de Guise.
From the Castle of Edinburgh – in great haste –
Sir my Uncle,
Having so favourable an opportunity of writing to you by this gentleman, who is on the point of setting off, I would not omit to inform you that the Queen my wife has just been delivered of a son – an event which, I am sure, will not cause you less joy than ourselves; also to let you know that I have written on my part, as the Queen my wife has on hers, to the King [of France], begging him to be pleased to oblige and honour us by standing Godfather for him, whereby he will increase the debt of gratitude I owe him for all his favours to me, for the which I shall always be ready to make every return in my power. So, having nothing more agreeable to inform you of at present, I conclude, praying God, Monsieur my Uncle, to have you always in His holy and worthy keeping.
Your very humble and obedient nephew,
Henry R.

Please to present my commendations to Madame the Dowager de Guise.

21. This was probably a record, until, thirty-seven years later, Sir Robert Carey rode from London to Edinburgh in three days, to bring James VI of Scotland news of his accession to the throne of England on the death of Queen Elizabeth.

22. Melville, op. cit., p. 56. He reported Elizabeth's words in the third person: 'The Queen did sit down, with her hand upon her cheek, bursting out to some of her ladies that the Queen of Scots was lighter of a fair son while she was but a barren stock'.

23. Ibid.

24. Elizabeth to the Countess of Argyll, 31/10/66, CSP (Scottish) Vol. 2, p. 302. If Lady Argyll were prevented by sickness from acting as proxy, then her place was to be taken by the Countess of Moray.

25. De Silva to Philip II, CSP (Spanish) Vol. 1, p. 562.

26. Bedford to Cecil, 3/8/66, BL Cott. Caligula BX Vol. 2 fol. 396; Stevenson, *Selection of Unpublished Manuscripts* (Maitland Club, 1837), p. 165.

27. Nau, op. cit., p. 28.

28. Hence the legendary hardihood of Leander's swimming the Hellespont to visit Hero; *vide* Marlowe, *Hero and Leander*, in which the swim is represented as the ultimate folly: 'What is it now but mad Leander dares?' (*Hero and Leander*, Sestiad 2, line 146); and his near-drowning is imagized as the dangerous passion for him of the sea god Neptune. In the sixteenth century going off alone to swim suggested disturbed emotions rather than athleticism, which was conventionally practised on dry land.

29. Nau, op. cit., p. 30.

30. Bedford to Cecil, 27/7/66, CSP (Foreign) Vol. 8, p. 110.

31. Ibid, p. 128.

32. Hume, *Love Affairs of Mary Queen of Scots*, p. 318.

33. Fraser, *Mary Queen of Scots*, p. 272.

34. Lords of Council to Catherine de Medici, 8/10/66, cit. Mumby, *Fall of Mary Stuart*, p. 116; Keith, op. cit., Vol. 2, p. 455.

35. Ibid.

36. Mumby, op. cit., p. 117; Keith, op. cit., p. 456.

37. 'They were three of the greatest lords of the kingdom . . .' Mumby, op. cit., p. 117; Keith, op. cit., p. 456.

38. Du Croc to Archbishop Beaton, 15/10/66, cit. Mumby, op. cit., p. 121; Keith, op. cit., Vol. 2, p. 450.

39. Ibid, p. 122; ibid, p. 451.

40. Lords of Council to Catherine de Medici, 8/10/66, cit. Mumby, op. cit., p. 120; Keith, op. cit., Vol. 2, p. 459.

41. This is one of the most controversial episodes of Mary's career, and there are widely differing interpretations of it. Buchanan represented her as dashing madly off to visit her lover in the midst of winter and with a disreputable escort. On this fabrication Professor Gordon Donaldson contented himself with a caustic comment: 'October is not exactly the heart of winter, and Mary's entourage on her ride included the Earl of Moray, whom it was careless of his client Buchanan to class as one of the "thieves and traitors" who accompanied her'. Donaldson, *Mary Queen of Scots*, p. 96. Lady Antonia Fraser saw the Queen's visit as purely political: '. . . when her business [the Justice Ayre at Jedburgh] had been completed, she decided to pay Bothwell a visit, not so much to express her sympathy, as for the practical reason that he was her lieutenant and one of her chief advisers, especially on the perennially vexed border questions, and she needed to consult with him'. Fraser, op. cit., p. 274. This at least provided an excellent pretext for the visit, if not the whole reason.

42. M. H. Armstrong Davison, op. cit., p. 38, and pp. 311–12.

43. Ibid.

44. Lethington to Beaton, 24/10/66, cit. Mumby, op. cit., p. 127.

45. *Diurnal of Occurrents*, p. 101. But the Bishop of Ross, who wrote to the Archbishop of Glasgow on 27/10/66, said that Darnley had been in Glasgow all the time: 'The King all this time remained in Glasgow, and yet is not come toward the Queen's Majesty'. Keith, op. cit., Vol. 3, p. 288 (spelling anglicized).

46. De Silva to Philip II, 13/11/66, CSP (Spanish) Vol. 1, p. 59, cit. Mumby, op. cit., pp. 133–4.

47. Du Croc to Archbishop Beaton, 6/12/66. Ibid, p. 144.

48. Donaldson, *The First Trial of Mary Queen of Scots*, p. 35.

49. 'The Protestation of Huntly and Argyll', cit. Keith, op. cit., Vol. 3, p. 291; Mumby, op. cit., p. 139.

50. Ibid, p. 292; ibid, p. 140.

51. Lord Herries, *Memoirs*, p. 80.

52. Melville, *Memoirs*, p. 59.

53. 'The Protestation of Huntly and Argyll', cit. Keith, op. cit., Vol. 3, p. 292; Mumby, op. cit., p. 140.

54. Ibid, p. 293; ibid, p. 141.

55. Ibid.

56. Hume, *Love Affairs of Mary Queen of Scots*, pp. 344–5. The author argues that Mary was aware that murder was the intended solution.

57. Du Croc to Archbishop Beaton, 6/12/66, Mumby, op. cit., p. 144.

58. William Rogers to Cecil, 5/7/66, CSP (Scottish) Vol. 2, pp. 293–4; 'Examination of William Rogers', 16/1/67. Ibid, p. 310.

59. Mary Queen of Scots to Archbishop Beaton, 20/1/67, Keith, op. cit., Introduction p. c (in original Scots); Mumby, op. cit., p. 154 (spelling anglicized). Though Mary wrote of this discovery in January 1567, she described a detailed investigation of the rumour, so probably received first intimations in the autumn of 1566.

60. Robert Pitcairn, *Criminal Trials in Scotland*, Vol. 1, pp. 511–12.

61. CSP (Venetian) Vol. 7, p. 387; also Bedford to Cecil, 25/11/66, CSP (Foreign) Vol. 8, p. 151, reports that there was an attempt to ambush the fabulous gift *en route* for Scotland: 'Certain who had heard of the fount [font] laid wait in a place not far from Doncaster, but missing it thought not to trouble themselves with baser things, and did no harm'.

62. CSP (Venetian), loc. cit.

63. Keith, op. cit., Vol. 2, p. 486.

64. *Diurnal of Occurrents*, p. 104.

65. Karl Pearson, *The Skull and Portraits of Henry Stewart, Lord Darnley*, p. 87 and fn; G. M. Thomson, *The Crime of Mary Stuart*, p. 48.

66. Keith, op. cit., p. 487.

67. Queen Elizabeth's Instructions to the Earl of Bedford, 7/11/66, BL Cott. Caligula B X (16)1 Vol. 2 fols 399–401; Keith, op. cit., Vol. 2, pp. 477–83.

68. Fraser, *Mary Queen of Scots*, p. 281.

69. This point is made by Dr Jenny Wormald, in *Mary Queen of Scots: A Study in Failure*, p. 161.

70. Du Croc to Archbishop Beaton, 23/12/66, cit. Strickland, *Letters of Mary Queen of Scots*; Mumby, op. cit., p. 145.

71. BL Cott. Caligula B IV fol. 149; Stevenson, Nau's *History of Mary Stewart*, Introduction, pp. cxlvii–cxlviii.

72. Karl Pearson, op. cit., p. 11.

73. Melville, op. cit., p. 60.

74. Bedford was entertained by Moray at St Andrews before returning to England.

75. Melville, op. cit., p. 61.

76. Donaldson, *Mary Queen of Scots*, pp. 98–9.

77. Ibid, p. 98.

78. Knox, *History of the Reformation*, Bk V, pp. 349–50.

79. This is the conclusion of both Karl Pearson and M. H. Armstrong Davison. Pearson investigates the matter thoroughly, op. cit., pp. 89–93, and many fns to these pages.

CHAPTER EIGHT: THE MURDER OF THE KING AND ITS AFTERMATH

1. Frederick Schiller, *Mary Stuart*, Act 1, Scene IV, trans. Joseph Mellish, *Dramas of Schiller* (1898), p. 217.
2. William Camden, *Annales* (1625), p. 116.
3. Barberini MSS XXXII 210 (1197), cit. Stevenson, Nau's *History of Mary Stewart*, Appendix 1, p. 120.
4. *The Lennox Narrative*, cit. Mahon, *Mary Queen of Scots: A Study of the Lennox Narrative*, p. 124.
5. Ibid.
6. Lord Herries, *Memoirs*, p. 81. Herries mistakenly places Darnley's illness after his visit to the Queen at Craigmillar, but before the baptism of the Prince. Melville also reverses the order of the Craigmillar Conference and the baptism.
7. Karl Pearson, op. cit., p. 95.
8. Ibid, pp. 96–7. Pearson said that the infection might have been due to Darnley's conduct before he reached Scotland, but did not know of Darnley's visit to France as a fugitive, which adds to the possibility, as it provided his first taste of complete independence.
9. M. H. Armstrong Davison, op. cit., Appendix A, 'The Maladies of Mary Queen of Scots and Her Husbands', pp. 314–15.
10. De Silva to Philip II, 17/2/67, said that Darnley was 'in so bad a state with the eruptions on his face that he begged her [the Queen] not to see him till he was somewhat better . . . after crisis of his malady was past she saw him'. CSP (Spanish) Vol. 2, p. 618. Silva believed the malady was smallpox.
11. Hay Fleming, op. cit., Itinerary, p. 540.
12. Bedford to Cecil, 9/1/67, CSP (Foreign), Vol. 8, pp. 103–4.
13. 'Les Affaires du Conte [sic] de Boduel' (Bannatyne Club, 1829), p. 12; Fraser, *Mary Queen of Scots*, p. 282.
14. Bedford to Cecil, 9/1/67, CSP (Scottish) Vol. 2, p. 163.
15. *The Lennox Narrative*, para. VIII, Mahon, op. cit., p. 125.
16. Mary Queen of Scots to Archbishop Beaton, 20/1/67, Keith, op. cit., Vol. 1, Introduction, p.c (in original Scots); Mumby, op. cit., p. 154 (anglicized spelling, here quoted).
17. Keith, op. cit., Introduction, p. ci; Mumby, op. cit., pp. 155–6.
18. T. F. Henderson, 'Thomas Crawford, or Craufurd, of Jordanhill', DNB, Vol. V, pp. 53–5.
19. 'Thomas Crawford's Declaration', ? February 67, CSP (Scottish) Vol. 2, p. 314.
20. Ibid, loc. cit.
21. Ibid, p. 315.

22. Ibid. Crawford's Declaration was not written until after Darnley's death (though he may have taken notes of what Darnley claimed he had said to Mary – or, indeed, may have eavesdropped). It is difficult not to suspect an element of dramatization in it, for example in the dramatic irony of Darnley's boast that if anyone attempted to harm him 'they should buy it dear unless they took him sleeping', and of his declaration that 'he would put himself in her [Mary's] hands though she should cut his throat'.

23. *The Lennox Narrative*, para. IX, op. cit., p. 126. It was contrary to his father's mind that Darnley went with the Queen at all.

24. Mary did not want him to come anywhere near the Prince; and Darnley was very sensitive about his disfigurement, *vide supra* ref. note 10.

25. Fraser, op. cit., p. 289: 'there is general agreement that the choice was his, not the Queen's.'

26. Melville, *Memoirs*, p. 62: 'a place of good air, where he might best recover his health'.

27. *The Lennox Narrative*, loc. cit.; 'The Deposition of Thomas Nelson', Pitcairn, op. cit., p. 501.

28. *Registrum Secreti Sigilli*, 1566, Vol. XXXV, fol. 95, cit. Robertson, *Inventaires de La Royne Descosse*, Introduction, p. xcviii, fn 1.

29. Mahon, op. cit., p. 126, fn 1; Hay Fleming, op. cit., Itinerary, p. 541, fn discusses alternative dates; Fraser, *The Lennox*, Vol. 1, p. 517.

30. *The Lennox Narrative*, para. IX, Mahon, op. cit., pp. 126–7.

31. All the buildings at Kirk o' Field have been demolished, and the site is now occupied by buildings belonging to the University of Edinburgh. The layout of the sixteenth-century site and the construction of the Old Provost's Lodging were researched by Major-General Mahon, and are described in *The Tragedy of Kirk o' Field* (1923).

32. Robertson, *Inventaires de La Royne Descosse*, p. 177: 'Decharge de meubles que javoye fect porter au logis du feu Roy ... Lesquelz meubles ont estez perdu sans en rien recouvrer ...' ('Discharge of furnishings which I caused to be carried to the lodging of the late King ... which furnishings have been lost without anything having been recovered.' Note by Servais de Conde, countersigned 'Marie R'). The substitution of one bed for the other was variously reported. Darnley's servant Nelson said that the black bed was new, and that Mary had an old bed substituted for it (Pitcairn, op. cit., p. 501); but this was obviously a misunderstanding, as the bed substituted was a far grander one, probably Darnley's own bed, previously given him by the Queen, from his own bedchamber in Holyroodhouse.

33. Robertson, op. cit., pp. 177–8.

34. On the whole, sixteenth-century houses had little furniture; the King's Bedchamber in the Old Provost's Lodging was comparatively crowded.

The Presence Chamber could have been left empty except for the tapestries, since no one would necessarily sit down in it.

35. *The Lennox Narrative*, para. XI, Mahon, op. cit., p. 127.
36. Ibid. Obviously this was told to Lennox by the messenger who witnessed it – unless one chooses to believe that Lennox invented the detail to heighten the drama of the narrative.
37. 'The Declaration of Thomas Crawford', CSP (Scottish) Vol. 2, p. 315.
38. Melville, op. cit., p. 62.
39. Ibid. Buchanan made this into a more dramatic episode, saying that Darnley and Lord Robert Stewart gave each other the lie, Mary screamed for Moray to come and stop them fighting, but really in the hope that there would be a general mêlée in which Darnley would be killed. Discussed by Donaldson, in *The First Trial of Mary Queen of Scots*, p. 167.
40. Captain Cockburn to William Cecil, 27/2/67, CSP (Foreign) Vol. 8, p. 181.
41. *The Lennox Narrative*, para. XII, Mahon, op. cit., p. 128.
42. *The Lennox Narrative*, loc. cit.; Giovanni Correr (Venetian Ambassador in France) to the Signory, 1/3/67, CSP (Venetian) Vol. VII, p. xx. Correr's informant was Moretta, who did not leave Scotland until 11 or 12 February, and would have been informed by one of those present.
43. Nau's original French narrative gives ' "Jesus, Paris, tu est noirci", dont il rougist bien fort', cit. Stevenson, op. cit., p. 243.
44. *The Lennox Narrative*, para. XII, Mahon, op. cit., p. 128.
45. Ibid.
46. The Bishop of Mondovi to the Cardinal of Alessandria, 16/3/67, cit. Mumby, op. cit., p. 194.
47. Correr to the Signory, 1/3/67, CSP (Venetian) Vol. VII, p. 389, cit. Mumby, op. cit., pp. 194–5. Other versions of events were reported. The anonymous author of the *Diurnal of Occurrents* thought that Darnley and Taylor had been strangled in their beds by murderers who entered the house with false keys, then carried the bodies outside before returning to blow up the house, 'to caus the pepill understand that it was ane suddane fyre', op. cit., pp. 105–6. Presumably by 'suddane fyre' he meant some sort of natural disaster such as being struck by lightning. On the other hand, the contemporary diarist, Robert Birrel, thought that Darnley had been in the house when it exploded, and had survived the blast, only to be strangled outside: 'If he had not been cruelly vyrriet [strangled] after he fell out of the aire, with his own garters, he had leived [lived]', 'Diary of Robert Birrel, Burgess of Edinburgh', in John Graham Dalyell, *Fragments of Scottish History* (1798), no pagination.
48. Lord Herries, *Memoirs*, p. 84. Herries thought that they then fired the

fuse, but this was obviously wrong. Those who later told the story of the transportation of the gunpowder, the laying of the fuse, the firing of it, etc., were Bothwell's kinsmen and servants, not Darnley's kinsmen, and they also assumed that they had blown him up; *vide* 'The Confession of the Laird of Ormiston', 13/12/73: 'As I shall answer to my God, I knew nothing but that he was blown up; and did enquire the same most diligently at [of] John Hepburn and John Hay . . . who swore unto me they never knew no other thing but that he was blown up . . .' Pitcairn, op. cit., Vol. 1, p. 512 (spelling anglicized).

49. M. de Clarnault, 16/2/67, 'Report of the K. of Scottes death', CSP (Scottish) Vol. 2, p. 313.

50. Lord Herries, *Memoirs*, loc. cit.

51. Ibid.

52. Only he could have provided the details of the psalm-singing, etc. for Lennox to report, or improve upon.

53. *The Lennox Narrative*, para XI, Mahon, op. cit., p. 127. Lennox even imagined that Mary had attended the murder of Darnley in male disguise, 'which apparel she loved oftentymes to be in, in dancings secretly with the King her husband, and going in masks by night through the streets'. Ibid, para. XV, p. 130.

54. De Silva to Philip II, 22/2/67, and 1/3/67, CSP (Spanish) Vol. 1, pp. 620, 623.

55. Ibid, p. 623.

56. *Accounts of the Lord High Treasurer of Scotland*, Vol. XII, p. 41; and Appendix E, 23/3/23, p. 398.

57. Queen Elizabeth to Mary Queen of Scots, 24/2/67, CSP (Scottish) Vol. 2, p. 316.

58. Sir William Drury to Cecil, 28/2/67, CSP (Foreign) Vol. 8, p. 182.

59. Child's *English and Scottish Popular Ballads*, No. 174, 'Earl Bothwell', pp. 423–4. In this highly fictive ballad the tree under which Darnley's body was laid becomes the instrument of his execution – a pear tree on which he is hanged. For other propaganda verses, see Appendix, 'Note on unpublished Verses concerning the Murder of Darnley'.

60. Wormald, op. cit., p. 162. Dr Wormald points out that sixteenth-century rulers did survive and recover from great scandals. Queen Elizabeth recovered from the scandal of the murder of Amy Robsart, and later in the reign from that of the execution of Mary Queen of Scots. Catherine de' Medici recovered from the even worse scandal of the Massacre of St Bartholomew. Mary should have been able to overcome the scandal of the murder of Darnley: 'The problem, therefore, was not the murder. It was the infinitely unwise behaviour of his widow.' Wormald, loc. cit.

61. Sir John Forster to Cecil, 15/4/67, CSP (Foreign) Vol. 8, p. 206.

62. 'Trial of the Earl of Bothwell', 12/4/67, CSP (Scottish) Vol. 2, pp. 319–20.

63. *The Heroicall Devices of M. Claudius Paradin*, p. 263; 'Allegorical Sketch' described in CSP (Scottish) Vol. 2, p. 332. The original coloured drawing is in the Public Record Office, PRO, SP/52/13, No. 60 – No. 61 is a cruder, uncoloured version of it, but with Paradin's Latin motto, which is omitted in the coloured version. If I have conjectured correctly that John Stuart d'Aubigny gave Darnley a copy of the first edition of *Symbola Heroica*, it could have been the very volume that was the source of the pasquil.

64. CSP (Scottish) Vol. 2, p. 320.

65. Nau, in Stevenson, op. cit., p. 36.

66. 'Band of Nobility to Bothwell', 19/4/67, CSP (Scottish) Vol. 2, p. 322. On this copy the Earl of Moray is listed as a signatory, but in fact he was still abroad.

67. Melville, op. cit., p. 64.

68. Kirkaldy of Grange to Bedford, 8/5/67, CSP (Scottish) Vol. 2, p. 327.

69. Ibid.

70. Fraser, *Mary Queen of Scots*, p. 331.

71. 'Deux enfants' was Nau's description, information which must have been given him by Mary herself. Fraser suggests that Mary's pregnancy should have been described as 'five weeks', not 'five months'. Ibid, p. 343. But in that case the miscarriage would not have been recognizable as twins at all. 'Deux enfants' indicates twin foetuses quite well developed.

72. 'Coronatio Ja 6 in Castro Striuelensi 29 Julii 1567', in Dalyell, *Fragments of Scottish History*, Appendix XIII.

73. Holy Bible, Chronicles, Bk 2, Ch. 23, vv. 20–21.

74. Donaldson, *The First Trial of Mary Queen of Scots*, p. 67.

75. Donaldson, *Mary Queen of Scots*, p. 124.

76. 'Documents Illustrative of the Murder of King Henry Darnley', Pitcairn, op. cit., Vol. 1, pp. 493–513; G. M. Thomson in *The Crime of Mary Stuart* attempted to create a coherent narrative out of these confessions, and wrote very effectively, but unfortunately without giving reference notes.

77. Donaldson, *The First Trial of Mary Queen of Scots*, p. 137.

78. Wormald, op. cit., p. 176. The author makes a strong case for the genuineness of the Casket Letters, and also makes the point that James VI must have believed them genuine, or he would not have destroyed them. With his desire to vindicate his mother's reputation, he would have preferred to prove them forgeries if he could. On the other hand, one could also argue that if he were unsure, to destroy them at best might help them to oblivion, or at worst would maintain their mystery.

79.. '... you make me dissemble so much, that I am afraid thereof with horror, and you make me almost to play the part of a traitor. Remember that if it were not for obeying you, I had rather be dead; my heart bleedeth for it.' Casket Letter No. 2, CSP (Scottish) Vol. 2, Appendix 2, p. 725 (spelling modernized).

80. Duncan Thomson, *Painting in Scotland, 1570–1650*, pp. 18–19, catalogue notes on 'The Memorial of Henry Stewart, Lord Darnley, King of Scots'; Dana Bentley-Cranch, 'Effigy and Portrait in Sixteenth Century Scotland', in *Review of Scottish Culture*, No. 4 (1988), pp. 9–23. Bentley-Cranch categorizes the Darnley Memorial as a 'vendetta picture', designed to inspire and encourage vengeance: 'The Darnley Memorial is a carefully organized picture into which have been crammed as many references as possible, both pictorial and literary, to the death of Darnley to form a dramatic and yet strangely subdued "history" ... The purpose of this "vendetta picture" is achieved by the device of accumulation: the spectator, rather in the manner of a visitor to a church or a museum, slowly "goes round" the exhibits, reading and observing until he has absorbed the whole of the tragic "history"'. Loc. cit., pp. 13–14.

81. Strickland, op. cit., Vol. 2, p. 441.

82. Hugh Tait, 'Historiated Tudor Jewellery', in *The Antiquaries' Journal*, Vol. XLII (1962), p. 241.

83. It was described as follows, by Dr Joan Evans: 'The jewel itself is a gold pendant two and a half inches long shaped as a heart, the cognizance of the house of Douglas. One side is set with a large heart-shaped cabochon sapphire between wings enamelled in red, blue and green, beneath a jewelled crown. Round this are figures of Faith with her cross and lamb, Hope with her anchor, Victory with the olive branch, and Truth with a mirror. The crown opens to disclose two hearts united by a gold knot and cipher of MSL. The sapphire heart opens also to show two clasped hands and other emblems and another motto. Round the pendant runs the legend QUHA HOPIS STIL CONSTANTLY VITH PATIENCE SAL OBTEIN VICTORIE IN YAIR PRETENCE [Who continues to hope constantly with patience shall obtain victory in their claim]. The reverse of the pendant is enamelled with the sun in glory and the moon, a crowned salamander in flames, a pelican in her piety, a phoenix, and the figure of a man between a sunflower and a laurel bush. The inner meaning of all these emblems is lost to us with the secret history of Margaret Lennox's intrigues for her son Darnley ... The locket opens; it once held a miniature, presumably of the Regent Lennox ...' Evans, *A History of Jewellery* (1953), p. 126. (If my suggestion is correct, that the jewel was made in memoriam of Darnley, then the lost miniature would have been of him.) Agnes

[241]

Strickland also wrote a detailed description of the jewel, and the reptile which Evans described as a salamander Strickland saw as the Rouge Dragon of the Tudors. Strickland, op. cit., Vol. 2, pp. 427–8.

84. '. . . the statements that he passed his latter years in insanity are made by so many contemporaries – Buchanan, Sir James Melville, De Thou, Lord Herries, etc. – that they must be accepted as conclusive'. T. F. Henderson, DNB, Vol. IX, p. 607; see also Robert Gore-Browne, *Lord Bothwell* (1937).

85. Accounts of the career of Esmé Stuart can be found in Cust, *Some Account of the Stuarts of Aubigny* (1891); Bingham, *The Making of a King: the Early Years of James VI and I* (1968) and *James VI of Scotland* (1979); Cassavetti, *The Lion and the Lilies* (1977). Esme's eldest son, Ludovic, second Duke of Lennox, was given Temple Newsam by James, shortly after his accession to the English throne; Ludovic sold it to Sir Arthur Ingram, who extensively rebuilt it in its present form.

86. Cit. J. E. Neale, *Queen Elizabeth I*, p. 284.

87. The body of Darnley rested in peace until the 'Glorious Revolution' of 1688, when a mob broke into the Royal Vault of Holyrood Abbey, and forced open the royal coffins; the bodies, however, were not desecrated, but remained in situ for another century. Then, in 1768, the roof of the Abbey church collapsed, and the vault was entered again. This time 'the head of Queen Magdalene [Madeleine of France] . . . and the skull of Lord Darnley, were also stolen' – H. Arnot, *Monastery of the Holy Cross* (1779), p. 255. In 1798 it was reported by Alexander Campbell that 'the skull of this debauchee is preserved among the curiosities of the Antiquarian Society of Scotland, – it exhibits a melancholy proof of the effects of his incontinence', i.e. the cranial caries of syphilis, already recognized for what they were – Campbell, *An Introduction to the History of Poetry in Scotland* (1798), p. 66 fn (in which Darnley was mentioned as having been a poet). The skull changed hands thrice, and in 1869 was presented to the Museum of the Royal College of Surgeons, where it was eventually examined by Karl Pearson, who incorporated the foregoing history and references into his *Skull and Portraits of Lord Darnley* (1928), pp. 43–7. The whereabouts of the skull were not known for a period during the first half of the nineteenth century, but the skull that reappeared and was sold at Sotheby's in 1865 was, in Karl Pearson's view, beyond reasonable doubt the genuine skull of Darnley.

EPILOGUE

1. David Mathew, *James I* (1967), p. 13.
2. John Knox (continuator), *History of the Reformation*, BK V, p. 352.
3. 'Thomas Crawford's Declaration', CSP (Scottish) Vol. 2, p. 314.

APPENDIX

1. CSP (Scottish) Vol. 2, p. 329.
2. PRO SP/52/13 No. 47. Broadsheet, blackletter.
3. PRO SP/52/13 No. 48. Broadside, blackletter. English versions by CB.
4. D. Hay Fleming, 'Notes on the Darnley Cenotaph', in *Scottish History and Life* (1902), pp. 66–9.

BIBLIOGRAPHY

A. Manuscript Sources.
B. Primary Printed Sources.
C. Secondary Sources.
D. Periodicals, Pamphlets, Catalogues, Guides.
E. Reference Books.

A. MANUSCRIPT SOURCES
(I) BRITISH LIBRARY

ADD. MSS 17492 'The Devonshire Manuscript'.
(Contains Darnley's poem 'My hope is yow for to obtaine'. The holograph manuscript, never previously photographed, is illustrated on plate nine, and quoted in full in Chapter Four. The Devonshire Manuscript also contains poems by Lady Margaret Douglas and Lord Thomas Howard, quoted in Chapter One).
ADD. MSS 19401
(Contain's Darnley's letter to the Earl of Leicester, illustrated on plate eight and quoted in Chapter Four).
COTTON MSS CALIGULA B X (16)
(Contains an illumination of the arms of Mary Queen of Scots quartered with the arms of England; the oath sworn by Darnley to the Queen of Scots on his creation as Earl of Ross, quoted in Chapter Four; the names of the men knighted by him on that occasion; the instructions of Queen Elizabeth I to the Earl of Bedford on his attending the baptism of Prince James).
COTTON MSS VESPASIAN F III 'Royal and Noble Autographs'
(Contains Darnley's letter to Mary I of England, illustrated on plate two, and quoted in Chapter Two).
EGERTON MSS 2805
(Contains Darnley's letter to Charles IX of France, illustrated on plate thirteen and quoted in Chapter Seven).

HARLEIAN MSS 6815
(Contains 'Orders of Service belonging to the degrees of a duke, a marquess, and an erle used in there owne howses', cited in Chapter Two;
and the form of the oath sworn by a recipient of the Order of St Michael,
quoted in Chapter Six).

ROYAL MSS 18 A XXXVIII
(The manuscript of John Elder's 'Proposal' addressed to Henry VIII, advo-
cating a union of Scotland and England).

ROYAL MSS 18 B VI
(Contains a contemporary copy of a letter written jointly by Mary and
Darnley to Pope Pius V, referred to in Chapter Seven, note seven).

(II) PUBLIC RECORD OFFICE

SP/12/23
(Contains the 'Deposition of William Forbes' and the 'Confession of
Arthur Lallart', quoted in Chapter Three).

SP/52/13
(Contains the drawings of events at Kirk o' Field, the design of the Confederate Lords' banner, and the scene at Carberry Hill, illustrated on
plates eighteen and nineteen; and the previously unpublished poems on
the murder of Darnley, quoted in the Appendix).

B. PRIMARY PRINTED SOURCES: RECORDS, MEMOIRS, COLLECTIONS OF LETTERS, ETC.

ACCOUNTS OF THE LORD HIGH TREASURER OF SCOTLAND. ed. Sir
James Balfour Paul. Vol. XI 1559–1566. (HMSO, Edinburgh, 1916).

BANNATYNE, George, *The Bannatyne Manuscript*, Writtin in Tyme of
Pest, 1568. ed. W. Tod Ritchie.   (Blackwood, Edinburgh and London,
1928).

*BANNATYNE MISCELLANY: Containing Original Papers and Tracts,
chiefly relating to the History and Literature of Scotland.* Vol. 1. (Bannatyne Club, 1827).

BIRREL, Robert, The Diarey of Robert Birrel, Burges of Edinburghe, Containing Divers Passages of Staite, and Uthers Memorable Accidents,
1532–1605, printed in Dalyell's *Fragments of Scottish History*, vide infra.

BLACKWOOD, *Adam, Martyre de la Royne D'Escosse*, 1588. ('English
Recusant Literature 1558–1640' ed. and select. D. M. Rogers. Vol. 391,
facsimile of original edition).

BLACKWOOD, Adam, *History of Mary Queen of Scots: A Fragment* (anon. trans.) (Maitland Club, Edinburgh, 1834).

BOTHWELL, James Hepburn, 4th Earl of, *Les Affaires du Conte de Boduel*, l'an MDLXVIII. (Bannatyne Club, Edinburgh, 1829).

BRANTÔME, Pierre de Bourdeille, Abbé de, *The Book of the Ladies –* Illustrious Dames: with elucidations of some of those ladies by C-A Sainte Beuve. trans. Katharine Prescott Wormeley. (William Heinemann, 1899).

BUCHANAN, George, *Rerum Scoticarum Historia*, books XVII, XVIII and XIX, and *Detectio Mariae Reginae Scotorum*. trans. and ed. W. A. Gatherer as 'The Tyrannous Reign of Mary Stewart'. (Edinburgh University Press, 1958).

BUCHANAN, George, *A Detection of the Actions of Mary Queen of Scots . . . and a Defence of the True Lords, Maintainers of the King's Majesty's Action and Authority*. Written in Latin by G. Buchanan; translated into English by a Person of Honour of the Kingdom of Scotland. (London, 1721).

CALENDAR OF STATE PAPERS DOMESTIC 1547–1580. ed. Robert Lemon. (Longman, Brown, Green, Longmans and Roberts, 1856).

CALENDAR OF LETTERS AND STATE PAPERS relating to English Affairs, preserved principally in the Archives of Simancas. Vol. 1, Elizabeth, 1558–1567. ed. and introd. Martin A. S. Hume. (PRO 1892; reprint 1971).

CALENDAR OF STATE PAPERS, FOREIGN SERIES, of the Reign of Elizabeth, Vol. VIII, 1566–68. ed. Allan James Crosby. (Longman and Co, and Trubner and Co, and others, 1871).

CALENDAR OF STATE PAPERS, Relating to Scotland and Mary Queen of Scots, Vol. I, 1547–1563; Vol. II, 1563–1569. ed. Joseph Bain. (H.M. General Register House, Edinburgh, 1898, 1900).

CALENDAR OF STATE PAPERS VENETIAN Vol. VII, 1558–1580. Ed. Rawdon Brown and G. Cavendish-Bentinck (HMSO, 1890).

CAMDEN, William, *Annales: The True and Royall History of the famous Empresse Elizabeth*. trans. Abraham Darcie. (London, 1625).

CHRONICLE OF QUEEN JANE and of Two Years of Queen Mary . . . Written by a resident in the Tower of London. ed. John gough Nichols. (Camden Society, 1850).

CRAIG, Sir Thomas, of Riccarton, Henrici Illustrissimi Ducis Albaniae, Comitis Rossiae etc. et Mariae Serenissimae Scotorum Reginae Epithalamium . . . 1565. trans. Revd Francis Wrangham, in *Epithalamia Tria Mariana*, vide infra.

DALYELL, John Graham, (ed.) *Fragments of Scottish History*. (Edinburgh, 1798).

DIURNAL OF REMARKABLE OCCURRENTS, that have passed within the

Country of Scotland since the death of King James the Fourth till the year MDLXXV, from a Manuscript of the sixteenth century in the possession of Sir John Maxwell of Pollock, Baronet. (Bannatyne Club, Edinburgh, 1833).

ELDER, John, *The Copie of a Letter Sent in to Scotlande, of the arrivill and landynge and moste noble marryage of the most Illustre Prynce Phillippe of Spayne, and the most excellente Princes Marye Quene of England* . . . (Black Letter tract, London, 1555).

HERRIES, Lord, *Historical Memoirs of the Reign of Mary Queen of Scots, and a portion of the reign of King James the Sixth*. ed. and introd. Robert Pitcairn. (Abbotsford Club, 1836).

INVENTAIRES DE LA ROYNE DESCOSSE, Douairière de France: Catalogues of the Jewels, Dresses, Furniture, Books, and Paintings of Mary Queen of Scots, 1556–1569. ed. and introd. Joseph Robertson. (Bannatyne Club, 1863).

KEITH, Robert, *History of the Affairs of Church and State in Scotland*. (3 Vols. Spottiswoode Society, 1844–50. Classified as a record source as it contains a vast number of documents reproduced in full).

KNOX, John, *The History of the Reformation of Religion in Scotland*. ed. and introd. William McGavin. (Blackie, Fullarton and Co, Glasgow, 1831).

KNOX, John, *The History of the Reformation of Religion in Scotland* revised and ed. Cuthbert Lennox. (Andrew Melrose, 1905).

KNOX, John, *The Political Writings of John Knox: The First Blast of the Trumpet against the Monstrous Regiment of Women, and Other Selected Works*. ed. Marvin Breslow. (Folger Books. Washington. The Folger Shakespeare Library. London and Toronto Associated University Presses, 1985).

KNOX, John, *The Works of John Knox*. ed. and coll. David Laing. (Bannatyne Club, Edinburgh, reprint AMS Press, New York, 1966).

LETTERS AND PAPERS, FOREIGN AND DOMESTIC OF THE REIGN OF HENRY VIII. ed. James Gairdner and R. H. Brodie. Vol. 18 parts 1 and 2. (HMSO, 1901, 1902).

MELVILLE, Sir James, *Memoirs of his own life*. (Bannatyne Club, Edinburgh, 1827).

MELVILLE, Sir James, *The Memoirs of Sir James Melville of Halhill*. ed. and introd. Gordon Donaldson. (The Folio Society, 1969).

MISCELLANEA ANTIQUA ANGLICANA, or a Select Collection of Curious Tracts Illustrative of the History . . . *of the English Nation*. Vol. 1. (Robert Triphook, London, 1816).

MISCELLANY OF THE SCOTTISH HISTORY SOCIETY, Vol. II. (Scottish History Society, Edinburgh, 1904).

NAU, Claude, *The History of Mary Stewart, from the Murder of Riccio until her flight into England, by Claude Nau, her Secretary.* ed. and introd. Revd Joseph Stevenson, S. J. (William Paterson, 1883)

NOSTREDAME, Michel de, [NOSTRADAMUS] *The True Prophecies or Prognostications of Michael Nostradamus ... One of the best Astronomers that ever were.* Translated and Commented by Theophilus de Garancières. (London, 1672).

ORIGINAL LETTERS ILLUSTRATIVE OF ENGLISH HISTORY: *including numerous Royal Letters with Autographs in the British Museum ...* 2nd Series. Vol. II. ed. Henry Ellis (Harding and Lepard, 1827).

PARADIN, Claude, *The Heroicall Devices of M. Claudius Paradin.* Translated out of Latin into English by P. S. (London. Imprinted by William Kearney ... 1591).

PARADIN, Claude, *Symbola Heroica M. C. Paradini ... de Gallica Lingua in Latinam Conversa.* (Antwerp, 1583).

PHYLLIPS, John, *A Commemoration of the Right Noble and vertuous Ladye Margrit Duglassis good grace, Countess of Lennox.* (Black Letter tract, London, 1578).

PITCAIRN, Robert, *Criminal Trials in Scotland, from AD 1488 to AD 1624, embracing the entire reigns of James IV and V, Mary Queen of Scots and James VI.* Vol. 1. (Bannatyne Club, Edinburgh, 1833).

REGISTER OF THE PRIVY COUNCIL OF SCOTLAND, Vol. 1, 1545–1569. ed. John Hill Burton. (Register House, Edinburgh, 1877).

REGISTRUM HONORIS DE MORTON: A Series of Ancient Charters of the Earldom of Morton with other Original Papers. Vol. 1 Original Papers. (Bannatyne Club, Edinburgh, 1853).

SELECTIONS FROM UNPUBLISHED MANUSCRIPTS in the College of Arms and the British Museum, Illustrating the Reign of Mary Queen of Scotland. (Maitland Club, Glasgow, 1837).

STOW, John, *The Chronicles of England, from Brute [Brutus] unto this present year of Christ, 1580.* (Ralph Newberie, London, 1580).

ZURICH LETTERS: Or the Correspondence of Several English Bishops and Others with the Helvetian Reformers, during the reign of Queen Elizabeth. Vol. 1. ed. Revd Hastings Robinson. (The Parker Society. Cambridge University Press, 2nd ed. 1846).

C. SECONDARY SOURCES

ADAMS, Simon, 'The Release of Lord Darnley and the Failure of the Amity', in Michael Lynch (ed.) *Mary Stewart, Queen in Three Kingdoms.* (Basil Blackwell, Oxford, 1988).

ANGLO, Sydney, *Images of Tudor Kingship.* (Seaby, 1992).

ARMSTRONG DAVISON, M. H., *The Casket Letters: A Solution to the*

Mystery of Mary Queen of Scots and the Murder of Lord Darnley. (the University Press of Washington D.C. USA, 1965).

ASHLEY, Maurice, *The Stuarts in Love: with some reflections on Love and Marriage in the Sixteenth and Seventeenth centuries.* (Hodder and Stoughton, 1963).

AUNGIER, George James, *The History and Antiquities of Syon Monastery.* (J. B. Nichols and Son, 1840).

BARBE, Louis A., *In Byways of Scottish History.* (Blackie and Son, 1912).

BARBE, Louis A., *Kirkaldy of Grange.* (Oliphant, Anderson and Ferrier, Edinburgh and London, 1897).

BAX, Clifford (ed.), *The Silver Casket:* Being Love-Letters and Love-Poems attributed to Mary Stuart, Queen of Scots, now modernised and translated, with an Introduction. (Hume and van Thal Ltd, 1946).

BELL, Robin ed. and trans. *Bittersweet within My Heart: The Collected Poems of Mary Queen of Scots.* (Pavilion Books, 1992).

BINGHAM, Caroline, *James V, King of Scots, 1512–1542.* (Collins, 1971).

BINGHAM, Caroline, *James VI of Scotland.* (Weidenfeld and Nicolson, 1979).

BLACK, J. B., *The Reign of Elizabeth 1558–1603.* ('The Oxford History of England', Vol. VIII, 2nd ed. 1959).

BRESLOW, Marvin (ed.). see Knox, Bibliography B.

BUCHANAN, Patricia Hill, *Margaret Tudor, Queen of Scots.* (Scottish Academic Press, Edinburgh and London, 1985).

BURTON, Elizabeth, and Felix Kelly, *The Elizabethans at Home.* (Secker and Warburg, 1958).

CAMDEN, Carroll, *The Elizabethan Woman.* (The Elsevier Press, Houston, New York, London, 1952).

CASSAVETTI, Eileen, *The Lion and the Lilies: The Stuarts and France.* (Macdonald and James/Book Club Associates, 1977).

CHALMERS, George, *Life of Mary Queen of Scots.* 2 Vols. (London, 1818).

CHAPMAN, Hester W., *The Last Tudor King: a Study of Edward VI.* (Jonathan Cape, 1958).

CHAPMAN, Hester W., *The Sisters of Henry VIII:* Margaret Tudor, Queen of Scotland (November 1489 – October 1541) Mary Tudor, Queen of France and Duchess of Suffolk (March 1496 – June 1533). (Jonathan Cape, 1969).

CHAUVIRÉ, Roger, *Le Secret de Marie Stuart.* (Paris, 1937).

CHAVREBIÈRE, Coissac de, *Histoire des Stuarts.* (Payot, Paris, 1930).

CHERRY, Alastair, *Princes, Poets and Patrons: The Stuarts and Scotland.* (National Library of Scotland/HMSO, Edinburgh, 1987).

CHILD, James Francis, *English and Scottish Popular Ballads* ed. from the Collection of J. F. Child by Helen Child Sargent and George Lyman Kittredge. (David Nutt, 1905).

COCHRAN-PATRICK, R. W., *Catalogue of the Medals of Scotland: from the Earliest Period to the Present Time*. (David Douglas, Edinburgh, 1884).

COCHRAN-PATRICK, R. W., *Records of the Coinage of Scotland: from the earliest period to the Union*. 2 Vols. (Edmondston and Douglas, Edinburgh, 1876).

COWAN, Ian B., *The Enigma of Mary Stuart*. (Victor Gollancz, 1971).

COWAN, Samuel, *The Lord Chancellors of Scotland, from the Institution of the Office to the Treaty of Union*. Vol. II. (W and A. K. Johnston, Edinburgh and London, 1911).

CUNNINGTON, C. Willet and Phillis, *Handbook of English Costume in the Sixteenth century*. (Faber and Faber, 1962).

CUST, Lady Elizabeth, *Some Account of the Stuarts of Aubigny, in France, 1422–1672*. (Privately Printed at the Chiswick Press, 1891).

DONALDSON, Gordon, *All the Queen's Men: Power and Politics in Mary Stewart's Scotland*. (Batsford Academic and Educational, Ltd, 1983).

DONALDSON, Gordon, *The First Trial of Mary Queen of Scots*. (Batsford, 1969).

DONALDSON, Gordon, *Mary Queen of Scots*. (The English Universities Press Ltd, 1974).

DONALDSON, Gordon, *Scotland: Church and Nation through Sixteen Centuries*. (Scottish Academic Press, Edinburgh and London, 1972).

DONALDSON, Gordon, *Scotland: James V to James VII* ('The Edinburgh History of Scotland', Vol. III. Oliver and Boyd, Edinburgh and London, 1965).

DONALDSON, Gordon, *Scottish Kings*. (Batsford, 1967).

DRUMMOND, Humphrey, *Our Man in Scotland: Sir Ralph Sadleir, 1507–1587*. (Leslie Frewin, 1969).

ELLIS, Henry, (ed.), see *Original Letters*, Bibliography B.

ERICKSON, Carolly, Bloody Mary. (J. M. Dent and Sons Ltd, 1978).

EVANS, Joan, *A History of Jewellery, 1100–1870*. (Faber and Faber, London, 1953).

FLEMING, David Hay, *Mary Queen of Scots: From her Birth to her Flight into England: A Brief Biography with Critical Notes, and a few Documents hitherto unpublished, and an Itinerary*. (Hodder and Stoughton, 2nd ed. 1898).

FRANCIS, Grant R., *Scotland's Royal Line: The tragic House of Stuart*. (E. P. Dutton and Company, New York, 1929).

FRASER, Lady Antonia, *Mary Queen of Scots*. (Weidenfeld and Nicolson, 1969).

FRASER, Lady Antonia, *The Six Wives of Henry VIII*. (Weidenfeld and Nicolson, 1992).

FRASER, William, *The Douglas Book*, Vol. 2 Angus Memoirs; Vol. 4 Correspondence. (Edinburgh, 1884).

FRASER, William, *The Lennox*, Vol. 1 Memoirs; Vol. 2 Muniments. (Edinburgh, 1874).

FREEMAN, Rosemary, *English Emblem Books*. (Chatto and Windus, 1948).

GARANCIÈRES, Theophilus de, see Nostredame, Bibliography B.

GATHERER, W. A. (ed.), see Buchanan, Bibliography B.

GIROUARD, Mark, *Life in the English Country House: A Social and Architectural History*. (Yale University Press, New Haven and London, 1978).

GOODARE, Julian, 'Queen Mary's Catholic Interlude', in Michael Lynch (ed.) *Mary Stewart, Queen in Three Kingdoms*. (Basil Blackwell, Oxford, 1988).

GORE-BROWNE, Robert, *Lord Bothwell: A Study of the Life, character and Times of James Hepburn, 4th Earl of Bothwell*. (Collins, 1937).

GRIFFITHS, Ralph A., and Roger S. Thomas, *The Making of the Tudor Dynasty*. (Alan Sutton, Stroud, 1985; paperback edition Alan Sutton and St Martin's Press, New York, 1993).

HAMILTON, Angus, Duke of, *Maria R: Mary Queen of Scots, the Crucial Years*. (Mainstream Publishing, Edinburgh and London, 1991).

HARDY, B. C., *Arbella Stuart: A Biography*. (Constable, 1913).

HENDERSON, T. F., *Mary Queen of Scots: her Environment and Tragedy*. (2 Vols. Hutchinson, 1905).

HENDERSON, T. F., *The Royal Stewarts*. (Blackwood, Edinburgh and London, 1914).

HÉRITIER, Jean, *Marie Stuart et le Meutre de Darnley*. ('Les Énigmes de l'Histoire' . . . Librairie Felix Lican, Paris 1934).

HODGES, J. P., *The Nature of the Lion: Elizabeth I and our Anglican Heritage*. (the Faith Press, 1962).

HUME, Martin, *The Love Affairs of Mary Queen of Scots: A Political History*. (Eveleigh Nash, 1903).

HUME BROWN, P., *George Buchanan: Humanist and Reformer*. (David Douglas, Edinburgh, 1890).

HURSTFIELD, Joel, *Elizabeth I and the Unity of England*. (the English Universities Press Ltd, 1960).

JENKINS, Elizabeth, *Elizabeth the Great*. (Victor Gollancz, 1958; Methuen University Paperbacks, 1965).

JENKINS, Elizabeth, *Elizabeth and Leicester*. (Victor Gollancz, 1961; paperback, 1972).

KENDALL, Alan, *Robert Dudley, Earl of Leicester*. (Cassell, 1980).

KLARWILL, Victor von, *Queen Elizabeth and Some Foreigners: Being a Series of hitherto unpublished Letters from the Archives of the Hapsburg family* (authorized trans. Professor T. H. Nash). (John Lane and The Bodley Head Ltd, 1928).

LAING, David (ed.), see Knox, Bibliography B.

LANG, Andrew, *The Mystery of Mary Stuart.* (Longmans, Green and Co, 1901).

LAVER, James, *Nostradamus, or the Future Foretold.* (Penguin edition, 1952).

LEE, Maurice, Jr., *James Stewart, Earl of Moray: A Political Study of the Reformation in Scotland.* (Columbia University Press, USA, 1966).

LEVINE, Mortimer, *The Early Elizabethan Succession Question, 1558–1568.* (Stanford University Press, USA, 1952).

LYNCH, Michael, (ed.), *Mary Stewart, Queen in Three Kingdoms.* (see Adams and Goodare, contribs.) (Basil Blackwell, Oxford, 1988).

MADDEN, Frederick, *Privy Purse Expenses of the Princess Mary, daughter of King Henry the Eighth, afterward Queen Mary.* (William Pickering, 1831).

MAHON, Major-General R. H., *Mary Queen of Scots: A Study of the Lennox Narrative.* (Cambridge University Press, 1924).

MAHON, Major-General R. H., *The Tragedy of Kirk o' Field.* (Cambridge University Press, 1930).

MARSHALL, Rosalind K., *Elizabeth I.* (HMSO, London, in association with the National Portrait Gallery, 1991).

MARSHALL, Rosalind K., *Queen of Scots.* (HMSO, Edinburgh, 1986).

MARSHALL, Rosalind K., *Virgins and Viragos: A History of Women in Scotland from 1080 to 1980.* (Collins, 1983).

MATHEW, David, Archbishop, *James I.* (Eyre and Spottiswoode, 1967).

MAXWELL, Sir Herbert, *A History of the House of Douglas, from the Earliest Times down to the Legislative Union of England and Scotland.* (Freemantle and Co, 1902).

MITCHISON, Rosalind, *A History of Scotland.* (Methuen, 1970).

MUMBY, Frank Arthur, *Elizabeth and Mary Stuart: The Beginning of the Feud.* ('History in Contemporary Letters', Constable, 1914).

MUMBY, Frank Arthur, *The Fall of Mary Stuart: A Narrative in Contemporary Letters.* (Constable, 1921).

MCGAVIN, William, (ed.), see Knox, Bibliography B.

MCKERLIE, E. Marrianne H., *Mary of Guise-Lorraine, Queen of Scotland.* (Sands and Co, London and Edinburgh, 1931).

MACKIE, Charles, *The Castles, Palaces and Prisons of Mary of Scotland.* (C. Cox, and others, 1849).

MACNALTY, Sir Arthur Salusbury, *Mary Queen of Scots: The Daughter of Debate.* (Christopher Johnson, 1960).

MCNEILL, F. Marian, *The Scots Kitchen: its Traditions and Lore.* (Blackie and Son Ltd, London and Glasgow, 1929; 2nd edition, 1963).

MACQUEEN, John, (ed. and introd.), *Ballattis of Luve: The Scottish Courtly Love Lyric, 1400–1570*. (Edinburgh University Press, 1970).

NEALE, J. E., *Elizabeth I and her Parliaments*. Vol. 1, 1559–1581. (Jonathan Cape, 1953; paperback ed. 1965).

NEALE, J. E., *Queen Elizabeth I*. (Jonathan Cape, 1934; paperback ed. 1971).

NICHOLS, John Gough, (ed.), see Chronicle of Queen Jane, Bibliography B.

PARKER, Geoffrey, *Philip II*. ('Library of World Biography', gen. ed. J. H. Plumb; Hutchinson, 1971).

PARRY, His Honour Sir Edward, *The Persecution of Mary Stewart: The Queen's Cause: A Study in Criminology*. (Cassell and Co Ltd, 1931).

PEARSON, Karl, *The Skull and Portraits of Henry Stewart, Lord Darnley, and their bearing on the Tragedy of Mary Queen of Scots*. ('Biometrika', July 1928, bound as volume, Cambridge University Press, 1928).

PHILLIPS, James Emerson, *Images of a Queen: Mary Stuart in Sixteenth Century Literature*. (University of California Press, USA, 1964).

PITCAIRN, Robert, (ed.), see Herries, Bibliography B.

PLOWDEN, Alison, *Two Queens in one Isle: The Deadly Relationship of Elizabeth I and Mary Queen of Scots*. (The Harvester Press, Sussex, 1984).

PURVEY, P. Frank, *Coins and Tokens of Scotland*. (B. A. Seaby, 1972).

READ, Conyers, *Mr Secretary Cecil and Queen Elizabeth*. (Jonathan Cape, 1955).

RIDLEY, Jasper, *John Knox*. (Clarendon Press, Oxford, 1968).

RIDLEY, Jasper, *The Tudor Age*. (Constable, 1988).

RITCHIE, W. Tod, (ed.), see Bannatyne Manuscript, Bibliography B.

ROBERTSON, Joseph, (ed.), see Inventaires, Bibliography B.

ROBINSON, Revd Hastings, (ed.), see Zurich Letters, Bibliography B.

SEMPLE, David, *The Tree of Crocston: being a refutation of the fables of the courtship of Queen Marie and Lord Darnley, at Crocston Castle, under the Yew Tree*. (J. and J. Cook, Paisley, 1876).

SHIRE, Helena Mennie, *Song, Dance and Poetry of the Court of Scotland under King James VI*. (Cambridge University Press, 1969).

SITWELL, Edith, *The Queens and the Hive*. (Macmillan, 1962).

SMITH, Lacey Baldwin, *The Elizabethan Epic*. (Jonathan Cape, 1966).

SMITH, Lacey Baldwin, *Henry VIII: The Mask of Royalty*. (Jonathan Cape, 1971).

STANLEY, Arthur Penrhyn, *Historical Memorials of Westminster Abbey*. (John Murray, 5th ed. 1882).

STEVENSON, Revd Joseph, S. J., (ed.), see Nau, Bibliography B.

STRICKLAND, Agnes, *Lives of the Queens of Scotland and English Prin-*

cesses connected with the Regal Succession of Great Britain. (William Blackwood, Edinburgh and London, 8 Vols, 1850–59).

STRONG, Roy, and Julia Trevelyan Oman, *Mary Queen of Scots.* (Secker and Warburg, 1972).

STRONG, Roy, *Tudor and Jacobean Portraits.* (HMSO, London, 2 Vols, 1969).

SWAIN, Margaret, *The Needlework of Mary Queen of Scots.* (Van Nostrand Reinhold and Company, 1973).

TEULET, A., *Lettres de Marie Stuart:* Lettres au Comte de Bothwell; Documents relatifs au Meutre de Darnley; Lettres et Écrits Divers de Marie Stuart; Documents Relatifs à Sa Mort et à ses Dispositions Testamentaires. (Librairie de Firmin Didot Frères, Fils et Cie, Paris, 1859).

THOMSON, George Malcolm, *The Crime of Mary Stuart.* (Hutchinson, 1967).

TILLYARD, E. M. W., *The Elizabethan World Picture.* (Chatto and Windus, 1943; paperback edition, 1963).

TYTLER, Patrick Fraser, *An Account of the Life and Writings of Sir Thomas Craig of Riccarton.* (W and C Tait, Edinburgh, 1823).

TYTLER, Patrick Fraser, *History of Scotland,* Vol. 5. (William Tait, Edinburgh, 3rd ed. 1845).

WALDMAN, Milton, *Elizabeth and Leicester.* (Collins, 1944).

WILLIAMS, Neville, *Elizabeth, Queen of England.* (Weidenfeld and Nicolson, 1967).

WILLIAMSON, Hugh Ross, *Catherine de' Medici.* (Michael Joseph, 1973).

WORMALD, Jenny, *Court, Kirk and Community: Scotland 1470–1625.* ('The New History of Scotland' Vol. IV, Edward Arnold, 1981).

WORMALD, Jenny, *Mary Queen of Scots: A Study in Failure.* ('Monarchs and Monarchy' gen.ed. David Starkey; George Philip, 1988).

WORMALD, Jenny, (ed. and contrib.), *Scotland Revisited.* (Collins and Brown, 1991).

WORMELEY, Katharine Prescott, (ed. and trans.), see Brantôme, Bibliography B.

WRANGHAM, Revd Francis (trans.) *Epithalamia Tria Mariana.* (Chester, 1837).

ZWEIG, Stefan, *The Queen of Scots.* (Cassell and Co Ltd, 1935).

D. PERIODICALS, PAMPHLETS, CATALOGUES, GUIDES.

BARWICK, G. F., 'A Sidelight on the Mystery of Mary Stuart: Pietro Bizari's Contemporary Account of the Murders of Riccio and Darnley'. (*Scottish Historical Review,* Vol. XXXI, 1924).

BENTLEY-CRANCH, Dana, 'Effigy and Portrait in Sixteenth Century Scotland'. (*Review of Scottish Culture*, 4, 1988).

BINGHAM, Caroline, 'The Poems of Mary Queen of Scots'. (*Royal Stuart Papers X*, The Royal Stuart Society, 1976).

CROSSLEY, F. W., 'A Temple Newsam Inventory, 1565'. (*Yorkshire Archaeological Journal*, Vol. XXV, 1918–19).

DAWSON, Jane E. A., 'Mary Queen of Scots, Lord Darnley and Anglo-Scottish Relations in 1565'. (*International History Review*, Vol. VIII, 1986).

DOLPHIN COINS, Fixed Price List No. 1 (Dolphin Coins, London, 1991).

DUNCAN, Thomas, 'The Queen's Maries'. (*Scottish Historical Review*, Vol II, 1905).

DUNCAN, Thomas, 'Relations of the Earl of Murray with Mary Stuart'. (*Scottish Historical Review*, Vol. VI, 1909).

FAWCETT, Richard, 'The Early Tudor House in the Light of Recent Excavations [Temple Newsam]' (*Leeds Arts Calander*, No. 70, 1972).

FRASER, Lady Antonia, 'Mary Queen of Scots and the Historians'. (*Royal Stuart Papers VII*, the Royal Stuart Society, 1974).

GENT, Frank, 'The Coffin in the Wall: an Edinburgh Castle "Mystery"'. (*Chambers's Journal*, September/October, 1944; and reprint as pamphlet).

GIROUARD, Mark, *Hardwick Hall*. (The National Trust, 1989).

MARSHALL, Rosalind K., *Costume in Scottish Portraits, 1560–1830*. (Scottish National Portrait Gallery, 1986).

MARSHALL, Rosalind K., (ed.), *Dynasty: the Royal House of Stewart*. (Contributors: Duncan Thomson; Rosalind K. Marshall; David H. Caldwell; Hugh Cheape; George Dalgleish). (National Galleries of Scotland and National Museums of Scotland, 1990).

MUIR, Kenneth, Unpublished Poems in the Devonshire MS. (Proceedings of the Leeds Philosophical and Literary Society, Vol. VI, 1944–52, Part IV, 1947).

MACALPINE, Ida; Hunter, Richard, and Professor C. Rimington, 'Porphyria in the Royal Houses of Stuart, Hanover and Prussia'; published in *Porphyria – A Royal Malady*. (British Medical Association, 1968).

MACDONALD, Alasdair A., 'The Bannatyne Manuscript – A Marian Anthology'. (*Innes Review*, Vol. XXXVII, No. 1, Spring, 1986).

POLLEN, J. H. 'The Dispensation for the Marriage of Mary Stuart with Darnley, and its date'. (*Scottish Historical Review*, Vol. IV, No. 15, April 1907).

STRONG, Roy, *Hans Eworth: A Tudor Artist and his Circle*. (Leicester Museums and Art Gallery, 1965).

TAIT, Hugh, 'Historiated Tudor Jewellery'. (*The Antiquaries' Journal*, Vol. XLII, 1962).

BIBLIOGRAPHY

TEMPLE NEWSAM, *Guide* (anonymous authorship). (Leeds City Art Galleries, 1989).

THOMSON, Duncan, *Painting in Scotland, 1570–1650*. (Trustees of the National Galleries of Scotland, 1975).

TREVOR-ROPER, Hugh, Queen Elizabeth's First Historian: William Camden and the beginnings of English 'Civil History'. (Neale Lecture in English History, 1971, Jonathan Cape, 1971).

E. REFERENCE BOOKS

DICTIONARY OF NATIONAL BIOGRAPHY eds. Sir Leslie Stephen and Sir Sidney Lee. (XXI Vols, Oxford University Press, reprint of 1921–22).

HANDBOOK OF BRITISH CHRONOLOGY eds. E. B. Fryde; D. E. Greenway; S. Porter and I. Roy. (Royal Historical Society, 3rd edition, 1986).

SCOTS PEERAGE ed. Sir James Balfour Paul. (IX Vols, David Douglas, Edinburgh, 1904–11).

SCOTTISH KINGS: A Revised Chronology of Scottish History 1005–1625, by Sir Archibald H. Dunbar, Bart. (David Douglas, Edinburgh, 1899).

SCOTTISH TEXTS AND CALENDARS: An Analytical Guide to Serial Publications by David and Wendy Stevenson. (Royal Historical Society, London, and Scottish History Society, Edinburgh, 1987).

WHO'S WHO IN HISTORY Vol. II England 1485–1603 by C. R. N. Routh. (Basil Blackwell, Oxford, 1964).

WHO'S WHO IN SCOTTISH HISTORY by Gordon Donaldson and Robert S. Morpeth. (Basil Blackwell, Oxford, 1973).

INDEX

NOTE ON INDEX

The subject of this book appears in the index as 'Darnley', this being the title of the book and the most familiar form of his name, and not as 'Henry King of Scots'. Other Kings and Queens are entered under their Christian names, eg 'James V, King of Scots' and 'Mary Queen of Scots'. The mother of Darnley, who figures in the narrative as 'Lady Margaret Douglas', 'Margaret, Countess of Lennox', 'Margaret Lennox' and 'Margaret', is entered under 'Margaret'. Other people whose names change are entered under the form more frequently used or better known, eg Lord Robert Dudley is entered under 'Leicester', with a cross reference. The spelling 'Stewart' is used for the earlier Royal Stewarts and their Scottish kindred; the Gallicized form 'Stuart' is used for Mary Queen of Scots, for Matthew Stuart, Earl of Lennox, who took French nationality, for his son Darnley, who wrote his name 'Hary Stuart', and for the Franco-Scottish Stuarts of Aubigny. French Catherines are entered under 'C' and English Katherines under 'K' – but including Katherine of Aragon, who used a K monogram.